SOUL
SCHOOL

SOUL
SCHOOL

Taking Kids on a Joy-Filled
Journey Through the Heart of
Black American Culture

AMBER O'NEAL JOHNSTON

A TarcherPerigee Book

tarcherperigee

an imprint of Penguin Random House LLC
penguinrandomhouse.com

TarcherPerigee with tp colophon is a registered trademark of Penguin Random House LLC

Most TarcherPerigee books are available at special quantity discounts for bulk purchase for sales promotions, premiums, fund-raising, and educational needs. Special books or book excerpts also can be created to fit specific needs. For details, write: SpecialMarkets@penguinrandomhouse.com.

Library of Congress Cataloging-in-Publication Data

Names: Johnston, Amber O'Neal, author.
Title: Soul school: taking kids on a joy-filled journey through the heart of Black American culture / Amber O'Neal Johnston.
Description: New York: TarcherPerigee, [2025] | Includes bibliographical references and indexes.
Identifiers: LCCN 2024044620 (print) | LCCN 2024044621 (ebook) |
ISBN 9780593716823 (trade paperback) | ISBN 9780593716830 (epub)
Subjects: LCSH: African American children—Books and reading. | African American teenagers—Books and reading. | American literature—African American authors—Bibliography. | English literature—Black authors—Bibliography. |
Children's literature—Bibliography | Young adult literature—Bibliography. |
African Americans—Juvenile literature—Bibliography. | Blacks—Juvenile literature—Bibliography. |
African Americans—Social life and customs. | African Americans—Intellectual life. | LCGFT: Literary criticism.
Classification: LCC Z1039.B56 J65 2025 (print) | LCC Z1039.B56 (ebook) |
DDC 016.305896/073—dc23/eng/20241030
LC record available at https://lccn.loc.gov/2024044620
LC ebook record available at https://lccn.loc.gov/2024044621

Printed in the United States of America
1st Printing

Book design by Angie Boutin

The mystery of storytelling is the miracle of a single living seed which can populate whole acres of human minds.

BEN OKRI, *A WAY OF BEING FREE*

CONTENTS

FOREWORD

Unsurprisingly, when I began reading *Soul School*, I gasped in recognition. Of myself, my daughter, friends, family, my students. Of my *story*. Of *our* story together. Amber O'Neal Johnston writes, "There was a separation between who I was and the world I was expected to thrive in." I know this tension, the Du Bois "double-consciousness" that leaves us vulnerable to dehumanization and despair. But, like Amber, I also know the restoration and renewal that can come through the transformative nature of children's literature.

Amber writes about Black Joy, not as a simplistic and fleeting happy place but as the "summoning of a protected healing space inside ourselves" that trauma cannot destroy. She shares lessons from witnessing how story nourished her children's profound understanding of Black resilience with the same humor, grace, thoughtfulness, and honesty that struck me when I first encountered her online. There she was, the book-loving Black mom friend I was always seeking, a kindred spirit who used story to illuminate paths so her children could find their way. When she writes about her childhood yearning for soul, her lifelong desire to be saturated in the fullness of our story, and her deep desire to expand our reading lives—and, by extension, our imaginations—you know that she means what she says.

In writing about the Black American story, Amber crosses boundaries of time and travels across geographical borders, reminding us not to close ourselves off or retreat but to claim the rich kaleidoscope of our story and cling to it like an heirloom patchwork quilt. As a Jamaican Nigerian New Yorker (or "Afropolitan," as a friend once said with a dismissive hand flick) and child of storytellers and avid readers, I grew up reading the diaspora in a way I now recognize as a tremendous blessing. I zigged to Eloise Greenfield and

Maya Angelou, zagged to Virginia Hamilton and Julius Lester. I connected deeply with the African Writers Series and the story songs of Louise Bennett Coverley.

"Attempting to fully separate the experience of Black Americans from Africa, the broader Americas, the Caribbean, and other parts of the world is like watching my pickiest eater try to pluck each fleck of green seasoning out of my cooking," she writes. Not only is that *what we not gonna do*, we *are* going to celebrate our stories in various forms—oral, fiction, nonfiction, poetry, drama, and more. The multitude of books featured here is a deep and wide delight, serving up a smorgasbord of titles from the oft-celebrated to the less well known and equally valuable.

I was a fortunate young reader, exposed to a diverse array of literature; alongside Langston Hughes, Zora Neale Hurston, August Wilson, and Ca-mille Yarbrough, I forged relationships with Madeleine L'Engle and Judy Blume, Charles Dickens and Jane Austen. I read for joy, to process pain, to remember who I was, and to be transformed. I read between the lines and wrote my own. Amber's mission here is not exclusionary or narrow; *Soul School* is all *yes, AND*, offering to hold our hands as we leap into an expanded world of children's literature with open minds and hearts.

Throughout the book, I am reminded that it is a family, "framily," and community journey that Amber invites us to take along with our children, a gift for all who need to be restored and renewed by story. She "wished for an intimate survey of Black American culture and experience told through chil-dren's literature—a celebratory 'book of books' that I could follow while guid-ing my children's learning. I wanted to have something to hand the many parents and teachers of children who are missing an authentic connection to the Black literary experience. Or those who simply want more." *Soul School* is all that and so much more. It is both balm and tonic, remedy and recipe. It is tradition and innovation, jazz and hip-hop, soul food on the page.

With a quintessential blend of meticulous scholarship, dynamic story-telling, and practical, concrete tips, Amber has created something extraordi-nary, both innovative and grounded in tradition, inviting us to honor and offer Black children's literature. This is a book for underlining and margin notes, for talking to yourself and sharing with friends as you read and reread, discover and remember. Amber says that *Soul School* is not a "deconstructed textbook" or step-by-step plan to learn everything there is to know about Black children's literature; it is a rich resource that tells its own story.

Amber reminds us that books are not just for lesson plans, lists, or even language acquisition but for life, community, culture, and capacity-building. As she guides us from stories of ancient African kingdoms to Black Reconstruction, Black Power, Black Arts, and Black Lives Matter, through fantasy and folktales, sports, beauty, food, and biography, she affirms that our many, many stories form one truth: "Our DNA tells a fact-based story that our hearts and minds corroborate, and for as long as we have breath, our history will endure . . . We bear witness through our stories."

On school visits and at conferences, I tell readers: Your story is precious. With *Soul School*, Amber O'Neal Johnston communicates that and more, delivering an empowering and enriching treasure that is sure to resonate deeply with young readers of all ages and the grown-ups who love them.

You are beautiful, she says. You are powerful.
You have a creative legacy that cannot be stolen.
Your story is multi-faceted, ever-changing, and firmly rooted.
You have survived, and you can thrive. You can claim the possibilities.
You have stories.
You have so many wonderful, magnificent, glorious stories.

—OLUGBEMISOLA RHUDAY-PERKOVICH, AUTHOR OF *OPERATION SISTERHOOD* AND *YOU'RE BREAKING MY HEART*

INTRODUCTION

I plucked my soul out of its secret place.[1] The first time I encountered this line, I felt it had been written just for me. Even though the poet Claude McKay died nearly thirty years before my birth, the words were as familiar and present as any I'd ever read. I know the feeling of harboring a hidden self. For years, part of my identity felt buried. I couldn't point to a specific issue, but I felt incomplete. Inexplicably so.

While growing up, I yearned for a deeper connection to Black cultural identity and expression, and the continued lack fed my discontent. I longed for tangible representation of my life, family, and community, but there was no way to ask for something I didn't even know existed. Yes, I was in relationship with Black people and had plenty of experiences pointing me toward African American culture. Still, I didn't have the framework to organize or unpack the disparate cultural inputs I sporadically picked up along the way.

There was a separation between who I was and the world I was expected to thrive in. Specifically, I was aware of my culture on Sundays at church and during family gatherings, but I learned not to expect any glimpses during the week. People like me weren't integral enough to the fabric of American education to be studied and appreciated in its classrooms beyond passing mentions of slavery or civil rights.

We weren't significant enough to be celebrated during the school day or included in field trips, assemblies, or class projects. I didn't actively wrestle with this reality then because I didn't know that my days could or should be different. Black stories weren't a big deal; it just was what it was.

I've always loved a good story, and I know I would have thrived on Black books. Yes, at school, but also in my leisure time, family time, and the hours I spent entrenched in my community. Fictional characters and real-life ordinary and extraordinary people would have answered many of my questions through literature. I would have been absorbed in their stories and discovered my own story along the way. Most of all, I would have danced to the pulse of a rich culture that happened to be my own.

In young adulthood, I encountered the fringes of Black American literature for the first time, and the taste I got was exhilarating but fleeting. It wasn't until I started raising a family that I recognized how perceptive I'd been as a child, even in my ignorance. The nagging part of me was onto something.

While reading aloud to my children, day after day, year after year, I realized what I'd missed: a childhood filled with Black stories. Even as a young schoolgirl, I'd cried out for some *soul*. I wanted it. I needed it. The more I read to my kids, the more I noticed it. I saw their reactions and even felt my adult emotions gravitate toward it. But what was *it*?

It is the vibrant rhythm of a deeply rooted, ever-evolving Black American culture. Our music, food, and relationships. How we communicate through words, sounds, idioms, intonation, and body language. It's the stories our old folks share and the games we play on hot summer days. The shared history that binds us in ways we can't fully understand and the present-day manifestations of that past. Our creative spirit and style infuse everything we touch—poetry, dance, theater, art—and *it* is the emotions they provoke. It is achievement, resilience, and all the pieces of life we cling to as part of what makes us who we are.

There's a reason that the descriptor *soul* precedes so many things synonymous with African American culture. Soul music. Soul food. Soul sisters and brothers. Even *Soul Train*. It's not a mistake that we've come to describe elements of our culture not just by what they are but by how they make people feel. The emotions invoked by these various aspects are experienced so profoundly that it seems they awaken our very souls.

When I think of the life education I want for my children, I think of books. My kids are most alive and content when reading and hearing the words of Black authors telling their stories. Our stories. I want to honor our experience with Black literature and do my part to make it a big, hairy deal in other homes and classrooms, for children like mine and other kids who haven't had the opportunity to learn about African American culture through their books.

Over the years, I've done the work to curate exceptional books for my children and thousands of others as "Heritage Mom," an author and speaker dedicated to making Black voices the norm in our children's literature, broader education, and other aspects of their worlds. I create lesson guides for my family and package them up as Heritage Packs to share with the home-schooling world and far beyond. My goal is to raise awareness of the undeniable power, beauty, and impact of Black literature on children's hearts and to make it more accessible to kids everywhere.

While knee-deep in this work, I wished for an intimate survey of Black American culture and experience told through children's literature—a celebratory "book of books" that I could follow while guiding my children's learning. I wanted to have something to hand the many parents and teachers of children who are missing an authentic connection to the Black literary experience. Or those who simply want more. I searched and couldn't find anything that made it easy for parents to share Black Joy, resilience, achievement, history, culture, legacy, and everything in between with their kids. But along the way, I did encounter books that gave me hope and inspired me to keep going.

In 1941, Charlemae Rollins, a pioneering librarian at the Chicago Public Library, published *We Build Together: A Reader's Guide to Negro Life and Literature for Elementary and High School Use.* My copy of the third revision (1967) enthralled me because I saw glimpses of what I longed for in the annotated list of "really good books for children and young people that would present Negroes as human beings and not stereotypes."[2] The selections and some of the informing thoughts were obviously dated, but knowing that passionate book lovers have been singing the praises of picture books, nonfiction narratives, and novels featuring Black people for decades inspired me to no end.

I felt equally encouraged by *A Bibliography of Negro History & Culture for Young Readers*, edited by Miles M. Jackson, Jr., in 1968. Written for librarians and educators, the foreword suggests that adults can challenge children "with the ideas and the provocative thoughts the books contain" as they help young readers find "new, different roads to travel . . . into the many faceted worlds of the Negro."[3] The book was revolutionary for its time, but where was *this* generation's gem?

I sat up at night, flipping through the pages of these bibliographies and others I found in the dusty digital corners of the Web, wondering who would create something similar but more modern, expansive, and celebratory. I desperately wanted to hold a contemporary guide to Black children's literature in my hands. I wanted something that spoke directly to the hearts of families—not only professionals—and I especially wanted it to provide a fulfilling, exploratory, and fun journey.

Pursuing the ideal guide felt like searching for a needle in a haystack. Don't get me wrong. Plenty of popular books recommend children's literature (I own and enjoy many of them!), but none feature more than a very light sprinkling, if that, of Black stories. Books featuring Black characters are glaringly absent from these compendiums, considered universal offerings of the best of the best. It pains me to see how little is thought of Black stories and the children who need and want to hear them.

I anticipate some pushback to *Soul School* as a small, familiar few will predictably criticize my focus on Black books by Black people. Yet it will never occur to them that book guides filled with stories featuring white characters by white authors are the norm, and no one thinks twice. These books aren't titled "The Best of the Best in White Children's Literature," but that's what they are. Thankfully, authors can write about whatever they'd like, but let's call it what it is so we'll all understand what we're dealing with.

I've heard the arguments about "great" literature and why it doesn't matter that it's mostly white:

"We're all the same. Race shouldn't be a factor in choosing books."

Race will stop being a factor in books when it stops being a factor in society. I agree that it "shouldn't" matter, but it does. We're righting a wrong by adding books to our children's world that **should have always been there.**

"Great books transcend race and culture. They're universal, so everyone can relate to them."

That's true. But why do people of color *always* have to leap the farthest to make the connection? Are white stories the *only* universal stories? If books are just books and Black kids are expected to relate to white books, then white kids can relate to Black books, too. It makes no sense that the expectation would only run one way.

"Literature is meant to draw us closer to God, not to be a mirror."

This is typically followed by a litany of misused Bible verses condemning the idea of books as mirrors, a manipulative approach designed to apply God's stamp of approval to all-white booklists. First, not everyone agrees that "drawing closer to God" is the sole purpose of literature. Second, if you do believe that, who decided that only certain books (that "just happen" to be mostly white) written by a select few (who "just happen" to be mostly white) is *the* path to God? This is the antithesis of biblical thinking.

If I were suggesting that children and teens *only* read Black books, the backlash would be deserved. Books featuring people of color should be abundant and included *along with* "traditional" (read: white) stories—including many classics in the established canon. Many of these books are phenomenal, and I can't imagine children not encountering them. Rather, I'm seeking an *expansion* of literature. I want kids to read this and that. It's a pretty reasonable goal, and it's difficult not to respond incredulously when faced with opposition. When I started this work, I never imagined encountering people who think kids should *not* read books representing the breadth of humankind. But the critics condemning our children's freedom to read widely argue that nothing should change, and they sound like broken records. Or perhaps clanging cymbals?

Sometimes, I walk away to bury my weary disbelief in a pint of butter pecan.

On other days, I head to the bookstore and buy more Black stories in silent protest.

Today, I'm writing a book.

In the wise words of Toni Morrison: "If there's a book that you want to read, but it hasn't been written yet, then you must write it."[4] So here I am. *Soul School* is a journey through Black American culture, unboxed and explored, one book at a time. It captures much of what it means to be Black in the United States and culls it down to some of the best children's, middle grade, and young adult books available. The following pages will introduce African American culture through masterfully told stories or point the way to a necessary reconnection with our roots, depending on your child's background, age, or stage, and what they need most.

In part 1, we'll look at attributes and values held dear for generations and aspects of history that highlight the pride and pain of the Black American experience. We'll dive into the art of storytelling and how the lives of Black authors and illustrators can inspire children as much as the stories they tell. Part 2 offers a robust booklist. With hundreds of handpicked titles—all written by Black authors—it's a well-seasoned feast of ideas delivered through prose, verse, and visual art. And it's served with a heaping dose of down-home, irresistible, good old-fashioned Black *soul* to nourish, uplift, and inspire children everywhere.

PART ONE

PART ONE

1

BLACK IS BEAUTIFUL

Hard times require furious dancing. Each of us is proof.
—ALICE WALKER

*B*lack is beautiful. Popularized in the 1960s and '70s, this phrase encompassed a broad celebration of Black culture and identity. It urged the recognition of a valuable legacy and fostered a sense of pride in contemporary accomplishments. It also focused on the Black community's emotional health by changing beauty standards and affirming natural aspects of who we are and how we show up in this world.

Today, more than half a century later, the phrase bears repeating for a new generation of children who may not have gotten the message the first time around. Black culture is indeed beautiful. The beauty shows up in more ways than can be covered here (or anywhere, really), but children can find some vibrant facets in Black literature.

Culture is the way of life for a group of people, including customs, arts, achievements, social norms, language, and values. Cultures shift over time and can be experienced differently across generations, but the most closely held or valued parts of a culture are generally preserved even amid outside influences. This is true of people everywhere, and it's especially true of African Americans, as our culture is situated within the landscape of American society.

American and African American cultures are distinct but related. We easily understand the interrelationship when we watch how quickly music originating in the Black community is embraced and emulated by the mainstream scene, with or without credit. It's also apparent when witnessing the similarities between some aspects of Southern comfort food and the narrower designation of authentic soul food. While overlap is acknowledged and expected, Black Americans proudly preserve a distinct culture that has evolved over many generations and hundreds of years.

Relationships and geography impact the degree to which a person associates with, embraces, understands, or even recognizes African American culture. This makes sense when we consider that cultural exposure is one of the greatest influencers of cultural adoption. The more time someone spends immersed in our culture, the more opportunities they gain to learn the unique aspects that make us who we are. Family relationships, close friendships, and community ties help build awareness and comfort, making belonging easier to come by.

Some children are immersed from birth. They know what it means to be surrounded by people who understand the nuanced attributes of their culture, and they recognize the pieces of their lives that are firmly tethered to the African American experience. These kids have a solid attachment to their Black families and communities, and parents often (and sometimes mistakenly) assume they don't need anything more to help them embrace who they are.

Other children aren't exposed to African American culture beyond what they may catch on television or overhear in a conversation. These children often must rely on stereotypes, assumptions, and misinformation to fill gaps in their understanding. While they may grow after leaving home and interacting with a more diverse group of people in college or through work, they're generally left to their own devices.

Most children fall between the two ends of the spectrum. They have some understanding and exposure to Black American culture but haven't had enough experience to comprehend its fullness. These kids, and often their parents (including Black parents), don't know what they don't know, making it difficult to move forward. They're open to learning more; some may even long for a deeper connection or more context. They need opportunities to learn from and connect with Black voices to help them align what they already know with new inputs.

Personal relationships are the most effective way to meet children's need to explore our culture. Whether close ties are formed through familial or significant community interactions, the more a child is immersed in authentic and varied relationships with Black people, the more they will naturally understand.

Geography can significantly influence children's opportunities to witness and experience Black American culture, but it's also generally locked in. And sometimes, even the perfect confluence of people in just the right place still isn't enough. When children need and long for more, sometimes a fantastic story is just about the only thing that will hit the spot.

In my book *A Place to Belong*, I spoke extensively about using literary mirrors and windows while curating a home library. A mirror is a book that helps build a child's identity as it reflects their own culture or personhood. Children find themselves represented along with their families and communities, and their sense of belonging grows as they recognize characters like themselves moving through the world. Books as windows, on the other hand, provide a realistic view of how others live while simultaneously situating children within the context of a wider world. Providing books that give honest and varied views of different people's lives is like pulling back the curtains of a darkened room, allowing light to pour in.

Literature can be a fun and accessible tool for kids as they grow in their understanding of and love for Black American culture. Mirrors help Black children already comfortable in their skin feel validated and valued. For kids with limited exposure to African American culture, the same stories serve as windows, providing details they don't encounter elsewhere. In either case, children recognize and learn from disparate yet harmonized Black voices delivered across time and place.

These pages celebrate the beauty of Black American culture. Through entertaining tales smothered in caramel, dipped in chocolate, and sprinkled with Black Joy, our kids will examine cultural elements intrinsic to the Black experience via words and pictures penned and drawn by Black hands.

SONG AND MUSIC

Every culture has its own music. But the sounds of Black America are so recognizable, and the emotions they invoke so visceral, that it's impossible to define our culture without granting particular attention to our music. Our ancestors brought their music to America, and it survived because it was housed inside their bodies and could not be stolen. If I ever questioned how closely linked our immersive styles of Black American song and music are to that of West Africa, a trip overseas made me a believer. While visiting Accra, Ghana, with my children, I was keenly aware of the rhythms surrounding us at every turn. Though it was my first time on the continent, the music made me feel like I'd been there all along. I recognized the call and response, improvisation, and accompanying body movements. I saw a clear and undeniable connection between the music of the Motherland and the music I grew up hearing, and the correlation moved me.

Born of the music carried from Africa, combined with unfamiliar and traumatic experiences, enslaved people formed spirituals, a new genre of music. Some were work songs, while others were biblically rooted, and all were passed along orally in the folk tradition. Wisely, these songs were often used to communicate outside the bounds of the enslaver's understanding, especially when instructing freedom seekers. At other times, the spirituals helped enslaved people stand up under the heavy burdens of captivity as forms of creative resistance, self-expression, worship, or recreation.

Created by "a circumscribed community of people in bondage [spirituals] eventually came to be regarded as the first 'signature' music of the new American nation."[1] The sacred tradition of these spirituals evolved into gospel music. Spirituals were communal, carried forth orally by unknown composers, and fostered under group ownership. In comparison, Black gospel grew out of urban Northern churches in the 1920s to 1930s with recognizable artists and styles based on hymns with improvised and "bluesy" influences. Rich solos and intervals of enthusiastic worship were often embedded in this style.

As gospel grew and developed from the sacred side of the spiritual, its protest and social traditions birthed an eclectic mix of Black musical expression. Freedom songs, blues, jazz, rock 'n' roll, soul, funk, rap, and hip-hop grew from the roots of an unparalleled cultural and musical African

American heritage. When we speak of baseball and apple pie, we can proudly include African American music in the fiber of Americana. Indeed, the familiar sounds that undergird nearly all folk, religious, and popular music in this country would not exist without it.

Often imitated and appropriated, Black music in the United States is frequently seen in an adulterated state. Our children should know and appreciate authentic sounds and learn how they came to be. Given the incredible influence of our music and its infectious and "marrow-deep" (per Wesley Morris) legacy, there's no doubt that music should have a refrain in the books our children enjoy.

CUISINE

Whenever I write about our food, I get caught up in the sights, sounds, and smells. I envision a table filled to the brim with an obscene amount of delectable dishes. How can I describe soul food?

According to Sheila Ferguson, author of *Soul Food: Classic Cuisine from the Deep South*, it's just what the name implies. "It is soulfully cooked food or richly flavored foods good for your ever-loving soul." But there's more to it than that. "It is a legacy clearly steeped in tradition: a way of life that has been handed down from generation to generation, from one Black family to another, by word of mouth and sleight of hand. It is both history and variety of flavor."[2] This history, legacy, and flavor set soul food apart from the broader designation of Southern cooking.

In his book *Soul Food: The Surprising Story of an American Cuisine One Plate at a Time*, culinary historian Adrian Miller describes a traditional dinner: "entrées (fried chicken, fried catfish, or chitlins); sides (black-eyed peas, greens, candied yams, and macaroni and cheese); cornbread to sop it up; hot sauce to spice it up; Kool-Aid to wash it down; and a sweet finish with a dessert plate of banana pudding, peach cobbler, pound cake, and sweet potato pie."[3] Yep, I'd say that sums it up nicely.

But while Miller chooses not to focus on regional cuisines, I would add the many famed soul food dishes of Louisiana's celebrated Creole cuisine, the Chesapeake Bay area's seafood-centered menus, and the legendary

Lowcountry cooking of South Carolina and Georgia. I'd also describe well-seasoned vegan and vegetarian dishes of Black American kitchens that long preceded current plant-based trends. And no list would be complete without grits, okra, biscuits, ham hocks, neck bones, and, of course, sweet tea. I've lived in the American South my entire adult life, and I promise you that Black folks take their sweet tea very seriously.

Black Americans feast as an outpouring of love and a means of connection. One of the quickest ways to offend an elder is to refuse her cooking. Both sets of my grandparents lived on the same street, just a few blocks apart. When visiting, we'd sleep at one house, wake up, and enjoy a breakfast of scratch-made biscuits, fried potatoes and onions, thick-cut country bacon, and savory grits with a hint of garlic.

After sitting for a sufficient amount of time, we'd make our way down to the other house, for an entirely different meal of sliced ham, smoked sausage, buttermilk waffles, and more biscuits smothered with gravy. Learning to eat just enough at both homes to avoid offending either grandmother was a sport my siblings and I trained in from our earliest years. Navigating Black kitchens (and grandmothers) is an art.

We show our care for one another and our guests through delicious food. Our cuisine is the heartbeat of gathering times, whether Sunday dinners, church picnics, family reunions, weddings, or funerals. Food laces life's valleys as we share during illness and hard times, just as it plays a starring role in our most joyous celebrations. And it fuels our playful competitive spirits as we tease and jest over who makes the best thus-and-such and argue about which cousin can best re-create so-and-so's famous dish.

Black American cultural food is well seasoned, meticulously flavored, and lovingly savored. It's as much a part of who we are as our music, and teaching children to recognize and honor it involves much more than just recipes. They have to get the *feel* of it, the energy and emotion behind the dishes, and the history of a people whose creativity turned scraps into delicacies. Kids can soak up this understanding from words and imagery as they hear stories from Black kitchens teeming with life.

VISUAL AND PERFORMING ARTS

The design and style aesthetic of Black American art is expansive. To box it into a tight space is to disregard the gifts and work of generations of artists. There's no artistic style that children need to imagine as singularly representing our culture. Instead, exposure to the movement and images conceived by Black faces, hands, and bodies will give them a steadfast appreciation for the creativity pulsing through our art.

Dance, music, and theater fueled some of our most defining eras, including the Harlem Renaissance of the 1920s and 1930s, during which Langston Hughes wrote, "We younger Negro artists who create now intend to express our individual dark-skinned selves without fear or shame. If white people are pleased we are glad. If they are not, it doesn't matter. We know we are beautiful. And ugly too . . . If colored people are pleased we are glad. If they are not, their displeasure doesn't matter either. We build our temples for tomorrow, strong as we know how, and we stand on top of the mountain, free within ourselves."[4]

Much like oral song, other performing arts traveled across the Atlantic and made their way into drum circles, cake walks, and pattin' juba (aka hambone, the slapping of hands, legs, arms, chest, and cheeks to create complex rhythms) on slave labor camps. These forms of entertainment, along with other instrumental performances, accompanying dances, and dramatic recitations, paved the foundation for today's collection of Black American arts across our nation.

My family once visited a museum exhibition called *The Dirty South: Contemporary Art, Material Culture, and the Sonic Impulse.* Unlike anything we'd previously witnessed in a traditional art museum, it captivated my children's attention, from the oldest to the youngest. The works highlighted the contributions of the American South and Black culture to the art world while showcasing how critical they are to comprehending America's past, present, and future.[5] The curators told a story of Black genius, through sculpture, painting, drawing, photography, film, and visual imagery. It gave necessary due to African American works often relegated to the back of the room in favor of "real" art.

Afterward, my oldest daughter began to see how she could use mixed media to define art on her own terms. Within months, she'd created a large-scale collage featuring pages of literature, broken porcelain, flea market antique jewelry, floral imagery, and old photographs of Black women. One of her Black handmade cloth dolls is affixed to the center of the wood-backed piece. She entered the work in a competition, and on the tag for the judges, she wrote, "I designed this doll entirely from fabric scraps as the centerpiece to this vintage-inspired work that imagines generations of women who enjoyed tea parties with dolls just like her."

I was nervous for Nina. Her piece embodied all it was meant to convey, but I was uncertain whether the judges would "get" it. But Nina walked away with a first place ribbon for our state and fourth place on the national stage. The lesson learned will be with her and me for a long time. And it's a lesson that I want all children to consider: There are no bounds to the creative energies of Black artistry.

Whether Black artists pull from their own experiences or the joys and struggles of our people, their work deserves to be seen. Seen for its unique expression rather than in comparison to an arbitrary European standard. It should be seen on the walls of art museums around the world, shared with students launching artistic, academic, and tech careers, and shown to our kids in our homes as we lay a foundation of what art is, can, and should be.

Art historian and curator Janet Dees says, "Art does not necessarily directly change things, but art can change people, and people change things. In providing a window unto perspectives that may be different from our own, it cultivates empathy; by being a mirror of our own or similar experiences, it provides solace."[6] Empathy and solace are worthy of pursuit, and the fact that art is engaging and inspiring to behold only adds to its allure.

Illustrations birthed from Black hands are embedded in many of the *Soul School* books, so the very act of reading them will naturally put engaging Black art in front of our children's eyes. Beyond that, some books showcase visual and performing artists whose stimulating work embodies our culture. Children will walk away knowing that Black people have always created and will continue to create art.

· · · · · · ◇ · · · · · ·

COMMUNICATION AND LANGUAGE

African Americans have a strong sense of culture and heritage, and language has been a significant means of cultivating our distinct identity. Black American cultural practices have impacted American popular culture and even global culture to an incredible degree, and language has been a tremendous component of this influence. The language of Black America has been given various names over time, including Ebonics, African American Vernacular English (AAVE), African American English (AAE), Black English, and African American Language. But regardless of how linguists choose to refer to it, our language has been incorporated into music, art, literature, and many other areas in which "standard American English" was once the only norm.

Black English, as I choose to call it, is not static. Regional varieties span our country, particularly the American South and major cities. From my experience living in metro Atlanta, I can attest that even within the same region, Black English varies between urban centers and outlying rural areas. As with other areas of cultural innovation, the creativity found within our language and style of communication is boundless.

Some Black Americans mostly or solely speak Black English, while many others style shift ("code switch") depending on their mood, environment, or the company they're keeping. Even Black people who choose not to use much Black English, or those who never learned to speak it, can typically understand and easily recognize when it's being mocked or spoken incorrectly because there are rules and grammatical structure to our language, as with any other.

My husband and I weave in and out of Black English with ease, as it's something we've always done. We intentionally use it around our children because we want them to learn and appreciate the intricacies of our cultural language as they grow so they, too, can enjoy using it as they see fit. We also use Black English with friends and family outside of our home. And then again, sometimes we don't. The fluidity of language is a unique asset that most African Americans possess. Despite the prejudices often targeting Black English from outside, and even within the Black community, I consider it a rich part of our history and heritage.

Linguist Chi Luu writes, "It's ironic that Black English speech is still dismissed and devalued as being linguistically broken, and at the same time is one of the richest sources of lexical innovation in English. It's clear that the linguistic creativity of Black English and African American vernacular speech, which across history has contributed so much to standard American English and American culture, is something to celebrate, not despise."[7] The *Soul School* books featuring Black English are meant to be celebratory. Though the language itself is never explicitly called out, its casual and intermittent use will help destigmatize our speech and prevent children from seeing it as inferior, uneducated, or ignorant.

Tip: If you or your child struggle with pronouncing some of the texts featuring Black English or African American vernacular, lean on read-aloud videos (often found on YouTube) and audiobooks to see you through.

SCIENCE AND SPORTS

African Americans have made a distinctive mark in both science and sports, yet only one is regularly associated with our people.

If they haven't already, children will quickly pick up on the dominance of Black athletes in some of America's most popular sports, including football and basketball. And for Black children, especially boys, that recognition can lead to great heights or down dangerous paths. Some feel the shame of misplaced expectations because they don't want to play or can't play sports. Others feel the burden of being a gifted athlete who gets stereotypically labeled as "just another Black jock."

By celebrating the achievements of Black athletes in the same way that we celebrate artistic, scientific, musical, academic, literary, or any other types of accomplishments, we remove this ridiculous pressure. We also override the tendency for stereotypes to creep into children's minds as they try to make sense of what they see on TV without guidance from well-informed adults. Finally, stories of Black athletic success can build a foundation for our children's understanding of the behind-the-scenes finances and power dynamics of sports. Hopefully, they'll even begin to wonder why the people in charge of nearly all-Black teams are rarely ever Black.

Sports is just one area in which African Americans have excelled, and often, our top athletes use their fame to bring attention to social issues impacting our communities. We want to explore the hardships many of our athletes have endured on their way to the top as we celebrate their breakthroughs with joy.

Running alongside this honoring of Black American athletic achievement, kids will read the same inspiring stories about our scientists, naturalists, architects, designers, and others who have also used their minds to make a difference. These men and women led breakthroughs and helped solve societal issues through technological advancements, new findings or designs, and carefully executed research. Their numbers are not few, but their stories are rarely heard. We need to change that. A broad understanding of African Americans must include a balanced view of our drive, dedication, and proven passion for excellence across vast and varied fields.

THE BLACK CHURCH

The Black Church has played a vital role in the history and culture of African American people. From the teaching and preaching to the music and worship, Sunday services were a much-needed weekly respite for a community that spent the other six days fighting for the right to exist. It's been during these gatherings that Black people have had space to lead and breathe outside the gaze of those who would interfere with their expressions of life, liberty, and the pursuit of happiness. The building housed meetings and operations for social change before, during, and after the Civil Rights Movement.

"The Black Church was the cultural cauldron that Black people created to combat a system designed to crush their spirit. Collectively and with enormous effort, they refused to allow that to happen. And the culture they created was sublime, awesome, majestic, lofty, glorious, and at all points subversive of the larger culture of enslavement that sought to destroy their humanity,"[8] writes historian and professor Henry Louis Gates, Jr., in *The Black Church: This Is Our Story, This Is Our Song.*

The books selected for *Soul School* aren't meant to proselytize. Beyond the Black Christian church, there are books featuring Muslim characters and traditional African religious practices. Your family's choice of which, if any, faith to pursue is yours alone. The selected works are intended to display the undeniable role of the Black Church in our past and its impact on our present. To say that we're teaching children about African American culture without mentioning the church intentionally skews the narrative.

My family and I are Christ followers, and I draw strength from the historical record of faith rooted in our community. But even if we weren't, and I didn't, I would still read these same stories to my children. The books chosen are included to teach, not preach. I hope that all families will walk away with a greater understanding of how the Black Church, despite its faults, contributed to our resiliency, self-expression, and sense of hope.

HAIR, SKIN, AND BEAUTY SENSE

Trying to summarize the need for children to lovingly wrap their arms around Black hair and skin feels like a daunting task. Entire books and films have devoted hundreds of pages and hours of research and interviews to this topic. And here I am trying to explain its importance in our kids' lives in just a few short paragraphs. Knowing that my explanation only scratches the surface, here I go.

Black hair and skin, in all their wondrous varieties, have been systematically demonized on American soil. Even today, despite the increase in awareness and imagery, our hair continues to be labeled as unkempt and even indecent, as evidenced by the many dress code policies specifically targeting natural Black hairstyles in schools and other organizations. It's hard to wrap our minds around how natural hair, worn the way it grows from our heads, is still labeled as unprofessional or unacceptable. And worst of all is the contempt for Black hair that occurs within the Black community. It cuts deeper than the shame piled on from others because it reflects generations of self-hatred permeating our veins.

Alongside the drama associated with Black hair is the pervasive negative discourse over African American skin, ranging from the white carried by my paternal grandmother to the darkest of darks carried by my great-grandfather and every tone in between. Turn on the news on any given night, and you'll walk away with a story that enters the realm of race—skin color. Though artificially constructed by humankind, this idea of race once tore our nation apart, and some days, it looks as though some of the progress made since then is being eroded right before our eyes. Before the eyes of our children. On our watch.

These vestiges of bondage and chattel slavery are also reflected across the diaspora, where colonialism left a wake of collateral damage in the minds of our people. During our time in Ghana, I was struck by the pervasive colorism that my family experienced. My gorgeous, lighter daughter with loose corkscrew curls was happily acknowledged with wonder and admiration. My gorgeous, darker daughter with abundant tight curls was set aside and bombarded with questions about how she could possibly be her sister's "backbone" (younger sibling). Whether in the braiding shop or the market, we received regular reminders that a hierarchy had long been established, and sixty-plus years of independence from colonial rule hadn't even begun to rattle the lies.

Children need to know that Black hair and skin are phenomenal. We are not all the same. We look different from one another, and those differences are noticed even by infants. To deny this fact or try to ignore it is to deny our kids the opportunity to grow in wisdom and admiration for all humanity.

Beyond the most noticeable features of skin and hair, African American culture also carries its own sense of beauty. The dictionary defines beauty as "the quality or aggregate of qualities in a person or thing that gives pleasure to the senses or pleasurably exalts the mind or spirit."[9] When I move in predominantly Black spaces, I see different expressions of beauty through design, fashion, style, décor, and more. I'm unable to define it, but there is always a confident display of what *we* believe to be beautiful. That doesn't mean we don't recognize beauty in other people or places—quite the contrary. But we lovingly cradle the standards of beauty bursting through Black American culture because there are times when we are the only ones doing so.

There are two ways that our children can learn about and celebrate our defining physical characteristics: through subtle observation of the imagery and descriptions across nearly all of the books and direct teaching conducted in a subset of the works. This is not an area where we can fool around. Our kids should walk away with full recognition of the inherent beauty of Black bodies. They should be infected with what editor and author Hoyt Fuller called "a fever of affirmation."[10] Can I get an amen?

DEFINING CULTURAL IDENTITY

Food. Art. Language. Science. Sports. Church. Beauty. These things alone don't encompass all of who we are. "Culture of any kind can be grounding and comforting, creating a home for nourishment and rules for understanding ourselves. But at a certain point, a cultural identity too tightly defined keeps us from growing."[11] These words from film producer Justin Simien guide my work. No single expression of Blackness accurately defines us, but some threads are woven through a recognizable tapestry, and they're worthy of exploration.

A childhood of reading about Black American culture won't result in children understanding every manifestation of our identity. The idea isn't to say, "This is all we are." Instead, "This is our story. Add chapters, write in the margins, and rearrange things. Make it yours." I want kids to appreciate and embrace Black American culture as an empowering springboard, not a limiting box. The ideas they'll soak up are those defined by our people, not the stereotypes or commercial embodiments that someone else thinks we are or should be. And this is only the starting point.

As children dig in, they'll find that we are complex, multifaceted, dynamic, and FUN! Any attempt to encapsulate who we are through a single medium—literature—has limitations. Even so, what Black authors and illustrators have gifted us is one of the richest cultural journeys our children can take. I hope *Soul School* creates a hunger in children that will spur them through a lifetime of reading widely, including—and perhaps especially—Black stories.

2

INTANGIBLE ASSETS

*I am what time, circumstance, history, have made of me, certainly, but
I am, also, much more than that. So are we all.*

—JAMES BALDWIN

B lack is nuanced. The intangible assets that undergird Black American
culture are foundational to understanding what makes us unique.
Subtle expressions of our shared culture that naturally appear in daily
living are not usually taught. They're absorbed over time, making them harder
to grasp but all the sweeter when intimately understood. Let's move beyond
the most recognizable cultural markers into less noticeable expressions of the
Black American experience.

Like all cultural groups, Black Americans are not a monolith. We're a rich
tapestry of varying, sometimes even contradicting, viewpoints, behaviors,
and identities. Though we may joke about this or that being or not being
Black, we hold to the idea that Black people show up in myriad ways. There is
no single way to "be Black."

At the same time, deeply rooted and commonly held beliefs and values
help define our culture, even if they're not held or followed by everyone
equally or at all. They're influenced by geography, family structure, and economic conditions, but they've withstood the tests of time and trial. Nailing
down these values and ideas is no easy feat. It requires years of quiet studying,

noticing, observing, and paying attention to the things that repeatedly arise in specific contexts and not in others. Black people in America generally talk about, believe, do, and say things that aren't seen, acted upon, or experienced the same way by others.

I'll focus on a few areas that can most readily be identified in children's literature. Remember, it's not any one of these ideas or *ingredients*, if you will, taken individually that Black Americans can claim as their own. Instead, it's the recipe itself: the combination of common ingredients mixed in specific ratios and cooked in a particular way by hands that have been stirring the same pot for generations.

INTERGENERATIONAL BONDING

The role and respect of elders in Black American culture cannot be overstated. Our oldest family members and seniors are regarded with the utmost respect. Grandparents, especially grandmothers, are seen nearly as royalty, always deserving of absolution and our highest regard. A part of the deference our elders receive is based solely on age and social authority, as we honor them as legacy keepers. These ingrained feelings toward older generations are also rooted in reverence, for the hardships and pervasive racism we know they endured, and gratitude for their past (and continued) sacrifices that buoy our lives today. We want to honor them. We want them to be proud of us and know their suffering was not in vain. We especially want to remove as many emotional, physical, or financial burdens as possible so they can enjoy their days. In short, we seek to give them back some of what they poured into us (and our parents) to the best of our abilities.

Speaking or acting disrespectfully to an older adult is a huge no-no. I've seen even the roughest and toughest among us remove his hat and quickly give up a seat to a grandma or auntie. Titles of respect or endearment ("Mama," "Mother," "Sister," "Brother," "Aunt," "Uncle," "Ma'am," and "Sir") are frequently used.

But this esteem is not one-sided; Black people adore their children and grandchildren. Alex Haley once said, "Nobody can do for little children what grandparents do. Grandparents sort of sprinkle stardust over the lives of little children."[1] If you're ever in doubt, do or say something ugly to a little one in front of an old Black granny, and you'll find out "real quick," as folks say. And just as the matriarchs and patriarchs in Black families are known for their fierce love and attachment, they're also known for saying things that no one else could get away with. At times, we sigh, snicker, or stare in mortification, but those moments are usually seen as endearing in their way.

I used to take the presence of older women and their advice for granted. I had grandmothers and a slew of older aunts and family friends who were always up for a visit and never more than a phone call away, which I considered the norm. But age, illness, distance, and time whittled away at my little circle. By the time I became a mother, I was left to muddle through alongside my peer group with few intimate ties to previous generations. I lamented the void their missing attention and wisdom left in my life, and at times, I felt helpless trying to reclaim some of what they'd shown me as I worried and rejoiced over my husband. My babies. Myself.

In Maya Angelou's first autobiography, *I Know Why the Caged Bird Sings*, she says she was told to "listen carefully to what country people called mother wit. That in those homely sayings was couched the collective wisdom of generations."[2] In that passing sentence, I found direction pointing me to a new understanding of how to reclaim a portion of what I so profoundly missed. I realized that my real-life heroines had left me with "mother wit" that I could cherish as I grew my own family and eventually became a mentor to those behind me.

"Always cook extra so you never have to turn away a friend or foe."

"Wear an apron when you're working so folks know not to pester you when you take it off."

"Don't let anyone borrow more than you're willing to lose with a smile."

"Marry a man who lets you overhear him telling others how much he loves you."

"Don't ever mistake service for weakness."

And my personal favorite, delivered by my maternal grandmother, Mabel Louise Meeks, as I sat on her sofa at twenty-two years old: "Keep a dime between your knees until he adds an 'r' to your title." That was well before Beyoncé reminded us to "put a ring on it." Leave it to old Black women to tell it like it is.

The bonds formed between grandparents and their grandchildren, between great-aunts and -uncles and their cherished nieces and nephews, and even among cross-generational cousins are influencers of Black culture across the globe. Wisdom and advice are doled out from older people as younger ones offer new understandings to their elders in an interplay that closes the generational gap. Intergenerational ties guide us and sometimes even define us, and young readers will see these precious relationships reflected in much of the *Soul School* literature.

EXTENDED KINSHIP

Family ties are undeniable, and the branches of Black family trees are often expanded, condensed, and blurred. Grandfamilies, households in which children are primarily raised by grandparents, are common. Cousins are seen as close relatives, even if they're third cousins or cousins twice removed and the such. The elusive "distant relative" designation is reserved for people we don't know rather than for how far away a person may sit on the family tree.

The term cousin (or aunt, uncle, etc.) doesn't even have to refer to a blood relative. Fictive kinship, or unrelated people with such a close emotional relationship that they're considered family, is a vibrant part of Black American life. Playfully known as "framily" (friends as family), the history of claiming relatives with whom we share no bloodline is so common that sometimes we forget it's even a thing. These relationships are apparent in everyday dealings; they appear during significant life events and can be found amid major traditions, including family reunions. For many Black families, their large annual or biannual gatherings are essential rituals that contribute to the strength and endurance of family (and *framily*) relationships.

What constitutes family and community is flexible and can be expanded to create safe spaces for socializing, living, and creating support systems. The extended kin network is a salient structure for Black families, and children will see this interconnectedness in our stories.

AFRICAN DIASPORA CONNECTIONS

Black people worldwide carry aspects of a common culture based on their shared experiences of enslavement, persecution, colonialism, exploitation, oppression, and abuse. This is an undeniable reality that can't be reworked or sugarcoated. Despite these connections rooted in hardship, these groups share artistic expressions, cuisine, storytelling, and values.

Relationships between African, African American, Afro-Caribbean, and Afro-Latino people can be complicated by racism (external and internalized), colorism, stereotypes, cultural ignorance, competition, financial hardship, social class, and dysfunction. At the same time, those relationships are often laced with joyful cultural exchange, camaraderie, friendship, and sometimes close family ties. The quest for more of the latter leads many families, including mine, to pursue learning from, about, and within global Black communities.

According to a 2021 report from the Pew Research Center, most Black immigrants in the United States are from only two regions of the world: "Almost nine-in-ten (88 percent) were born in African or Caribbean countries . . . The remaining 12 percent of Black immigrants are from other parts of the world, with Guyana, Mexico, and Honduras as the top three countries of origin."[3] Historically, Black immigrants and U.S.-born Black Americans haven't held close bonds (though many individuals within those populations indeed forged strong relationships). This tension persists, but technology, globalization, and enhanced cultural awareness have inspired individuals and, to some degree, entire groups to embrace one another. Connections within the global diaspora are growing stronger.

Cooperation among Afrodiasporic people is essential to the emotional and financial well-being of Black people, and enhanced education around shared history, cultural norms, and common traditions is a necessary step toward thriving relationships. By experiencing early positive representations of various Black cultures through experiences, relationships, literature, and storytelling, children will quickly see beyond stereotypes and misrepresentations as they engage in honest dialogue and life-giving relationships with Black people worldwide.

Attempting to fully separate the experience of Black Americans from Africa, the broader Americas, the Caribbean, and other parts of the world is like watching my pickiest eater try to pluck each fleck of green seasoning out of my cooking. It's just not going to work. And why would we even want to try? Black American culture doesn't exist in a vacuum. We influence and are influenced by our African roots and sisters and brothers throughout the Caribbean and beyond. Our interrelated cultures and parallel histories have created joy-filled bonds that will continue to withstand the strain of past and present struggles as we increasingly choose to share our lives.

OUR RELATIONSHIP TO THE LAND

Complicated and beautiful. That's how I would characterize Black Americans' relationship with the environment. Historically, we were forced to work lands for little or no pay through slavery, sharecropping, and tenant farming. Segregation and racial violence impacted how we moved and where we spent time, and the "public" lands of the great outdoors haven't always been available to us in the same ways or at all. These experiences, coupled with our movements away from the lush American South, have colored the collective experiences of African Americans and the outdoor world.

"For black people, navigating both city streets and hiking trails can be charged; at worst, they are fraught terrains where we are at the mercy of someone else's interpretation of our presence."[4] These thoughts from storyteller and cultural geographer Carolyn Finney echo the ideas found in her book *Black Faces, White Spaces: Reimagining the Relationship of African Americans to the Great Outdoors.*

We lack representation in many organizations charged with nurturing and communicating care for the environment and promoting how people engage with it. These groups are often not speaking to Black people with their messaging or don't know how to communicate in ways that align with our values and priorities. We're regularly seen as a low priority due to the fallacy that we don't want to be outdoors.

Even a cursory survey reveals many reasons Black people have a reputation for avoiding time outside, especially in uncultivated spaces. At the same time, precolonial Africans and African American enslaved people had a deep knowledge of the natural world that served them well for foraging, harboring, and more. Black folks have long been involved in environmentalism, herbalism, and horticulture as scientists, activists, healers, growers, and just around-the-way purveyors of goodness for their families. This history of voluntarily working the land and enjoying nature points to our ongoing, close, and intimate knowledge of the natural environment rarely portrayed in literature, media, or elsewhere.

Our great-grandmothers had gardens before it was fashionable, even in urban settings. My grandfather farmed acres of land my family still owns, but it was some miles from the family home, so my grandmother grew her bounty in a tiny dirt strip just to the left of my grandparents' back-alley carport in small-town USA. It wasn't much, but it was hers, and I have fond memories of watching her snap green beans and pick turnip greens. Homegrown and farm-raised fresh food have been Black folks' thing since forever.

As I write this, a corner of our basement is filled with gear as we prepare for a tent camping excursion with ten families from our homeschooling group. We'll be on an eighty-acre Black-owned property with a fishing pond and walking trails. We've already reserved our next camping trip at a local state park. My husband and I didn't grow up camping. My childhood didn't involve doing anything outside beyond walking from an air-conditioned or heated car to an air-conditioned or heated building and back again. But as an adult, I saw the limitations in that mindset and wanted so much more for my kids.

In *A Place to Belong*, I share ideas for families interested in finding meaning in their own contexts at the intersection of the land, nature, and history. Whether you live in the country, suburbs, or the city, there's beauty to be found. Across the nation, Black people work the land they own, make much of abandoned inner-city plots, and find joy in nature. We relish our connections to our ancestors and the legacies we build with and for our children. We regularly socialize outside with friends and family, and our engagement in outdoor recreation is rapidly increasing. Most importantly, we're having fun!

Soul School books show children that history impacts our relationships with each other and the environment. They'll understand that Black people engage with, and belong in, the natural world despite the complexities of the human-nature bond. By absorbing these messages early and often, I hope the next generation will grow up with more informed thoughts about who does and does not belong outside.

SOUTHERN ROOTS AND INFLUENCES

The South is unlike any other region of the United States. Its culture of stories, customs, music, expressions, and foodways is recognizable to anyone who has spent significant time there. I grew up in suburban Chicago, but I've spent my adult life below the Mason-Dixon Line. I was initially exposed to Southern culture through summers and holidays with extended family in southern Illinois, where my parents were raised.

I understood the vernacular and was accustomed to eating grits, so I thought I knew the South. But I discovered just how much I had to learn as a college student in Tallahassee. Mentions of the Sunshine State call up pictures of Mickey Mouse and Miami Beach, but Tallahassee is in northern Florida, and it's best to think of it as an annexation of Georgia. I arrived with an unprecedented level of naiveté regarding the people, their mannerisms, and the unwritten codes and mores of the area.

By graduation, I'd finally started to feel comfortable with the lingo and different pace of life. I knew that a buggy is a shopping cart, not a horse-drawn carriage, and cars piled up on the road are in a wreck, not an accident. I understood that college football is a religion and "bless your heart" isn't actually a blessing. I moved to North Carolina and Virginia before settling in Georgia, where I've lived for nearly twenty years. In each of these locales, I picked up vital clues on how the South has impacted and been impacted by African American culture, along with the ins and outs of Southern hospitality. Living down here is a "whole thing," as my neighbor used to say, and though I've been frustrated at times by my lack of understanding, there's nowhere I'd rather be.

More than a third of all U.S. residents call the South home, making it our nation's most populous region. Despite the Great Migration in the first half of the twentieth century, most Black people live in the South, and the influences formed in Southern states have remained the bedrock of Black American culture. Today, roughly 55 percent of the Black American population resides in the Southern United States. The balance is split between the Midwest (18 percent), the Northeast (17 percent), and the West (10 percent).[5]

Southern heritage is diverse. It includes significant African, Native American, and European influences, and its land is just as diverse as its people. Many of the stories shared in Soul School reflect the lived experiences of Black people in the South. Against this backdrop, children will learn of the music, food, history, and people that have come together to form much of what we consider Black American culture.

However, careful consideration is given not to overrepresent this area because Southern culture is not synonymous with Black culture. The urban centers and suburban outposts in other parts of the United States have contributed to and continue to pour into the ever-changing vibrancy of African American life. They, too, deserve recognition and exploration.

CULTURAL COMMUNICATION, MANNERISMS, AND IDIOMS

How we communicate extends beyond pronunciation, grammar, and inflection. Black Americans have distinctive forms and styles of expression that enhance intragroup comprehension and connection. Our mannerisms, sayings, and delivery techniques have been abusively mocked and denigrated for laughs. Still, misuse and disrespect haven't changed our love for and use of culturally rooted idioms, creative wordplay (sometimes called *signifyin'*), and expressive language delivery.

Henry Louis Gates, Jr., explored the history and usage of signifyin' in his book *The Signifying Monkey: A Theory of Afro-American Literary Criticism*, where he discussed its use in Black literature and music. Signifyin' is the "practice of representing an idea indirectly, through a commentary that is often humorous, boastful, insulting, or provocative."[6] Encoding a message with double meaning requires cultural knowledge or experience to reinterpret the intended message accurately.

For example, having grown up around relatives and others sharing commonly understood idioms and folk sayings, loud-talking (saying something loud enough for the intended party to hear but indirectly enough that they won't necessarily respond), playing the dozens (casually trading insults with someone about their family members, especially their mothers, in front of an audience), and participating in other wordplays, all of it feels second nature to many Black people. Though some of these practices may sound mean-spirited or inappropriate to an uninformed outsider, seasoned participants fully recognize that traditions like playing the dozens are typically considered affectionate play and aren't meant to be taken seriously.

I experienced the potential misunderstandings of cultural wordplay directly when I recommended *Lies and Other Tall Tales* in the Melanated Tales Heritage Pack lesson guide shared on my website. The book is filled with exaggerations and playful insults collected by late author and anthropologist Zora Neale Hurston and adapted and illustrated by Christopher Myers. It's one of the most direct examples of embellished quips that I've seen in children's literature, and I included it as an example of such with the assumption that it would be read aloud and edited on the fly as needed. Examples included:

> *"I knowed a man so smart, he had the seven-year itch and scratched it out in three months."*

> *"You is sho' nuff strowin' it."*

> *"Once I seen wind so hard till it blowed a man's nose off his face and onto the back of his neck, and if he got a cold, every time he sneeze, he blow his hat off."*[7]

Within weeks, I received the first complaint. A parent who didn't understand the book, the language used, or any of its contents felt let down by the recommendation. I tried to explain the cultural relevancy and the book's importance as an anthropological artifact, but she couldn't wrap her mind around it. I learned firsthand how cultural exposure and knowledge are imperative for extracting meaning and relevance from communication devices that aren't mainstream in the broader American culture.

Nonverbal gestures are also a way to communicate thoughts and feelings. The up nod acknowledges the familiar presence of another Black person. It's a way of saying "Hey" or "I see you." Giving dap is a quintessentially Black handshake that is much more than it seems on the surface. Black soldiers developed it during the Vietnam War as a creative way to convey solidarity. Originally standing for "dignity and pride," the dap has evolved into a universal communication for brotherhood between close friends and even strangers. Along with the up nod, dapping is another method of demonstrating belonging and acceptance within the Black community.

So, whether it's through a traditional tall tale, familiar call-and-response language, African-rooted storytelling devices, signs and signals, or other elements of Black American culture exposed through literature, kids will gain a familiarity with not only how we speak but also how we play with and deliver words to convey meaning to eyes and ears who understand. In most cases, this type of learning is subtle and more caught than taught.

THE POWER OF BLACK JOY

Black Joy is the summoning of a protected healing space inside ourselves that occurrences of traumatic and disturbing racialized encounters cannot pierce. It's not an invented superpower, but we certainly did make it up "here on this bridge between starshine and clay,"[8] and it's a controllable internal response that offers solace and restricted access to our hearts. Black Joy is an empowering and boundless source of whatever we need in a given moment: quiet rest, uplifting inspiration, boisterous celebration, rhythmic dancing, joyous song, happy tears, lively discussion, peaceful silence, and so on.

Black people have endured suffering while smiling, singing, dancing, and gathering. This behavior is not a denial of hardship or our lived experiences. Instead, it's a reclamation of control over our spirits and emotional health. It's an actively resistant "You-can-do-this-and-that-but-what-you-won't-do-is-rob-me-of-my-joy" (*clap, clap, clap, clap, clap*) type of thing. The idea that Black people can experience goodness despite . . . everything . . . is Black Joy. It's individual, it's collective, and the well never runs dry.

These are but a handful of the intangible assets and values at work behind the scenes of Black American culture. There are limitations in defining an entire culture with a collection of children's books. Black American culture is a deeply rooted yet constantly morphing set of beliefs, actions, and values that permeate millions of people. A single story will never demonstrate the fullness of who we are and what we value, and this book should not be seen as a static and definitive statement. Still, the blended tapestry of literary voices, images, histories, and stories presents an authentic and intimate view of ideas we hold dear. Please consider *Soul School* the beginning of a lifelong exploration of an ever-evolving work of art.

3

PAIN, PROTEST, AND PRIDE

No man can know where he is going unless he knows exactly where
he has been and exactly how he arrived at his present place.

—MAYA ANGELOU, *THE NEW YORK TIMES*
(APRIL 16, 1972)

lack is resilient. The story of our lives—from Africa to North America, from long ago and just the other day—is constantly being challenged. Black history is seemingly optional to most curricula, and as we've seen lately, even undisputed facts are on the chopping block if it's determined that they may make children think critically about the past and how it impacts our present day.

These issues are making headlines, but they're nothing new. Black parents have always worried about what their children are (and are not) learning in school. Even before Black history became contentious in classrooms, parents charged with raising Black children were lobbying for a more diverse curriculum. They've fought for their children to be seen by teachers, administrators, and other students, and they've longed for their kids to see themselves in their schoolbooks and other resources.

In some ways, the efforts to erase Black people from the main thread of American history have been overwhelmingly successful. Campaigns to sanitize school textbooks, suppress compelling parts of our story, and create a mandatory body of general educational knowledge that isn't dependent on knowing much about our existence or influence are remarkably well-executed.

There's an ongoing effort to contain our history and culture, but it has proved unsuccessful. Many want to sweep the brutality we've experienced in the Americas under the rug, hoping that we can all move on without full reckoning. But how much of the past is really in the past? And why, despite the full-court press, do the stories of our ancestors continue to rise from the ashes?

When I recently ran across this 1935 quote from W.E.B. Du Bois, I was stunned. I can't believe that nine decades ago, Du Bois—a historian, sociologist, and author—was saying something as piercingly relevant:

> If history is going to be specific, if the record of human action is going to be set down with that accuracy of faithfulness of detail which will allow its use as a measuring rod and guidepost for the future of nations, there must be set some standards of ethics in research and interpretation. If, on the other hand, we are going to use history for our pleasure and amusement, for inflating our national ego, and giving us a false but pleasurable sense of accomplishment, then we must give up the idea of history either as a science or as an art using the results of science, and admit frankly that we are using a version of historic fact in order to influence and educate the new generations along the way we wish.[1]

The history of Black Americans has been labeled divisive, debatable, political, and polarizing. But our presence prevents it from being eradicated. Our very bodies are an ever-present reminder of what happened on this soil, and no amount of rearranging and cleansing will change that. Our DNA tells a fact-based story that our hearts and minds corroborate, and for as long as we have breath, our history will endure.

Cultural anxiety is rattling our nation, and our children are suffering. They're stuck between warring adults who can't decide whether to ignore our traumatic past or hang it out for all to see. As school boards, teachers, politicians, and parents jockey for power over curriculum and narratives, our kids are left to make sense of the world without a cohesive message from the people they trust most. This issue impacts children across our country, regardless of background or ethnicity, and given the intensity of the heated debate, a widely accepted solution can't reasonably be expected anytime soon.

In James Baldwin's *Collected Essays*, he wrote, "It took many years of vomiting up all the filth I'd been taught about myself, and half-believed, before I was able to walk on this earth as though I had a right to be here."[2] This is what many parents are trying to avoid: years of their children having to work through and undo the false messages they've received about Black people. About themselves. About others. It sounds like something that should be easy, but common ground is elusive; parents are increasingly concerned, and rightfully so.

But within our homes, we have the sole say in what our children learn. We can drown out lies of ignorance, fear, and hate. And we can fill the void left by lies of omission. We have the right to give our kids an expansive and honest view of the past alongside a hopeful sense of the future, and we're responsible for doing both well. It's our job. Having the support of school boards and politicians would be mighty nice, but their stamp of approval is unnecessary. They only control the ordinary and are unable to contain the extraordinary.

It's impossible to tell the story of America without including Black people. Not a little, but a lot. Our sacrifices and contributions—those stolen and those freely given—are so inextricably woven into the genesis and rise of the United States of America that anything less than complete integration into the fabric of the historical record is unsatisfactory. Ideally, Black history would flow through American history as a fundamental and integral inner-working rather than be set apart as a "nice-to-have" for people who are into it.

Carter G. Woodson, the "father of Black history," famously said, "We should emphasize not Negro History, but the Negro in History. What we need is not a history of selected races or nations, but the history of the world void of national bias, race hatred, and religious prejudice."[3]

That ideal still holds today. That's what we *should* have. It's what we need. But Woodson also established Negro History Week, the precursor to Black History Month, in 1926 as he championed this idea of a fully integrated history. Let's follow in his footsteps with a departure from either/or in favor of both: continued and relentless efforts toward the inclusion of Black people and our experiences permanently embedded in the American and global history canons AND a targeted and persistent study of Black history, specifically, independent of other efforts and inquiries. We don't have to choose.

Starting with Africa's great kingdoms and encompassing the Black experience on American soil from the 1600s to today, *Soul School* gives a taste of the significant swaths of time to be covered in an ideal survey of Black American history for children and teens. From the transatlantic slave trade and America's peculiar institution of chattel slavery to Reconstruction, Jim Crow, and World War I. From the Great Migration and the explosive Harlem Renaissance to the Great Depression and World War II. From the Civil Rights Movement to the Black Power Movement and the years since, there is much to be explored through literature as we help children understand the past and how it impacts our collective present and future.

Soul School is not a deconstructed textbook, and the books that cover major historical events and the people who lived through them are not presented in a neat chronological box. Instead, the history is intermingled with inspiring poetry, uplifting storytelling, incredible fantasy and sci-fi worlds, and stunning art as part of a grand story. This book presents history as a natural flow of ideas that children will engage with consistently but not exclusively. History is embedded in Black culture, but it alone does not speak to who we are today.

Soul School books tell readers what Black people were doing and experiencing during early and modern historical eras. Some people covered are well-known, even famous, while the world has been much more silent about others. Whether told through nonfiction narrative or historical fiction, some books most certainly include hardship and tragedy, but the history is shared age-appropriately and redeemed with truth and triumph. The stories are told through the eyes of Black people who met the challenges of their day and left a legacy of hope, not despair. Their accomplishments, sometimes just their existence, are celebrated and included in books for every age group.

Among the tougher topics are uplifting stories of creativity, ingenuity, and joy. We have an expansive history. We were thinkers and doers before, during, and after the worst times. Black American culture is dynamic and innovative, and for every story of struggle and pain, we have a counter-story of perseverance and progress. Pride and pain characterize our history, and to tell one side without the other would leave far too much unsaid.

While the *Soul School* literature can create affection and informed curiosity while whetting the appetite, it alone is not enough to encompass the fullness of Black American history. However, it serves as an excellent foundation and jumping-off point for further exploration. The following pages will help you connect with the historical content and ideas your children will encounter in some of the history books in part 2.

AFRICAN KINGDOMS

When children learn of the Middle Ages, they typically only hear of European powers and knights in shining armor. During these same years, the West African kingdoms of Ghana, Mali, and Songhai were flourishing with well-organized societies, established family structures, lucrative trade routes, and thriving industry. There are thousands of years of recorded history, including these and other African civilizations, and this is where the study of Black history should begin for our children. Not with enslavement.

In *The Mis-Education of the Negro*, Carter G. Woodson expresses how detrimental it is for African history to be ignored in favor of teaching only European history. He warns that not learning African history while consistently admiring European history can "lead the negro to detest the man of African blood—to hate himself . . . With the truth hidden, there will be little expression of thought to the contrary."[4] Teaching children the historical accomplishments, achievements, and ordinary stories of Africa is a critical aspect of Black American history, perhaps even the most important.

Sadly, some of the best young people's books focusing on African kingdoms are out of print and, therefore, not included in my booklists. If you're inclined to seek them out, I recommend *The Royal Kingdoms of Ghana, Mali, and Songhay: Life in Medieval Africa* (1994) by Patricia and Frederick McKissack or *A Glorious Age in Africa: The Story of Three Great African Empires* (1965) by Daniel Chu and Elliott Skinner.

TRANSATLANTIC SLAVE TRADE, CHATTEL SLAVERY, AND REBELLION

For many children, most of their meager Black history education will come from this era. They learn that Black people were captured in Africa, brought to the United States and other places against their will, forced to pick cotton, and eventually freed. That's all true, but it's grossly oversimplified, and the details matter.

African people did not just spontaneously appear on North American shores. There's a story there. Chattel slavery didn't accidentally evolve. There's a story there. And African Americans didn't just sit and take it. They rebelled in various ways, including feigning ignorance, sabotaging tools and plans, sending messages and sharing information, learning to read and write, revolting, and emancipating themselves. There are so many stories there. (Many are told in *Resistance Stories from Black History for Kids* by Rann Miller.) This isn't an aspect of history that can be quickly gobbled up in a book or even a school year. This nation was built on the backs of enslaved African and African American people, and their stories emanate from every direction we take when discussing United States history. The stories must be told.

THE CIVIL WAR

With more than six hundred thousand deaths (more than both World Wars combined), the Civil War was the deadliest in American history, but I was well into my adult years before I even began to understand its complexities. The myth of the Lost Cause, the Confederate South's warped version, is a story that continues to be perpetuated. The Confederate flag is flown high across the United States as a symbol of hate and racism, despite the claims of "Southern pride." Children need to hear from primary sources, free from political agenda, as they understand why brother stood against brother, resulting in the end of legally sanctioned slavery. They need to be sure that the United States is united under only one flag, and many people fought and lost their lives for it to be so. Along these lines, narratives about how Black people participated in and were impacted by the Revolutionary War and World Wars are eye-opening areas of American history that aren't typically investigated in children's literature.

RECONSTRUCTION

Reconstruction was the period following the Civil War when America struggled to integrate millions of newly freed Black people into public life and the existing systems governing the land. At the same time, former Confederate states rejoined the Union and attempted to rebuild. It provides a glimpse at what almost was and why it wouldn't be.

During Reconstruction, some Black people received free education and land and were elected to state and federal governments, but the gains were short-lived. Violence and oppressive "Black Codes" choked out progress, and with the support of federal troops withdrawn, Southerners were once again free to terrorize Black people. This was a critical time in American history, encompassed in what historian Benjamin Quarles called the "decades of disappointment"[5] in his seminal text *The Negro in the Making of America*. Digging into Reconstruction gives kids a glimpse at what could have been and helps illuminate the whys and hows of racial segregation and the Jim Crow era.

THE GREAT MIGRATION

The Great Migration refers to the multiple waves of Black people who moved from the South to other parts of the United States in search of economic opportunities and relief from the South's unique brand of oppression. The initial wave in the first half of the twentieth century saw Black Southerners relocating to cities like Chicago, New York, Detroit, and Pittsburgh. World War II kicked off another big wave north and west. In all cases, Black Americans were met with continued racial disparity and various injustices, including discriminatory housing and employment practices. Still, the movement of Black ideas, customs, and talents profoundly affected American culture.

THE HARLEM RENAISSANCE

These are some of the most exciting years to study. The Great Migration and its resulting Northern Black communities fed explosive growth in music, literature, theater, photography, and other art forms in multiple cities, especially Harlem, New York. This cultural and intellectual boom of the 1920s and 1930s (declining amid the Great Depression) gave way to some of the most revered works in American history, and many of the ideas birthed during those years continue to flourish today.

The period was marked by the flowering of artistic life and a literary tradition lovingly held and fiercely protected by multiple leaders, including Langston Hughes. In his landmark essay, *The Negro Artist and the Racial Mountain*, Hughes writes of his reaction to a young Black man who told him that he wished to write like white poets:

> *But this is the mountain standing in the way of any true Negro art in America—this urge within the race toward whiteness, the desire to pour racial individuality into the mold of American standardization, and to be as little Negro and as much American as possible . . . This young poet's home is, I believe, a fairly typical home of the colored middle class. One sees immediately how difficult it would be for an artist born in such a home to interest himself in interpreting the beauty of his own people. He is never taught to see that beauty. He is taught rather not to see it, or if he does, to be ashamed of it when it is not according to Caucasian patterns.*[6]

What Hughes describes is precisely what we must avoid: that any child would believe that the words, art, thoughts, and ideas of Black people are unworthy of exploration and celebration. Appreciation of Black creativity and art does not magically appear; children must be taught to value such things. *Soul School* books offer a glorious opportunity for our kids to chase beauty because exposure breeds taste, and affection is born of familiarity.

THE GREAT DEPRESSION

The energy of the Harlem Renaissance came to an abrupt end in the face of the Great Depression, which worsened an already bleak financial existence for African Americans, who were "last hired, first fired." Black people disproportionately lost jobs and faced a much higher unemployment rate than any other group in the country. Some charities, especially in the South, refused to supply food to needy Black families, and attempts to gain employment were met with resistance and sometimes violence. Ultimately, the Second World War and the millions of defense-related jobs it provided proved to be the necessary turnaround for Black people and the entire country.

THE CIVIL RIGHTS MOVEMENT

If most of our children's Black history exposure exists within the realm of slavery, the rest of it is squeezed from the work of Martin Luther King, Jr., and Rosa Parks. Depending on the home or school, some kids know a bit about one or two other people who lived during this time, but most children's books are silent on specifics. Here, readers will find stories of freedom fighters who were young and old, teachers and students. They'll read firsthand accounts of school integrations, protests and marches, and the many attempts to resist progress at every turn. Throughout each story, the sounds of persistence, justice, and freedom will ring.

THE BLACK POWER AND BLACK ARTS MOVEMENTS

The Black Power Movement of the late 1960s and 1970s is usually ignored in history studies despite its size and influence. Part of this erasure is due to the legacy of the Black Panther Party, a nationwide organization of civil rights activists, community organizers, and militant revolutionaries. Their advocacy of self-defense in response to persistent oppression and recorded acts of violence against and by their members and communities has always been controversial. The U.S. government's targeting and repression of their efforts are equally contentious.

Ignoring the Black Power Movement is a form of suppression and is directly related to wanting to silence the history of organized resistance promulgated by Black Americans. Thinking back to Du Bois's quote earlier in this chapter, selectively choosing which stories to tell our children based on our fears or opinions of their morality is disingenuous indoctrination. The United States was founded by revolutionaries willing to shed blood to gain the humanity they felt was owed to them. They won and, therefore, got to manage the storytelling, so they are considered heroes. Those who do the same and don't (or can't) stand to tell their story will be condemned by the ones who silenced and thwarted their efforts. Exploring complicated history is not scary; it's refreshing because the past illuminates the present and gives us a greater sense of humanity.

The Black Power Movement's artistic and cultural sister, the Black Arts Movement (BAM), is sometimes called the Black Aesthetics Movement. During this time, the term *Black aesthetic* was used "to describe works of art, literature, poetry, music, and theater that centralized black life and culture. In acknowledging the historical usage of the term and understanding blackness to be iterative—something that is evolving, abundant, and prolific—we can begin to understand that the creativity of black people contributes, always, to a black aesthetic."[7]

Leroi Jones, later known as Amiri Baraka, relocated to Harlem following the murder of Malcolm X in 1965 to start the Black Arts Repertory Theatre/School (BARTS), which is often seen as the beginning of BAM. Among other things, Black Americans wore clothing, jewelry, and hairstyles associated with their African heritage. The creators used their talents and platforms to ignite a cultural revolution as young Black people were consistently and unapologetically affirmed.

BLACK LIVES MATTER

In 2013, three radical organizers—Alicia Garza, Patrisse Cullors, and Opal Tometi—created #BlackLivesMatter in response to the acquittal of Trayvon Martin's killer. In their own words, "Black Lives Matter is an ideological and political intervention in a world where Black lives are systematically and intentionally targeted for demise. It is an affirmation of Black folks' humanity, our contributions to this society, and our resilience in the face of deadly oppression,"[8] and it may be the largest movement in U.S. history.[9] That alone warrants our attention and serious study.

And since study isn't the same as agreement, how one individually feels about BLM is irrelevant when it comes to teaching our children about what it is, why it started, and how it's shaping the landscape of American society. A recent Pew Research Center survey indicates that there are significant differences in opinion on the relevancy and support of BLM. About eight in ten Black Americans (81 percent) support the movement, compared with 63 percent of Asian, 61 percent of Hispanic, and 42 percent of White Americans. Democrats and those who lean toward the Democratic Party are about five times as likely as Republicans and Republican leaners to support Black Lives Matter (84 percent vs. 17 percent). And whereas most adults ages 18 to 29 (64 percent) support the movement, 41 percent of those ages sixty-five and older do.[10]

There's no *Soul School* book dedicated to explaining BLM to children, but there are books that will help them understand the atmosphere in which it was birthed, most explicitly for high schoolers.

BUT ISN'T BLACK AMERICAN HISTORY TOO COMPLEX AND TRAUMATIC FOR KIDS?

My family likes to purchase bookish gifts for our fellow bookworm friends, and sometimes, my kids want to snag a little swag as well. After we ordered a string of custom book cover necklaces for others, my youngest daughter asked if I would purchase one for her. I thought this would be an easy yes until she informed me that the book cover necklace she planned to wear was *A Picture of Freedom: The Diary of Clotee, a Slave Girl* by Patricia C. McKissack. I had a significant issue with her wearing anything that says "slave girl" on a chain around her neck (for obvious reasons), so I proceeded to delve into her love for such a complicated book:

"I don't want you wearing jewelry that says 'slave girl,' and I'm concerned about you reading that book so many times. How many times has it been anyway?"

"I just finished reading it for the thirteenth time."

"Sasha! Why on earth do you keep reading that book?! Stories focused on the lives of enslaved people can be traumatic, and I'm worried about you constantly taking in this type of literature."

"Traumatic? I don't see it that way at all, Mama. I love reading this book because every time I do, I feel stronger. Reading it reminds me of how resilient our ancestors were and how they continued to survive no matter what was done to them. It makes me feel proud of who I am. Plus, I just like reading about the 1800s in general. And I really want that necklace."

"Wow. I never considered that perspective. You teach me so much, girl. How about if we compromise? I'll buy you the necklace as a keepsake and reminder of a book that means so much to you, but I'd prefer you not wear it. Deal?"

"Deal!"

This conversation helped me internalize the value of "hard" history (stories that are difficult to process or accept). I'm the one who purchased the book, so I knew it was an important story, but I didn't recognize that it would or even *could* elicit such positive emotions. Hearing Sasha's thoughts reminded me not to assume that my children will always experience complex history or even traumatic stories in a negative or problematic way.

Children have a fantastic ability to interact with complicated narratives, and I regularly find myself learning to see things anew through their eyes. They crave heroic tales, and they're able to see heroism where our jaded adult eyes find only hardship. Our stories are ours to know and tell, and if children feel downtrodden or hopeless after hearing them, it's not the story we need to reevaluate but rather the heart of the storyteller.

We can't shy away from Black American history just because every story isn't sugarcoated with rainbow sprinkles. Among and between the grand and sometimes difficult historical times are beautiful moments worthy of study and celebration. Battle-weary and joyful Black people and their tragic and triumphant stories. Innovators and athletes. Creators and caretakers. Revolutionaries and ordinary folks. We've reinvented and birthed new stories, relationships, and revolutions from the voids and scars left by everything taken and denied. We've withstood inexplicable and pervasive pain, but we're still standing and dancing, shouting and protesting, reading and growing, exploring and laughing. We are resilient and insightful, and thoughtful explorations of our history are priceless treasures to pass on to all children.

4

BIRDS WITH WINGS

One who sees something good must narrate it.
—UGANDAN PROVERB

*B*lack is creative, and Black storytelling has always held power. Our true stories, imaginative tales, poetry, lore, and myths celebrate expressions of childhood, culture, and place. Some of the accounts contain pain and struggle, but even they speak in loving exaltation of who we are and the many ways we show up in this world. As John Lewis said, "The movement without storytelling is like birds without wings."[1] *Soul School* is bubbling over with stories, and they undoubtedly are birds *with* wings, laced with rhythm, tradition, and joy.

We bear witness through our stories. Witness to what, you ask? Well, everything. The mundane, spectacular, heartbreaking, and priceless. The hilarious, spontaneous, confusing, and comfortable. We sing our stories and rap them, too. We bear witness through painting, photography, dance, and spoken word. We shout, whisper, and laugh while we cry them. And more than anything, we write them. The content of our stories is an immense part of what makes them unique, but the delivery situates Black storytelling in a class of its own.

"A story told by a black person, especially one who has roots in the South, could be about crossing the street, but it is never just about that. Somewhere, there is going to be something about God and grits and blue lights in the basement. There is going to be a song that includes a long-ago heartbreak and a dance, and somebody is going to tell you about the best food (or the worst) they have ever tasted. Sometimes there is a dog. It is our tradition."[2] These words by journalist Andrea Collier conjure up all sorts of connections and nostalgia. The effortless familiarity sends warm waves of solace through my body as I smile and nod in agreement. But as accurate as this is, it only represents one slice of the Black American storytelling pie.

Black literature is wide-ranging and constantly evolving. Authors often engage deeply with African, Caribbean, or African American history or cultural experiences. Still, plenty of prose (and perhaps especially verse) departs from this convention to explore vast oceans of interests and passions across time and place. Our stories may call attention to the injustices Black Americans have faced, or they may never mention any such thing.

Virginia Hamilton, the late author of *M. C. Higgins, the Great*, heralded for preserving Black oral tradition through children's literature, once said that storytelling was the first opportunity for Black folks to represent themselves as anything other than property.[3] Considering the weight of that sentiment, it's easy to see why soulful storytelling is in our bones. *Soul School* draws on this legacy of telling stories in our own words, trusting that the fullness of our voices will ring clearly in every direction.

TYPES OF LITERATURE

"For while the tale of how we suffer, and how we are delighted, and how we may triumph is never new, it always must be heard. There isn't any other tale to tell, it's the only light we've got in all this darkness."[4] The narrator in *Sonny's Blues* by James Baldwin voices the idea that tales of trauma or hard times aren't particularly original, but they provide connection and understanding that can offer a reprieve from suffering. They represent an authentic part of life, and to say otherwise is disingenuous because it sets an expectation that stories should ignore some of the lived realities of Black people. But the Black experience can't be defined by a single emotion or vantage point. All readers need to see Black characters outside the realm of racism, slavery, Jim Crow, and police brutality, and *Soul School* explores various paths toward that goal.

Some of the books weave in those necessary and valuable matters in age-appropriate, insightful ways to intrigue and inform children. To empower them to participate in the struggle and triumph alongside the characters. However, others are everyday stories where children live free of physical and emotional violence. These tales are dominated by the sweet simplicity of daily living, without assuming that delightful moments are only believable outside the context of Black family life. This is not to say that they're just white stories colored brown (which is what I think many people regard as "Black" stories). Instead, the characters are culturally, socially, and (authentically) visually Black but aren't directly addressing racially motivated drama.

Both avenues convene to create an expansive literary journey that includes Black people in every realm, where past, present, and future represent a circularity that collapses when one part is ignored. *Soul School* addresses the fullness of storytelling by exposing kids to many genres within Black American and diasporic literature. Through a mix of fiction, nonfiction, graphic novels, poetry, and prose, young readers will experience and enjoy many iterations of Black culture explored through various types of literature, including:

Afrofuturism and Africanfuturism

The Smithsonian National Museum of African American History and Culture defines Afrofuturism as an evolving concept expressed through a "Black cultural lens that reimagines, reinterprets, and reclaims the past and present for a more empowering future for African Americans . . . Black writers and artists utilize themes of technology, science fiction, fantasy, and heroism to envision stories and futures of Black liberation to convey an authentic, hopeful, and culturally expansive image of the Black experience."[5]

Nigerian American author Nnedi Okorafor defines Africanfuturism as a subcategory of science fiction that's similar to Afrofuturism but more deeply "rooted in African culture, history, mythology, and point-of-view as it then branches into the Black diaspora, and it does not privilege or center the West."[6] The distinction she makes expresses more than simply a change in locale from America to Africa; it also speaks to the fundamental structure of the story, its characters, and how they exist in the world.

These highly imaginative stories are steeped in Black culture and often history. Technology and evocative characterization assist in imagining a future of Black liberation that accounts for but moves beyond historical fact and present-day conventions. To read this type of literature opens children's minds to ideas, structure, and language they're unlikely to encounter elsewhere.

Biography and Memoir

Reading accounts of how Black individuals or groups moved through society is a spectacular way to understand the past and make sense of today. Biographies delve into tangible experiences, allowing kids to gain insight into prominent figures and ordinary individuals. They often provide valuable glimpses into the routines and experiences of fascinating people and their profound contributions to and reception from society. Whether in chapter or picture-book form, biographies and memoirs are invaluable resources for helping children comprehend people's behaviors, motivations, and the environments in which they operated. Importantly, *Soul School* includes but moves far beyond the typical Black history figures children are exposed to most often.

Drama

Drama is a form of artistic expression that permits the writer to interpret and convey ideas and emotions in refreshing ways. Stories relying on dialogue and action to share human experiences are often ripe for performance, and reading plays versus watching them can be underwhelming for kids in some circumstances. To account for this, *Soul School* uses dialogue-driven dramatic literature sparingly but intentionally, so kids (especially teens) don't miss out on seminal stories or the craft by which they were created.

Folktales

In her essay on bicultural mythology, Celestine Woo writes, "A people displaced from its homeland necessarily establishes a different relationship with its mythology, and the mythology must change to accommodate and incorporate the displacement."[7] This superbly encapsulates why African American myths and folktales share elements of traditional African tales. But they were creatively reinvented to preserve a distinctive culture while accounting for the disruption of place and experience unique to Black Americans.

Folktales, including fairy tales, tall tales, myths, and legends, enthrall children and adults alike, particularly when delivered with expressive energy. The ones selected for *Soul School* are especially attractive and culturally relevant to young people. Some are fun and playful, and others carry a more serious tone. In either case, they give voice to the joys and customs of the past while speaking into the present. Children are entertained by characters and imagery safely couched within inventive scenarios as they explore perceptions, beliefs, and ideas in some of Black America's most foundational stories.

Fantasy

Books with imaginary events, settings, or characters who rely on magic or supernatural means are essential for balancing the more realistic scenarios included in many Black stories. Fantasy books allow children to get lost in a world where our current realities don't have to be attended to, and society's rules no longer matter. The author sets up a new dynamic, and kids get to read about lots of Black people navigating the world through a storyline that isn't *about* being Black. The distinction seems inconsequential at first glance, but it's actually quite spectacular.

Books that centralize experiences around being Black, especially history and historical fiction, are vital. But books centered on Black characters nestled within their cultural landscape without maneuvering through race-based conflict are underrated gems. When our children's imaginations are fed this way, they can see a world where Black characters are self-actualized, and natural expressions of their humanity are the rule rather than an exception.

Ebony Elizabeth Thomas, author of *The Dark Fantastic: Race and the Imagination from Harry Potter to the Hunger Games*, shares that her childhood literary imagination was segregated: "Books and movies about children and teens who looked like me were read and viewed out of duty, to learn something about the past. Books and movies that showcased the pleasures of dreaming, imagination, and escape were stories about people who did not look like me. And yet I was most drawn to those magical stories, for I longed to dream."[8] This imagination gap, as Thomas calls it, in children's literature continues today, as most fantasy books don't include Black characters. When they are part of the story, they're typically billed as sidekicks. This is not the case with the fantasy books presented in *Soul School*.

These books are not white stories with the skin color changed to Black, and the Black characters are not sidelined. Instead, these tales are naturally steeped in Black culture and environments, where kids enter portals to other lands, encounter mythical creatures, and use magical powers in an imagined reality. *Soul School* fantasy books erase the "Black, serious, and realistic" vs. "white, fun-filled, and imaginative" dichotomy of Thomas's (and my) childhood.

Historical Fiction

I'm a sucker for historical fiction. I think it's one of the most powerful tools to give children a sense of the past with flavor, emotion, and interest. It situates fictional characters in historically accurate times and places while calling their humanity to the forefront. It gives our kids a glimpse at private conversations that could have been and the prevailing thoughts of the times without being entirely beholden to primary documents and cited works.

Historical fiction wraps history in recognizable story packaging that children are naturally drawn toward, and it presents the past as people-centric and connective. The language and latitude afforded by this genre fittingly offer many opportunities to examine the wholeness of the Black experience. It stands alone as a genre to keep close for a lifetime while hopefully piquing our kids' interest in delving into the nonfictional narratives that undergird their most beloved fictional stories.

"Then it was that books began to happen to me, and I began to believe in nothing but books and the wonderful world of books—where if people suffered, they suffered in beautiful language, not in monosyllables . . ."[9] Langston Hughes's idea of suffering in beautiful language speaks to me immensely. It points to the power of story to soften the blows of life's harsh realities, making the past comprehensible and showing, more directly, the redeeming qualities of humanity that always exist even amid the tempests of life's valleys.

Soul School booklists feature an abundance of historical fiction, and those books stand as a loving bridge between the imaginative and the factual, bringing clarity and cohesiveness to our children's reading experience.

Historical Nonfiction Narrative

When most people think about Black books for kids, historical nonfiction narratives come to mind. And for good reason. Despite my desire to root *Soul School* in joy-filled cultural storytelling, I've included nonfiction history books at every age level. This isn't a departure from the ideal; it's simply a broader path. Honest history is necessary and sometimes heavy, but hard doesn't mean bad. There are gems tucked between the pages of every story, even when they're not readily apparent. Learning about the past isn't always pleasurable in the traditional sense, but our role as adults is to protect and prepare our children, and the truth really does set us free.

An expansive view of our history can be joyful, and children deserve to explore the best and worst of what's transpired. They must understand that even horrible circumstances can be redeemed, and the truth is interpreted differently depending on who tells the story. "Until the story of the hunt is told by the lion, the tale of the hunt will always glorify the hunter." This African proverb adds verve to the idea that complex stories told well build character, and I'll take that over the easy button every time.

Many areas of Black history are *not* traumatic; they're naturally joyful and inspiring without any need for additional interpretation or the stretching of emotional bandwidth. To water Black history down to slavery, which, let's face it, is usually the correlation people make, is a cheapening of our story. *Soul School* books include true tales of entrepreneurs, scientists, fashion designers, athletes, dancers, musicians, artists, and more. We have imaginative stories of jubilation, liberation, and celebration that position novels and historical narratives well outside the realm of slavery and beyond the history of Black pain.

Mystery and Suspense

My oldest has always been disinterested in mystery. At least that's what she says. But it turns out that she just wants a friend along for the ride. It's like being able to grab the arm of the person next to you when a movie scene surprises or shocks you. Nina enjoys mysteries best when we read them aloud as a family.

On the other hand, her sister guzzles suspenseful books on her own.

Sasha will read them upon waking, on the couch in the middle of the day, or in bed at night. The setting matters not. She's okay if someone wants to join her in the adventure, but she's perfectly happy to meander solo through any and every type of mystery, ghost tale, or thriller. And my boys are the same way! They've never met a suspenseful story they didn't enjoy.

Some *Soul School* books center on Black characters facing mysterious dilemmas, puzzling circumstances, and suspenseful adventures. Stories with twists and turns appeal to many children; a good mystery delivers plenty of them to enjoy. Searching for clues alongside protagonists and trying to figure out whodunit and how they made it happen gives a story page-turning value. Watching seemingly disparate discoveries come together is just the type of thing that many kids relish.

Visual Storytelling

Black art extends in all directions. Much of it depicts hard times because, in the words of artist Horace Pippin, "If a man knows nothing but hard times, he will paint them, for he must be true to himself."[10] But Black art is not solely a vehicle to express disparity and loss; it's a fountain of delight and merrymaking. Images of and by Black artists are potent forms of communication that tell their own poignant stories. And when combined with prose and poetry, art becomes a priceless treasure, a sublime amusement for children to soak up and store in their hearts.

Visual storytelling is crucial for many of the stories in this book because Black people and aesthetics are rarely included in books of any kind, especially those given the highest regard within American society. In a letter to the editor of the January 1894 issue of *Southern Workman*, sociologist and author Anna Julia Cooper expressed concern that educated Black people, under the shadow of overwhelmingly white environments, may become ashamed of their "own distinctive features and aspire only to be an imitator of that which can not but impress him as the climax of human greatness, and so all originality, all *sincerity,* all *self*-assertion would be lost to him. What he needs is the inspiration of knowing that his racial inheritance is of interest to others and that when they come to seek his homely [friendly, unpretentious] songs and sayings and doings, it is not to scoff and sneer, but to study reverently, as an original type of the Creator's handiwork."[11]

Our children are still at risk of feeling shame and disregard when they think of Black culture. This path is inevitable unless we provide ample opportunity for our kids to see it as an inherent source of truth, goodness, and beauty.

The illustrations in *Soul School* books are enjoyable and entertaining. They're meant to convey meaning and bring pleasure, particularly to younger children. However, they're much more than just eye candy. These images of Black people and their environments address Cooper's concerns, which I share 130 years later, as they work to prevent the ideas of Black inferiority from forming. I know from experience that if kids don't see or read about Black people, they can mistakenly arrive at the idea that Black people aren't worth noticing. That their images and voices don't matter because they're mere deviations and distractions from the "standard."

I'm confident that your children will adore these illustrations as much as mine do. And for that, I'm grateful, but please make no mistake: The pictures exist for much more than visual gratification. They signify the intrinsic value of our culture in all its glory.

Literary Themes

For centuries, Black Americans have written about "beauty and injustice, music and muses, Africa and America, freedoms and foodways, Harlem and history, funk and opera, boredom and longing, jazz and joy."[12] These words from poet and scholar Kevin Young were part of the Lift Every Voice project, which identified key themes in African American poetry.[13] I see these same themes mirrored broadly across Black literature, including children's books, as a means for acknowledging and creatively addressing society's realities and irresistibly imaginative possibilities.

The Freedom Struggle

I often find myself backpedaling when it comes to discussing Black folks' struggle for freedom of movement, expression, and unhindered living. You may even notice the ever-present tension within this book. On the one hand, I want to continuously point out that we have so much more than "the struggle" to write about. That we *are* so much more. On the other hand, we can't expect authentic stories by and about Black Americans to exclude an entire strand of our collective cord. Ignoring a part of our experience is not something we desire, and it's not possible anyway.

Black Americans have stories of oppression, pain, and trauma. Not trauma triggered by hearing about the past but rather the trauma of having lived through it. Generational trauma directly resulting from chattel slavery and racism's pervasive and relentless pursuit of every aspect of our lives. The psychological and emotional wounds from the past, accompanied by today's steady beat of aftershocks, require us to remember and write.

I worked hard to ensure that the freedom struggle of Black Americans was not scrubbed out of these booklists. I worked just as hard to safeguard our collective children from harm. What does this mean? It means that *Soul School* stands for truthfulness and goodness in equal measure, and the unveiling of the most tender parts of our story is progressive and age-appropriate. The goal is to artistically reveal a story that unfolds over time versus shocking children with an onslaught of tragic vignettes. Progress is expected, but meandering fosters enjoyment, and our children's journey of discovery is not a race.

These books were selected because of how exquisitely they engage children. They're triumphant and celebratory while highlighting resistance, perseverance, and victory over victimization. Great care was taken to steer clear of oppressive language because as Toni Morrison stated in her 1993 Nobel Lecture, "Oppressive language does more than represent violence; it is violence; does more than represent the limits of knowledge; it limits knowledge."[14]

The freedom struggle is not a sad plight to avoid, but the stories must be told well. Reading and writing about it pays homage to the courageous Black people who stood (and still stand) tall in good times and bad. Our stories of struggle are liberatory claims to an inherent right to life, liberty, and the pursuit of happiness, birthrights our beloved but sometimes blinded country has often struggled to accept.

Black Identities

We must cast a wide net when discussing Black Americans. As I write, I'm gripped by the intricacies of our complementary and contradictory identities. I chuckle while attempting to present a concise picture of a dynamic, living people using a collection of static words coupled with a finite list. For every statement I make about who we are and what we do and value, I could spend an entire chapter exploring the nuanced dynamics that support and simultaneously call into question my assertions.

Rather than throw in the towel, I'm carefully wading through ever-changing literary expressions and interpretations of who we are and how we choose to move in this country. In this world. For every recognizable cultural marker of Black America described or referenced here, a juxtaposition exists in one text or another. These aren't errors or inconsistencies. They're lighthouses guiding us through the expansive oceans of Black identities. I hope that when our children's paths are lit, they'll thoroughly enjoy digging into the complexities of our identities.

Black Experience in History and Memory

As Evie Shockley writes, "Black poets have consistently used their poems to create a historical counternarrative, a corrective to the skewed one that has marginalized and denigrated Black people. Our poems regularly celebrate Black people's collective and individual achievements, shed light on figures and events whose importance is little known, record and remember injustices that have been swept under the rug, and elegize our tragedies."[15] This encapsulates what children will find throughout *Soul School*. The stories accurately share history in honest and uplifting ways. They highlight unheard voices and lesser-known events while introducing intimate portraits of our most familiar faces.

Family and Community

The *Soul School* stories of family and community are among my favorites, as they're based on memory, scholarly research, family lore, and lived experience. Familial stories and communal histories appear in so many books that you may begin to think the lists are born of my bias toward the lens of family life, but this is not the case. The reason for the range and multitude of books sprinkled and splashed with this theme is that relationships are the glue that holds stories together. Kids of all ages light up when they see their most treasured bonds personified on a page, and they have an insatiable drive to experience the coziness that comes from a book rooted in familial and communal bonds.

Dr. Rudine Sims Bishop, author of *Free Within Ourselves: The Development of African American Children's Literature*, examined the growth of Black books for kids and concluded that as a body of work, the literature:

(1) celebrates the strengths of the Black family as a cultural
institution and vehicle for survival;
(2) bears witness to Black people's determined struggle for freedom,
equality, and dignity;
(3) nurtures the souls of Black children by reflecting back to them,
both visually and verbally, the beauty and competencies that we as
adults see in them;
(4) situates itself, through its language and its content, within African
American literary and cultural contexts; and
(5) honors the tradition of story as a way of teaching and knowing.[16]

Soul School takes kids on a joy-filled journey through the heart of Black American culture, and along the way, they'll repeatedly encounter these themes and more.

5

ROCKSTARS AND READERS

A writer's life and work are not a gift to mankind;
they are its necessity.

—TONI MORRISON, *THE SOURCE OF SELF-REGARD*

Black is expressive. When Trevor Noah interviewed award-winning author Jacqueline Woodson on *The Daily Show*, he expressed his excitement over the audience's reaction to her, saying, "As someone who grew up *living* in books, nothing gives me more joy than seeing writers treated like rock stars."[1] *Soul School* celebrates essential names in Black children's literature. When reading books on African American culture, the storytellers are as meaningful as the stories themselves. The Black authors and illustrators that we've lost and the ones that are still gifting us today have personal histories that inform their works.

There's no possible way to explore every author and illustrator of the past and present, so please know that by sharing the work of specific creators, I'm not suggesting they are the *only* ones; this isn't an exhaustive list. It's merely a tasty sampling of the heroes I've encountered time and again when searching for beautiful Black stories, poetry, and images for children—mine and yours. These transformational authors and artists shared across the remaining chapters have encouraged and facilitated literary revolutions. They understood Black children because they remembered themselves. They know Black stories because they live them across every context.

In her autobiography, *Dust Tracks on a Road*, Zora Neale Hurston said, "The force from somewhere in Space which commands you to write in the first place, gives you no choice. You take up the pen when you are told, and write what is commanded. There is no agony like bearing an untold story inside you."[2] *Soul School*'s literary rockstars are determined to tell their stories. In doing so, they're offering up parts of themselves that speak to our children in profound ways. They've boldly chosen to write within and against the grain of traditional literary genres, themes, and devices. These creators changed the interpretation of "mainstream children's literature," making it no longer a desert devoid of Black voices. They're actively producing a body of work where children can swim in Black culture.

When we speak to our children about heroes, we name freedom fighters, scientists, athletes, and community leaders. But how would we know the greatness of these figures if not for the heroes penning and drawing their way through their stories? What about the lives of the artists, poets, and writers themselves? They are the keepers and communicators of the stories. Their work and lives are heroic. They *also* represent history. They are storytellers whose experiences and voices are integral to preserving the Black American story. These writers and illustrators saw a glaring need for Black children's literature, and they took up the mantle to do all they could to improve the literary landscape for our children.

In an article for the *New York Times* titled "Where Are the People of Color in Children's Books?" Walter Dean Myers shared his thoughts on why so many young people find solace in his books. "They have been struck by the recognition of themselves in the story, a validation of their existence as human beings, an acknowledgment of their value by someone who understands who they are. It is the shock of recognition at its highest level." A prolific author of more than one hundred books for children and young adults, Myers continued:

> *Books transmit values. They explore our common humanity. What is the message when some children are not represented in those books? . . . Where*

are black children going to get a sense of who they are and what they can be? And what are the books that are being published about blacks? . . . Black history is usually depicted as folklore about slavery, and then a fast-forward to the civil rights movement. Then I'm told that black children, and boys in particular, don't read. Small wonder. There is work to be done.[3]

On the same day that they ran his father's opinion piece, the *Times* printed a commentary by Walter's son, award-winning illustrator Christopher Myers, who echoed his father's thoughts:

We adults—parents, authors, illustrators and publishers—give them in each book a world of supposedly boundless imagination that can delineate the most ornate geographies, and yet too often today's books remain blind to the everyday reality of thousands of children. Children of color remain outside the boundaries of imagination. The cartography we create with this literature is flawed.[4]

Both father and son were able to articulate the issues at hand, and though these pieces were written more than a decade ago, they're more relevant today than ever. As we promote the need for more diverse literature, more storytellers add their work to the growing collection, but Black storytellers have always been a thing.

Starting with African griots, secret nighttime literacy schools, and slave narratives, we've had an insatiable drive to preserve our stories. This legacy can be seen through the lens of Black literary societies in the 1800s, the literature and art explosion of the Harlem Renaissance, the Black Arts Movement, and beyond. Tales told by Black Americans are often rooted in some aspect of shared experience. Though we aren't the only people group to have stories, we uniquely share ours as opportunities to remember and heal.

West African griots were (and still are) highly skilled storytellers, musicians, and oral historians. This esteemed role required extensive training and expertise in preserving the cultural traditions and histories of villages and families. Griots were pillars of West African society, holding records of important events such as births, deaths, and marriages spanning generations.

The importance of storytelling was carried to the Americas as enslaved Africans found creative ways to tell their stories.

Perhaps this commitment to accessing and sharing stories can't be seen more clearly than in the history of underground literacy schools. Before the Civil War, African Americans were forbidden from reading and writing for fear that they would gain ideas for liberation and navigate society more easily. After Nat Turner's rebellion in 1831, white people intensified their efforts to prevent education among enslaved and free Black people, and the anti-literacy laws of the time dictated stiff punishments for enslaved people learning to read and those caught assisting them. Despite this dehumanizing prohibition on learning, some Black people continued to find ways to gain knowledge, often at significant personal risk.

Following the Civil War, it became commonplace for Black people to teach each other, and the literacy rate soared. This new generation of readers and writers joined others who had been thriving in Black literary societies for decades. First organized within urban communities of the 1820s and 1830s, these societies served as places for members to discuss issues of importance.

Within these unique cultural institutions, literature and writing were appreciated forms of expression, social interaction, and activism in antebellum America. They were salient operations that directly fed the insatiable thirst Black Americans had for reading and discussing their thoughts and ideas. Eventually, this interest in growth through reading gave way to a small but vital body of work directed at the literary lives of Black American children. Early community leaders and creative visionaries understood that kids flourish when afforded an expansive reading life that includes stories and images of people like them. We can see these efforts in works that remain available to us today, including these landmark titles:

A NARRATIVE OF THE NEGRO. Leila Amos Pendleton (1868–1938), an African American teacher and activist, recognized the need to expand young people's limited view of Black history. In *A Narrative of the Negro* (1912), she aimed for a chronological history or "family story" of Black people across the African diaspora, especially within the United States of America. The twenty-two-chapter text (for which I had the honor of writing the foreword in the republished edition by

Smidgen Press) is a product of its time, and not without flaws. Still, it set a standard in establishing the importance of sharing a thorough examination of Black history.

THE BROWNIES' BOOK. Running monthly from January 1920 to December 1921, *The Brownies' Book* was the first magazine to speak directly to African American children. Born of *The Crisis*, the NAACP's magazine for adults, this publication is a pearl in children's literature. While expanding the canon, *The Brownies' Book* normalized being Black for children everywhere. It sought to cement positive images of culture and adventure in the minds of Black children, a radical act. It's a wonder that we're still discussing this same need more than a hundred years later.

POPO AND FIFINA. Langston Hughes and Arna Bontemps, renowned poets and noted contributors to the Harlem Renaissance, offered a treasure trove of literature to Black America. They sometimes collaborated on projects, including a children's book called *Popo and Fifina* (1932), which tells of a brother's and sister's adjustment to a new home by the sea in Cape Haiti. It was well received upon publication, with a review in the *New York Times* offering praise while stating that the book "tempts us to wish that all our travel books for children might be written by poets."[5]

GLADIOLA GARDEN. My quest for poetry with words or images of Black children's experiences and meanderings through fields and forests alongside the crickets and toads led to this treasure of poems that spoke to the little girl inside me who had longed to see herself within the pages of an extraordinary book. In 1940, poet Effie Lee Newsome and illustrator Lois Mailou Jones published *Gladiola Garden*. The book is likely the first volume of children's poetry ever published by a Black American woman, and I delightedly provided the foreword for the republished edition by Living Book Press.

These rich contributions are just a sampling of the works that paved the path carried forward by many Black authors and artists. Their books present a priceless opportunity for families to dive into rich African American cultural themes with the unmistakable goal of celebrating who we are. But as with many sweet treasures, there are a multitude of other benefits that come from taking this journey. One of the main ones is cultivating an enduring and gratifying literary life.

WHAT IS A LITERARY LIFE?

A childhood of exploring and enjoying the creative spirit of writers, poets, and artists is a gift. I consider a literary life one that unmistakably positions books as good friends and reading as an enjoyable way to grow and have fun. This may feel like an undertaking requiring more time and energy than the average family can devote. But that's the thing. It isn't something to do or achieve; it's just a way of being. There's no quality check to pass or time quota to satisfy. All it takes is a seed of intention, a sprinkle of motivation, an encouraging adult—and a phenomenal booklist. An indie bookshop and a library card are the only required tools, but some magnetic bookmarks and a Kindle will make the whole thing official.

Don't Underestimate Stolen Moments

Reading requires a time investment, but it doesn't have to be an intimidating block of hours. Every book is read one page at a time. And unless a child is under a homework deadline, there's no need to rush or feel overwhelmed. Teach children to carry a book wherever they go so later in life they'll always be prepared in waiting rooms, traffic, and customer service lines. Encourage nighttime reading by delaying "lights out" once your kiddos have been tucked in and play family-friendly audiobooks in the car. Minutes lead to hours, which lead to stacks of finished books.

Prioritize Reading Aloud for All Ages

My kids prefer me to read aloud because I'm fully committed to character voices, but sometimes, one of them will take the lead. It would be so easy for my family to let this habit slide, or for my teens to slip away from this family time, even though we've done it forever. But we prioritize reading aloud and keep our kids in the fold with alluring books and good snacks. Food always works.

Read Multiple Books at the Same Time

Reading more than one book at a time increases the connections our kids make in other areas of life, including relationships, and expands their ability to read continuously. Keeping a stack of books that are old, new, easy, and challenging (or some other combination) helps ensure that children will always have something on hand that matches their mood. Sometimes, young people want to dive headfirst into a high-interest, denser text they can savor and contemplate. At other times, they want to be entertained with a lighthearted tale that doesn't require too much of them. Kids benefit both from the perspectives of contemporary writers and the wisdom and experiences of authors who left their words behind. The goal is a mix of this and that.

Join or Start a Book Club

When I launched Heritage Book Club eight years ago in our local community, I had no idea that it would grow to be such a blessing to my family and others. At the first meeting, my young daughter led her friends through a book discussion about a little girl who finds a duck egg at a park as they sat by a pond surrounded by ducks and geese near our home. She read questions from index cards we'd prepared at home, and her friends piped in with their thoughts. Today, that same group of friends and newcomers are teenagers preparing to dig into juicy books like *Their Eyes Were Watching God*. I couldn't have known it at the time, but launching a youth book club has provided many unexpected benefits:

1. **It promotes a love of reading.** We have fun, and our only expectation is that kids enjoy the process. This freedom helps them associate reading with pleasure, and that's something that can be overshadowed when their only books are schoolbooks.

2. **It exposes kids to books they might not otherwise read.** Book club encourages kids to read widely, often outside their preferred genre or subject, providing opportunities to connect with new authors and ideas. I can't tell you how many times kids in our group, including my own children, have said

that they loved a book club book they initially had no interest in reading.

3. **It's fulfilling for every age group.** We now have groups for children in preschool through high school. The dynamics are different as the children grow. The younger ones tend to lean into book-related crafts and activities, while the older tweens and teens generally prefer to discuss the book more deeply (and eat).

4. **It encourages a more profound exploration.** Much is to be gained when children read alone for pleasure, but discussing their books with friends leads to deeper thinking and consideration of plot, characters, and ideas.

5. **It provides kids a safe space to share their honest thoughts.** I always remind my book club kids that they don't have to censor their views to please me or because their friends feel differently. I tell them, "You have every right to say you dislike a book, but only if you can articulate *why*." Having a platform to gush about a favorite character or scene or vent about how you think the author went wrong adds vibrancy to the discussion and gives children a voice.

6. **It's a meaningful way to add diverse voices to our children's thought life.** Our book club groups primarily read books written about Black people and other people of color, and this is an exceptional opportunity for our kids to swim in Black culture. Every kid involved knows they can count on the book club to offer mirrors and multicultural windows, and this is especially pertinent for those who aren't accessing these books in other contexts.

7. **It helps children form lasting friendships and view reading as a social activity.** Adults like to talk about what they're reading, and children are no different. Book club gives kids a reason to gather and provides plenty to discuss. They learn more about each

other and themselves and have opportunities to explore broader conversations with the same friends regularly.

These are just a few ideas that can illuminate the path of your child's reading journey. Readers are self-educated lifelong learners. The more we can encourage our kids along that path, the more years they'll have to fall hopelessly in love with turning (or swiping or listening to) the pages of books, glorious books.

The preceding chapters explored the nature of Black American culture and how creatively our storytellers convey its complexity and depth through their work. In part two, we'll move from the ideas and people behind the books to the stories themselves. You'll find curated lists of breathtaking literature for every stage of childhood and beyond. Hold on tightly. You're in for a magnificent ride!

PART TWO

. . . . ◇❖◇ . . . .

For all children, but especially for ours,
the Children of the Sun.

—W.E.B. DU BOIS, *THE CRISIS*, VOL. 18, NO. 6. (OCTOBER 1919)

INTRODUCTION

To children who with eager look
Scanned vainly library shelf and nook
For History or Song or Story
That told of Colored People's glory
—JESSIE REDMON FAUSET, THE BROWNIES' BOOK (JANUARY 1920)

Uniquely, I'm knee-deep in parenting children in nearly every category of books represented here—early elementary, late elementary, middle school, and high school. This is not only a list of books I'm recommending for your children as a passionate researcher and champion of Black children's literature (though it is undoubtedly that); these are the best of the best books that my family has enjoyed. The ones we talk about over Friday night pizza and laugh (or cry) with during road trips.

I sought to craft the most authentic and transparent story of my culture told through children's literature and to do so with the highest integrity and most nuanced communication. To claim that these delicate and delicious meanderings represent the very soul of my people, I needed to—*wanted* to—give deference to Black creators. This doesn't mean that the books are only for Black children, as author Derrick Barnes explains:

Because I write with Black children in mind does not mean that I don't write for other children. It's quite the contrary, actually. The more all children have an opportunity to see others being happy, being valued, being loved, laughing, solving the mystery, and saving the day, the closer we will all get to the type of society where we are lifting each other up, celebrating our differences, and hoping desperately to see joy in the faces of other human beings.[1]

First and foremost, these are outstanding stories. And while they're sure to hold a special place in the hearts of Black families, they are unequivocally and without hesitation for *all* children.

Age Recommendations

Soul School is an open-and-go resource for parents and teachers, but with a bit of preparation and informed reading, it can be a powerful tool in any space. The booklist is broken up into the following age-based categories:

Chapter 6: The Early Years	Ages 2–4	Illustrated young children's books
Chapter 7: Early Elementary	Ages 5–7	Illustrated children's books with a few early chapter books
Chapter 8: Late Elementary	Ages 8–10	A mix of illustrated children's books, elementary chapter books, and middle-grade chapter books geared to elementary children
Chapter 9: Middle School	Ages 11–14	More mature middle-grade chapter books with a sprinkle of text-dense illustrated books. Books rarely contain crude words, controversial issues, or overly mature references. Selected with older tweens and young teens in mind.
Chapter 10: High School	Ages 15–17	Young adult chapter books may contain profanity, romance, sexual innuendo, or historically accurate or plot-driven trauma, though care was taken not to saturate the list with these elements. Mature upper teen audience assumed.

The *Soul School* categories often align or overlap with the publisher's recommended reading ages, but sometimes I list books as being for children younger or older than the publisher for various reasons. I focus on who will likely enjoy the book most or who needs to hear a particular story at that point in their development. As much as I've tried to place each book within the best age range, the decision is inherently steeped in subjectivity, and no two readers are just alike. Never doubt your intuition to introduce a book to your child at an earlier or later age.

I call out potentially sensitive language or topics in some books on the lists, particularly within the young adult category. I either have shared or plan to share every book in *Soul School* with my own children because I see particular value in each selection. Still, I feel strongly about content being age appropriate. I include the information so parents can hold off on certain books or be prepared for discussions and out of respect for families with different preferences than my own. I know from experience that no parent or teacher enjoys being caught off guard.

Every core book is accompanied by "Second Helpings" or two related books with brief descriptions that your child will likely enjoy. Sometimes, the Second Helpings provide deeper insight to the core book. In other instances, they explore connected themes or invoke similar feelings as the core book. The connection may be direct, like books from the same author or illustrator, or less obvious, as with books in the same historical period or written in a similar style. In one way or another, there's a relationship between the core books and Second Helpings, and they work together to provide a more complete experience than any single book can deliver on its own.

Whatever you do, please don't mistake the Second Helpings for being second-rate!

If time and page counts were infinite, I would have expanded the details for every title. Add as many as you comfortably and naturally can and feel confident swapping them with core books as needed or desired due to book availability or preference. Like another spoonful of your favorite foods, they will satisfy and soothe your children's hearts, minds, and . . . souls, of course.

When I started writing *Soul School*, there were originally supposed to be a hundred books. But in the words of Nikki Giovanni in her introduction of *The 100 Best African American Poems*, "I cheated. The idea of *this* and no more would simply not work for me. I needed *these* plus *those*."[2] So, without further ado, I present this extraordinary selection of 360 books (120 core titles accompanied by 240 Second Helpings) to spice up your child's reading life while introducing them to the indomitable spirit of Black American culture.

6

THE EARLY YEARS (AGES 2–4)

EMILE AND THE FIELD

Written by Kevin Young

Illustrated by Chioma Ebinama

"There was a boy named Emile who fell in love with a field.
It was wide and blue—and if you could have seen it so would've you."

The words in this book are carefully chosen, while the watercolor images bring each season to life. Through lyrical text, readers are taken on a walk through a little boy's most beloved spot in nature. We see what he appreciates in his environment as his father helps him see that the most beautiful part of the field is that it can't be bought or belong to anyone. Not even Emile.

WHY I CHOSE THIS BOOK: A note in the back of the book from author Christopher Myers states, "There is a gift to being in different spaces. There is a way the earth can talk to you." I didn't grow up spending time outdoors, and raising my children differently has taken considerable, yet enjoyable, effort. First, I had to imagine my children falling in love with nature. Next, they needed plenty of time outdoors. With much intention, my family has learned to feel at home among forest trails, mountaintops, lakes, valleys, and the ocean air. This book epitomizes the freedom that comes to children who can dream, run, explore, and just be in nature. It recaptures a connection with the land that was once intuitive for African American families.

THOUGHT STARTERS

1. Where is your favorite outdoor space, and why do you love it? Describe what it looks like to someone who has never seen it. How do you feel when you're there? What do you like to do when you spend time in that space?
2. Which seasons are shown in the illustrations of the field, and how can you tell? What's your favorite season and why?
3. What areas of nature near you are available for everyone to enjoy?

DIGGING DEEPER

1. Draw a picture of a tree in every season. Show your four pictures to someone else and see if they can guess which tree represents winter, spring, summer, and fall.
2. Take a nature walk on a trail or in a park. Look up, down, and all around as you walk using all your senses. Listen carefully, pay attention to new scents, and notice how the air feels as you move. Try to see as many little details as possible. While walking, point out three things you find most interesting. Take photos or sketch your favorite finds.
3. What kind of land would you like to own when you grow up? Where will it be, and what kinds of things will be on it? Who will enjoy the land with you, and how will you take care of it? Find an adult who owns their land. Ask them how they got it and what it means to them.

SECOND HELPINGS

» *Jayden's Impossible Garden*
    Written by Mélina Mangal
    Illustrated by Ken Daley
» *The Thing About Bees: A Love Letter*
    Written and illustrated by Shabazz Larkin

NELL PLANTS A TREE

Written by Anne Wynter
Illustrated by Daniel Miyares

"Before a grip on a branch and a fall to the ground and a scrape and a leap and a reach for the top, before anyone finds out how high they can climb, Nell picks up a seed."

This heartwarming intergenerational story is told with alternating pages depicting young Nell's quest to plant a tree and her grandchildren's delight and joy while playing in and around that same tree decades later. Nell's carefully tended pecan tree grows as she becomes a young mother and a beloved grandmother. The tenderness with which she first handles her seed gives birth to priceless moments shared between loved ones under its expansive shade.

WHY I CHOSE THIS BOOK: The tree becomes a central gathering place for generations of a family and illustrates the importance of intergenerational relationships within the Black community. I appreciate Nell's relationship with the land and what it produces and her grandchildren's apparent comfort in and enjoyment of the outdoor world. The muted, smoky pen-and-ink illustrations, gouache, and collage combine perfectly.

THOUGHT STARTERS

1. How can we tell that planting the seed and tending the tree was important to Nell? What's something that means a lot to you? How can someone tell how much you care about it?

2. Of all the activities Nell's grandchildren do in the book, which one would you enjoy most and why? What are some of your favorite activities?

3. What does it feel like to have a grandparent, family member, or special friend with whom you can share things? What things can you show or share with your grandchildren someday?

DIGGING DEEPER

1. Plant a tree in your yard or somewhere else in your community where you can watch it grow. If this isn't possible right now, or if you want to see something happening quickly, plant a small herb like basil, rosemary, or mint in an indoor container. Tell a story about where it came from and how it will be used as it grows.

2. Work with your loved ones to create your actual family tree or an imaginary one based on Nell's family pictured in the book. Use visual elements from the book, like the patchwork end pages or soft color palette, to inspire decorations for your family tree.

3. One of the children in the book reads in a "too-noisy den . . . a too-squeaky chair . . . a too-scratchy field" and under the pecan tree. Find a book you love

(maybe this one!) and go outdoors where you can get comfortable and look at the pictures or listen to a grown-up read the book. If the weather is not cooperating, build a fort inside instead. Crawl in and curl up with a good story.

SECOND HELPINGS

» *The Old Truck*
  Written by Jarrett Pumphrey
  Illustrated by Jerome Pumphrey
» *The Last Stand*
  Written by Antwan Eady
  Illustrated by Jarrett and Jerome Pumphrey

MAX AND THE TAG-ALONG MOON

Written and illustrated by Floyd Cooper
"That ol' moon will always shine for you . . . on and on!"

Sadly, Max has to leave his granpa's house to head home, but he's comforted by Granpa's embrace and promise that the moon will always shine on him. As he travels down the road, the clouds cover the moon, and Max wonders what happened to it. He feels alone and misses his granpa until the moon peeks through, and he's reassured that his grandfather's words are true.

WHY I CHOSE THIS BOOK: As soon as I read this book, I knew Floyd Cooper had nailed it. He captured a warm, intimate moment between a boy and his grandfather and expertly carried their bond across time and space through soft, glowing illustrations and subtle narration.

THOUGHT STARTERS

1. Is there someone in your life that you often miss? It could be a friend you don't get to see as often as you'd like or a family member who has passed away. Is there anything that reminds you of that person, something special you can think about when you start to miss them?
2. What makes you know your family and other adults love and care for you?

3. Why does Max call his "magic ball of light" a tag-along moon? What do you think is another good descriptor or nickname for the moon?

DIGGING DEEPER

1. If Max had known that the moon was only hiding behind the clouds, he wouldn't have been worried. What are some other things that people don't have to worry about if they know the truth? Pick one of your ideas and make a short video of you teaching others about your topic so they'll be informed and understand that they have nothing to worry about.

2. Have you ever taken a long journey by car? Did you notice whether you could see the moon the entire way? The moon seems to follow us because it's so far away, and closer things appear to move between us and the moon (or sun). The next time you're in the car, try to spot the sun or moon.

3. Each evening before bed, look out your window or step outside to view the moon. Notice how its shape *appears* to change slowly over time. Investigate why that happens and how long it takes to see a full moon that looks like the one Max saw with his granpa.

SECOND HELPINGS

» *Peeny Butter Fudge*
    Written by Toni Morrison and Slade Morrison
    Illustrated by Joe Cepeda
» *My Nana and Me*
    Written by Irene Smalls
    Illustrated by Cathy Ann Johnson

BIG
Written and illustrated by Vashti Harrison
"The words stung and were hard to shake off."

• •

This book uses touching illustrations and few words to tell of a young girl and the adults in her life who love and affirm her when she's little. As she grows physically larger in spaces that value smaller bodies, their words become weapons that make her feel trapped and alone. Ultimately, she chooses to make space for herself by returning the unkind words to their speakers.

WHY I CHOSE THIS BOOK: Harrison shares details from her childhood in the author's note: "My size indicated to adults I was big enough to know better even though I was still just a kid." I can personally identify with this experience of being the biggest kid around, and I've also seen it play out with my children, one of whom has always appeared much older. While this may seem trivial to some, anti-fat bias and the adultification of Black girls are concerning societal issues that I've never seen tackled in a children's book, certainly not with such tenderness and empathy.

THOUGHT STARTERS

1. The girl in the book starts out happy, but then people begin to hurt her with their words. Has anyone spoken unkind words to you? How did that make you feel? Have you said hurtful things to others? How do you think that made them feel?

2. What would you say if you could talk to the girl in the book? What would you want someone to tell you if you were her?

3. What do you think the girl feels on the pages with no words? How can you tell that she may feel that way?

DIGGING DEEPER

1. People come in all different shapes and sizes. The next time you go to the store or somewhere else in your community, pay close attention to all the different types of bodies you see. When you get home, draw a picture of some of the people you saw, and be sure to draw their bodies just as you remember.

2. Try this experiment in kindness: For an entire day, say something kind to everyone you meet or speak with. At the end of the day, think about the experience and share whether it was easy or difficult and why.

3. Think of ten things that you love about yourself. Ask a grown-up to type the list or write it down for you and help you hang it somewhere you'll see often. Whenever you pass by the list, remind yourself of those things so you'll never forget them.

SECOND HELPINGS

» *Repeat After Me: Big Things to Say Every Day*
  Written by Jazmyn Simon and Dulé Hill
  Illustrated by Shamar Knight-Justice
» *I'm From*
  Written by Gary R. Gray, Jr.
  Illustrated by Oge Mora

INDIGO DREAMING

Written by Dinah Johnson
Illustrated by Anna Cunha
*"I wonder if somewhere there's a girl like me,
who spends every day beside the sea."*

....

This book is a poetic musing between a little girl in a white dress living off the coast of South Carolina and her counterpart in a blue dress on the shores of West Africa. Though the girls reside on different sides of the same ocean and have never met, they somehow sense there's someone like them in another part of this big, wide world. The story unfolds through little tales of the girls' meanderings peppered with detailed observations.

WHY I CHOSE THIS BOOK: I've fallen in love with these little girls separated by the sea, sharing the same indigo dream. The text is dotted with cultural references to sweetgrass, goobers, Frogmore Stew, and other meaningful sights and sounds that leave rich breadcrumbs to explore after each reading. The author's note ties together the references to Africans on the Continent, on the Sea Islands of South Carolina, and in the Brazilian region of Bahia. The illustrations invoke such a deep sense of beauty and connection that the book feels as much like an art gallery as a piece of literature.

THOUGHT STARTERS

1. What would you say if you had to describe yourself and your life to someone from a different country? What might you have in common with a child living on

the other side of the ocean? What are the possible differences between how you
live and what you enjoy?

2. If you could ask a child living in a faraway country three questions, what would
you ask?

3. What is your favorite part of this story and why? Which picture do you like most
and why?

DIGGING DEEPER

1. Reach out to someone you know in or from another country and ask them to
describe what they enjoy most about where they live(d). Then you take a turn
and tell them about the unique parts of your life—where you go, what you do,
who you enjoy, etc.

2. In the book, the child from the coast of South Carolina enjoys Frogmore Stew
with her family. Have you ever tried that dish? Ask an adult to help you make
Frogmore Stew. It's a simple, one-pot "Lowcountry boil" made with unpeeled
shrimp, corn on the cob, new red potatoes, and hot smoked sausage flavored
with Old Bay seafood seasoning. It's quite tasty, but sometimes it has a little kick
(it can be spicy), so be prepared to wash it down with some refreshing coconut
water or sweet iced tea like the little girl from West Africa. There are plenty of
recipes online to follow.

3. People in many parts of the world tell stories of Anansi the Spider, like the
grandmother in the book. Anansi is an African folktale character originating
from the Asante people in Ghana, and he's often portrayed as a trickster who
outsmarts the characters around him. Ask someone to read you a story about
Anansi (or watch one read aloud online) and see if you can determine the story's
moral. Then develop a short story that teaches a lesson using talking animals.

SECOND HELPINGS

» *Sleep Well Siba & Saba*
Written by Nansubuga Nagadya Isdahl
Illustrated by Sandra van Doorn

» *A Story About Afiya*
Written by James Berry
Illustrated by Anna Cunha

THE SUN IS SO QUIET

Written by Nikki Giovanni

Illustrated by Ashley Bryan

"Snowflakes ballet in my heart, warming me to crystal dreams."

· ·

These simple yet highly descriptive poems capture the attention of young listeners as the cheerful imagery exudes happiness on every page. Giovanni offers verses that capture wonderful childhood moments like twirling in the snow, riding rainbows, and playing hide-and-seek in a strawberry patch. Most of the poems focus on the seasons and nature, but one of my favorites highlights the thrill of licking chocolatey fingers.

WHY I CHOSE THIS BOOK: Some children immediately take to poetry, while others grow their appreciation for verse through continued exposure. This book combines playful ideas that young children find appealing with quality poetic writing, so it speaks to those who already love hearing words strung together beautifully and those who still need some convincing. Each page is bursting with fun, but the poems aren't silly, making it an excellent choice for introducing kids to the vivid descriptions, imagery, and emotions often found in poetry.

THOUGHT STARTERS

1. In the first poem, *Winter*, we learn many things that happen when the temperature turns cold. What other wintery things would you include? What about summer, spring, and fall? What are some ways that we know each of those seasons is near?

2. On page 10, the illustrator chose to paint different snowflakes over each child. Why do you think he did that? According to the poem, what are some similarities that the children share?

3. What is the mood of the girl in *November*? How can you tell? Have you ever danced in the snow? How did it feel, or how do you think it would feel?

DIGGING DEEPER

1. Have you ever been strawberry picking? Read *Strawberry Patches*, and plan to visit a garden or farm where you can see strawberries grow. If they're out of season, buy some at the store and see how many delicious things you

can make from them—smoothies, strawberry shortcake, jam, strawberries and cream, etc.

2. The boy in *The Reason I Like Chocolate* lists five things he enjoys. Which of those things do you like? Name five things that make you happy and share them with a friend. Ask friends or family members for five things that make them happy and see if you have any in common. Then, think of how you can enjoy your favorite things together.

3. The last poem in the book, *Connie*, describes many different quiet things. Think of an adjective (a word that describes things) and ask an adult to write down all the things you can think of that fit that word. For example, if you picked "wet," you could list fish dancing at the end of a pole, feet stepping out of the ocean, the kitchen floor after a mop swishes by, and Popsicles on a warm day.

SECOND HELPINGS

» *In Daddy's Arms I Am Tall: African Americans Celebrating Fathers*
   Written by twelve Black authors
   Illustrated by Javaka Steptoe

» *The ABCs of Black History*
   Written by Rio Cortez
   Illustrated by Lauren Semmer

BLACK IS A RAINBOW COLOR
Written by Angela Joy
Illustrated by Ekua Holmes
"Black is a rhythm. Black is the blues.
Black is side-walking in spit-shined shoes."

. . . .

In this unique story, a little girl thinks of all the pleasant things in her life that are black as she contemplates that black isn't a rainbow color. The poetic language is layered in meaning as the girl realizes that black isn't only a color but also a culture rich in history and experience. Very young children likely won't understand all the historical references baked into the story, but each listener will take what they can from the text while leaving an opening for further discussion and many rereads over time. With a song list, historical and cultural notes, three classic poems, and a timeline of Black ethnonyms in the back, plenty is available for parents and teachers to learn and share with their children.

WHY I CHOSE THIS BOOK: I love how the author communicates that the color black is beautiful while simultaneously celebrating that *being* Black is beautiful without ever needing to state either concept overtly. Black is a color and a culture, and the age-appropriate treatment of this complex notion is nuanced and artistic, making it easy for young children to grow in understanding.

THOUGHT STARTERS

1. What is your favorite thing that is the color black? Why is it your favorite?
2. Choose a bright color (red, orange, yellow, blue, or purple) and list everything you can think of that's the same color.
3. What's the difference between the color black and Black people?

DIGGING DEEPER

1. Grab your crayons and draw a picture of a scene that includes nice, happy things using your black crayon and other fun colors.
2. The girl with cornrows (braids close to her scalp) on page 6 is shown with a profile or side view. Draw or paint a self-portrait (a picture of yourself) profile and include some of the many things you enjoy doing in the background.
3. On page 18, the mother (or another family member) shows the children some pictures in a photo album. We can assume these are family photos based on the author's words. Look through your family photos and ask an adult to tell you a few stories about the people in the pictures. If you don't have a family album, start one today! Take photos of yourself doing things you're good at and paste them onto paper. Leave room for an adult to help you write a little caption that describes the photos. Add to your album by including pictures of your loved ones.

SECOND HELPINGS

» *Black Magic*
   Written by Dinah Johnson
   Illustrated by R. Gregory Christie

» *Beautiful Blackbird*
Written and illustrated by Ashley Bryan

ME & MAMA
Written and illustrated by Cozbi A. Cabrera
"I want to be everywhere Mama is."

. . . .

A spunky little girl and her mom share the sweetest bond as they spend a rainy day at each other's side. The daughter wakes to her smiling mama on the sewing machine as she tiptoes around the house, which smells like cinnamon, before getting dressed and sharing warm bowls of fruit-topped oatmeal. They style their big, thick hair and enjoy a walk in the rain before settling in for funny bedtime stories, loud kisses, and sweet dreams. The lush two-page spreads in acrylic further denote the relational connection with multiple images of mom-sized and kid-sized items like cups, dresses, toothbrushes, and boots shown side-by-side.

WHY I CHOSE THIS BOOK: This endearing story normalizes the natural desire of many young children to be with their mamas. Still in this stage with my youngest, I understand the intensity with which kids can demonstrate their healthy attachments, and I find Cabrera's take on it innocently refreshing. This is the kind of book you just can't read without smiling as each page demonstrates a mutually affirming relationship amid life's ordinary moments.

THOUGHT STARTERS

1. What similarities and differences do you see between the little girl and her mama? What about between you and your mom or loved one?
2. What kinds of things does the little girl in the story learn from her mama? What has your mama or caretaker taught you?
3. The detailed paintings in this book show us many little things that can be found in a home. What are some items that best represent your family or home?

DIGGING DEEPER

1. What do you usually do on rainy days? Have you ever played in the rain? Plan what you can do inside and outside the next time it rains.

2. Have you ever broken something that belonged to someone else? How did that make you feel? How did you handle it? What would you want someone to say or do if they broke something of yours? Pretend you've broken a loved one's item, and practice saying what needs to be communicated to make things right.

3. Turn to page 12 to see what the girl and her mom have for breakfast. Have you ever tried oatmeal? With the help of an adult, make yourself a bowl and choose a fun new topping to include.

SECOND HELPINGS

» *Saturday*
   Written and illustrated by Oge Mora
» *The Magic Doll: A Children's Book Inspired by African Art*
   Written by Adrienne Yabouza
   Illustrated by Élodie Nouhen

THIS IS THE ROPE: A STORY FROM THE GREAT MIGRATION

Written by Jacqueline Woodson
Illustrated by James Ransome

*"This is the rope my grandmother found beneath an old tree
a long time ago back home in South Carolina."*

· ·

Starting with a family's move from South Carolina to New York City during the Great Migration, this story centers on a rope that passes through several generations while being used for the most beautiful and mundane things. As the mother ages, she passes the rope to her daughter and granddaughter, grounding their memories and giving them a tangible connection.

WHY I CHOSE THIS BOOK: This story is a gentle introduction to the Great Migration, a significant historical experience often left out of children's books. By attaching the timeline to the rope and how it's been used through the years, young children can easily understand the passage of time and the changes within this loving family across the decades. Woodson's signature storytelling is brought to life with sentimental yellow- and brown-tinged oil paintings that further demonstrate the everyday activities of a family following their dreams.

THOUGHT STARTERS

1. Have you ever moved to a new house? If so, how did you feel about moving, and what are some important things you brought? If not, what might it be like to start a new life in a new place? Which three things would you most want to bring if you moved to a new city next week?

2. Beatrice's grandmother moved from the South Carolina countryside to the big-city neighborhood of Brooklyn, New York. What are some differences between the city and the country? How do you think Beatrice's grandmother's life changed when she moved? (Students can revisit the illustrations to compare the rural and city settings.)

3. The rope follows the girl's path from South Carolina to New York during the Great Migration, when millions of African American families relocated from the South, seeking better jobs, treatment, education, and opportunities. Look up these states on a map to see how far they traveled. Do you think it was good for them to leave the South, or should they have stayed there and tried to make things better where they lived? Why do you think so?

DIGGING DEEPER

1. The rope in this story was with the family for many years, and it was one of their most important treasures. Does your family have something important that you think should be kept forever? What is it, and why do you think it's special? If not, what can you think of in your home that could become a treasure to pass on to your kids someday? Find an empty box to turn into a memorable keepsake box for future generations of your family. Decorate it however you'd like and begin to keep your unique family treasures inside.

2. Several characters in this book sing jump-rope rhymes with family and friends. Ask your mom, grandmother, or another adult to share their favorite jump-rope rhyme with you or discover new ones online. If you don't have a jump rope, learn some new hand-clapping games instead.

3. Toward the end of the book, the little girl shares a rhyme that she made using the first letter of her name: "B, my name is Beatrice, I come from Brooklyn..." What is the first letter of your name? Think of a little song like Beatrice's using words that start with the same first letter as your name.

SECOND HELPINGS

» *Freedom in Congo Square*
   Written by Carole Boston Weatherford
   Illustrated by R. Gregory Christie
» *Tar Beach*
   Written and illustrated by Faith Ringgold

I LOVE MY HAIR!

Written by Natasha Anastasia Tarpley
Illustrated by E. B. Lewis
"I love my hair because it is thick as a forest, soft as cotton candy, and curly as a vine winding upward . . ."

Soft watercolor images bring the ritual of Black hair care and the magic of each unique hairstyle to life. Keyana's loving mother oils her daughter's scalp and gingerly combs out her hair as Keyana squirms between her knees. Mama tries to be gentle, but the tangled places hurt, and Keyana feels discouraged until she's reminded that her hair is beautiful because it can be worn in so many fabulous styles: puffy buns, cornrows, braids with beads, a big Afro, and even ponytails that serve as wings for flying high.

WHY I CHOSE THIS BOOK: If I'd had this book growing up, I would have known that my experience when having my hair combed was one shared by many little girls who looked like me and had a head full of big, thick hair, just like mine. And perhaps this would have helped me find joy in my natural hair much sooner. Keyana's story is my story. It was my mom's story, along with her mom before her and my daughters after me. Books that casually include the ordinary moments in the lives of Black children should not be so rare.

THOUGHT STARTERS

1. Do you have a favorite way to wear your hair or clothes? How does your style make you feel?
2. Keyana's mom helps her imagine her hair in many beautiful scenarios. What types of things do you think about when you daydream?
3. What kind words can you say to let someone know you noticed the effort they put into their hair or outfit? Share your compliment the next time you have the chance.

DIGGING DEEPER

1. Take a moment to touch your hair. What does it feel like? Use your imagination and describe yourself to someone who can't see you.
2. Getting her hair combed is a special time Keyana spends with her mom. Complete this sentence: My special time with my mom, family member, or friend is _____.
   Now, draw a picture of you enjoying that moment. If you have watercolors, use those to create your image like E. B. Lewis, the illustrator of *I Love My Hair!*
3. Go on a nature walk and find things that look like your hair. Create a self-portrait by gluing the items onto paper or flat wood.

SECOND HELPINGS

» *Bippity Bop Barbershop*
   Written by Natasha Anastasia Tarpley
   Illustrated by E. B. Lewis
» *Happy Hair* (and companion book *Cool Cuts*)
   Written and illustrated by Mechal Renee Roe

YELLOW DOG BLUES

Written by Alice Faye Duncan
Illustrated by Chris Raschka
"Sometimes life is a mystery. Love is a mountain climb."

．．

Bo Willie sets out on a journey along the Mississippi Blues Trail in search of his puppy. Along the way, he visits seven places with historical significance to the "Delta blues," a genre of acoustic music that gave way to rock and roll and early country music. The words flow like a blues song carried by the little boy's desperation before he makes a startling discovery about Yellow Dog's whereabouts. The incredibly unique illustrations were created with fabric paint and embroidery thread on raw canvas, and their impact on the artistic value of this story cannot be overestimated.

WHY I CHOSE THIS BOOK: My interest was piqued after seeing a review that said reading this book was "like listening to a blues record while wrapped up in a homemade quilt sipping sweet tea." I knew then that I had to have it, and it did not disappoint. Young children may not understand all the musical references in this book, but neither did I the first time, and I loved it anyway. The historical details in the back are necessary for understanding the book's significance, and the bluesy story coupled with one-of-a-kind artwork is enough to set it apart.

THOUGHT STARTERS

1. Blues music is all about expressing sad feelings (and sometimes good ones, too). Why do you think singing songs about sad times can make people feel better? What makes you feel better when you're sad?

2. Have you ever had a dog? If so, what did you name your pet, and how did you come up with the name? If not, what would you call your dog if you got one, and why?

3. What do you think about the pictures in this book? Have you ever seen anything like them before? Do you prefer these images or more traditional artwork?

DIGGING DEEPER

1. Do you think Yellow Dog will ever return to Bo Willie's house? Make a sequel to this book in which you tell what happens to Yellow Dog after he leaves home. You can tell it to an adult while they type or write it for you.

2. Hot tamales are famous in the Mississippi Delta, where this story takes place. Find a recipe and work with an adult to make your own version of this delicious meal made of meat and cornmeal wrapped in a corn husk and simmered in a savory spiced broth.

3. The title of this book comes from an old blues song. Listen to Bessie Smith (or someone else) sing "Yellow Dog Blues." Compare how the music makes you feel when you hear it to what you felt when reading the book. Do they give you similar or different feelings? Which do you prefer and why?

SECOND HELPINGS
» *Music Is a Rainbow*
   Written and illustrated by Bryan Collier
» *Max Found Two Sticks*
   Written and illustrated by Brian Pinkney

SOUL FOOD SUNDAY

Written by Winsome Bingham
Illustrated by C. G. Esperanza
*"I put the jug next to the mac 'n' cheese and greens
and ribs and chicken and sausages."*

Granny's house is the gathering spot for Sunday soul food dinners. Parents, aunts, uncles, and cousins come together to enjoy each other's company while Roscoe Ray operates the grill. While the other kids run outside and play video games, a little boy gets to help his grandmother grate cheese, pick greens, and skin the meat before making the most fantastic pitcher of sweet tea.

WHY I CHOSE THIS BOOK: The mere mention of a soul food Sunday brings up years of cherished memories for me and many others. Gathering with family around a large table filled with lovingly prepared soul food is a priceless experience well worth documenting. My children are being raised more than seven hundred miles from our extended families, and this book reminds me of why we prioritize getting them back for visits as often as possible.

THOUGHT STARTERS

1. Have you ever helped cook a meal? What did you prepare, and how did it feel to eat something you'd made?
2. Do you think that big family gatherings are (or would be) fun? Why or why not? What fun things can you do next time your extended family or friends get together?
3. Why do you think the boy wanted to be in the kitchen rather than playing with his cousins? What makes you say so? What lessons did the little boy learn while helping his granny?

DIGGING DEEPER

1. Prepare the mac 'n' cheese recipe at the back of the book. How does it compare to other macaroni and cheese that you've had? What other foods are considered soul food? If you can, prepare some of the things you've named, or the foods mentioned in the book, and see how you enjoy the flavors.
2. Who would you invite to a big dinner at your house, and what would you serve? Grab a piece of paper and create an imaginary invitation (or a real one!) that lets your guests know exactly what to expect.
3. Read the author's note to discover how she learned to cook. What new thing have you learned to do, and who taught you? What's something that you're good at and can teach others?

SECOND HELPINGS

» *Granny's Kitchen*
Written by Sadé Smith
Illustrated by Ken Daley
» *Full, Full, Full of Love*
Written by Trish Cooke
Illustrated by Paul Howard

JAKE MAKES A WORLD: JACOB LAWRENCE, A YOUNG ARTIST IN HARLEM
Written by Sharifa Rhodes-Pitts
Illustrated by Christopher Myers

"In the morning Jake watches the sun come up.
He makes a big stretch, and the sun stretches too."

This book offers an inspiring glimpse at the childhood of acclaimed artist Jacob Lawrence. The story ends before Lawrence becomes a working adult artist. Still, the author shows how the sights and sounds of Harlem and its people prompted him to create using the materials made available to him at a local studio. Little Jake uses his creative energy to experiment with different art mediums, even re-creating his vibrant street inside a shoebox.

WHY I CHOSE THIS BOOK: Jacob Lawrence was one of the most well-known Black American artists of his time. Learning how people use art to tell their stories helps young children grow confident in their voices and creative abilities. Regularly gazing upon and interacting with Black artistry helps render it beautiful in the eyes of our children, giving them another avenue of enjoyment and art appreciation throughout their lives.

THOUGHT STARTERS

1. This book tells of the childhood of a real artist named Jacob Lawrence. What kind of art do you like to see? What kind of art do you enjoy making?

2. When Jake moved to New York City, his mom placed things from their old house into the new apartment. This made his new home feel more familiar. If you were moving into a new home, what five things would you want to take from your current home? Why did you choose those items?

3. All types of people do various things on Jake's street. Who do you see when you walk or drive around your neighborhood, and what are they usually doing?

DIGGING DEEPER

1. Outside Jake's apartment building, men play chess and checkers. Have you ever played one of those games? Ask a friend or relative to teach you how to play. Checkers are usually easier for beginners, but people of all ages can pick up both games.

2. Try your hand at one of the projects that Jake loves so much at Utopia House: Carve a bar of soap with a plastic knife or vegetable peeler, sew scraps of leather or fabric together to make something new, paint patterns on paper using

watercolors, draw a face with a charcoal pencil, or create a mask using brown paper bags, glue, and paint.

3. The pictures on the book's last few pages are reproductions of Jacob Lawrence's paintings. They were part of a series, and you can see all sixty of the panels from the Migration series at phillipscollection.org. Draw or paint your own series of three or more pictures that go together to tell a story about something important to you.

SECOND HELPINGS

» *Take a Picture of Me, James VanDerZee!*
   Written by Andrea J. Loney
   Illustrated by Keith Mallett
» *Before There Was Mozart: The Story of Joseph Boulogne, Chevalier de Saint-George*
   Written by Lesa Cline-Ransome
   Illustrated by James E. Ransome

OCTOPUS STEW

Written and illustrated by Eric Velasquez

"Whaaaaaaaaat! Cook me? Take out my eyes and beak? Why?"

. . . .

A giant octopus catches Ramsey's grandma off guard after she gets the idea to make *pulpo guisado*, an octopus stew. Ramsey relies on ingenuity and his knack for drawing to save his grandma from harm just before she decides to rethink their dinner plans. The story spotlights an Afro-Latino family with primarily English dialogue mixed with Spanish and features a short glossary in the back.

WHY I CHOSE THIS BOOK: There is a lot to love about this book. On the one hand, it's a straightforward supernatural tale about an ordinary kid who loves his grandma, but when you look closer, you'll find that the author has hidden other gifts. Readers meet a Black family that looks like their own or someone they may know, but the family is bilingual, speaking both English and Spanish. For many kids, this may be their first introduction to Afro-Latino culture. We see Ramsey's family embracing the African oral storytelling tradition alongside their love for art and Puerto Rican food.

THOUGHT STARTERS

1. Were you surprised when you flipped open the pages and found that Ramsey was telling his family a story? Think of a story that you can relate to entertain your family. Gather them around and perform your tale out loud. Be sure to use different voices, facial expressions, and gestures (hand movements) to make it even more exciting.

2. The author uses a mixture of possible and impossible things in this story. Which parts of this story could actually happen, and which are entirely imaginary?

3. People who speak two languages are bilingual. Are you, or is anyone in your family, bilingual? What about any friends or other people you know in your community? If so, which languages are spoken? Flip to the back of the book and learn the Spanish words spoken by Ramsey's family. If you already know these words, look them up in a different language and try remembering them.

DIGGING DEEPER

1. Before leaving for the store with his grandma, Ramsey pretends to be a caped superhero named Super Ram. Who is your favorite superhero, and why? What kind of character would you be if you could have superpowers? Think of a name, costume, special powers, and more. Draw a picture or act out a story featuring the new you.

2. Ramsey tries to warn his grandma about the octopus, but she doesn't listen. What else could he have done to get her attention before it was too late? Pretend you're Ramsey and your busy grandma is standing a few feet away. Act out how you would get her attention and share your important news.

3. Have you ever tried octopus stew or some other form of soup containing seafood? Look at the recipe in the back of the book and ask your family if someone can help you make it (or take you to a restaurant that serves this dish). If you're not able to make octopus stew, try cooking a different Puerto Rican dish like *arroz con gandules* (rice with pigeon peas), *pasteles* (plantain cakes), *tostones* (twice-fried plantain slices), or *flan de queso* (cream cheese dessert).

SECOND HELPINGS

» *Islandborn*

Written by Junot Díaz

Illustrated by Leo Espinosa

» *Baby Goes to Market*

Written by Atinuke

Illustrated by Angela Brooksbank

THE ELECTRIC SLIDE AND KAI

Written by Kelly J. Baptist

Illustrated by Darnell Johnson

"Mama's words sound nice, and her hug is warm,
but I don't want my own rhythm.
I want the one everyone else has!"

Kai's family is excited when they receive an invitation to Aunt Nina's wedding, but he immediately begins to worry because he's never been a good dancer. Grandpa has given everyone else in the family a desirable nickname based on their dazzling dance moves, and Kai desperately wants to earn his unique name. After practicing for months, he almost misses out on his opportunity to shine, but in the end, his new talents are showcased during the family's traditional Electric Slide dance at the wedding reception.

WHY I CHOSE THIS BOOK: Food, music, and celebration are a big part of many Black wedding receptions. When the party gets into full swing, the DJ will inevitably play songs that pull everyone onto the dance floor. Social line dances like the Electric Slide are hugely popular at Black gatherings, and this book also sneaks in the common practice of nickname usage in the Black community, which I find endearing.

THOUGHT STARTERS

1. Have you ever been to a wedding? What are some of the things that typically happen during the ceremony and at the reception or party afterward?

2. Dancing is one of Kai's family traditions, which his family always or usually does when they gather. What would you like to start or continue as a tradition in your family?
3. Kai and his new uncle Troy are both nervous about doing the dance correctly but have more courage when they join the dance floor together. Why does doing something scary with a friend or helper make it easier? Have you ever helped someone do something hard? Has anyone ever helped you get through a tough time or task? Describe how you felt in both scenarios.

DIGGING DEEPER

1. The Electric Slide is a fun party dance that anyone can learn. Give it a try! Ask a grown-up to show you what it looks like in person or on a video.
2. In some families, everyone gets up and dances together whenever people hear the music that goes with the Electric Slide or other group dances. What are some of your favorite songs? What do you think about when you listen to them? Make a simple dance to go with one of your top songs and teach it to a friend or loved one.
3. The illustrator who drew the pictures for this book said that he discovered his passion for art while watching cartoons. Do his pictures remind you of cartoons? Describe your favorite picture in the book and tell why you like it. Compare the art in this book to the illustrations in other books you've read. What are some of the similarities? What are some of the differences?

SECOND HELPINGS

» *Family Reunion*
Written by Chad & Dad Richardson
Illustrated by Ashleigh Corrin
» *When My Cousins Come to Town*
Written by Angela Shanté
Illustrated by Keisha Morris

A DAY WITH NO WORDS
Written by Tiffany Hammond
Illustrated by Kate Cosgrove

*"Daddy's voice is like air, soft as a light summer breeze
that kisses my cheek, strong as the winds of hurricanes
that abandon ships at sea."*

....

This story follows a young boy, Aidan, and his mom through their day as they use tablets to communicate with each other and various people in their community. Written by an autistic mother of two autistic sons, the book provides an intimate look into the life of a family that communicates without speaking words. The illustrations offer a path to a deeper understanding of Aidan's experiences as a nonspeaking child surrounded by people who assume that everyone communicates through speech.

WHY I CHOSE THIS BOOK: The first time I read through this story, I was left to sit with my thoughts for a while before fully processing my emotions. The story is entirely different than what I expected, and that is where much of its power lies. The author provides a poignant and expansive view of language, words, and communication as seen through the eyes of a child. By demonstrating the power of accommodations, understanding, and love within our community, this story allows children to feel seen and see others in equal measure. It shows yet another dimension of family, creativity, connection, and acceptance while demonstrating the beauty and fun that can emanate from all children.

THOUGHT STARTERS

1. What surprised you most about this book? What lessons do you think the author wanted readers to learn?
2. If you could ask Aidan three questions, what would you ask?
3. If Aidan were your neighbor, what are some things you could do together for fun?

DIGGING DEEPER

1. Aidan enjoys staring through his parted fingers, hugging trees, spinning barefoot on the grass, jumping, and eating French fries, among other things. What do you like to do when you're happy? When do you feel most free to be yourself? Take a poll of your family and friends by asking them these two questions. What do you think about the answers you received?

2. Most people communicate nonverbally (without words) using facial expressions, body movements, pointing, etc. Nonspeaking people also express themselves through other forms of communication, including tablets and different actions or sounds. Communicating without speaking can take longer than speaking with words, and some people get very impatient and become irritable, selfish, or downright mean when they notice someone using a tablet or communicating without speaking. What would you say or do if you saw someone behaving this way toward Aidan or another nonspeaking person? Tell someone you know about *A Day with No Words*. Afterward, share your ideas for things they can do if they witness someone being unkind.

3. The author wrote this book about her real-life son, Aidan, who uses an app called Proloquo2Go (by AssistiveWare) on his tablet. Ask an adult to show you the website for this app, where you can watch a video about how it works and listen to how the words sound. It's very cool!

SECOND HELPINGS

» *Song in the City*
Written by Daniel Bernstrom
Illustrated by Jenin Mohammed

» *Many Shapes of Clay: A Story of Healing*
Written and illustrated by Kenesha Sneed

MAGNIFICENT HOMESPUN BROWN: A CELEBRATION

Written by Samara Cole Doyon
Illustrated by Kaylani Juanita

"Cozy brown. Like hot cocoa, a comfortable cup of liquid dreams sliding lazily over contented lips."

· ·

The text in this book alternates between a poem about a type of brown ("feathery brown like the jagged shadows of hemlock branches") and a spread relating the color to a girl's image ("Feathery brown . . . like my lashes"). This celebration of life and the many browns encountered while living well is combined with an admiration for each narrator's image. The images feature little brown girls in various shades with different hairstyles experiencing joy found in the natural world and their everyday environments. There are girls wearing hijabs, a child with vitiligo, another kiddo in a wheelchair with a service dog, and an adult with one hand. Throughout the book, similarities and differences are beautifully tucked into everyday life without fanfare.

WHY I CHOSE THIS BOOK: Every page offers a feast for the eyes and ears, and though the rich vocabulary will stretch young ones, they'll understand the meaning and emotion of the poetic lines in context. From the Afros, locs, and pigtails to the laughter, leaves, and quilts, this book is a stunning celebration of the beauty of seeing, experiencing, and being brown.

THOUGHT STARTERS

1. Look around your room, step outside, or look out the window at the world around you. What kinds of things do you see that are brown? If you were given the job of naming each shade of brown you see, what would you call them?

2. Start at the beginning of the book and tell an original story based on the pictures as you turn each page.

3. Was there anything in this book that surprised you? What was it, and why do you think you were surprised? If nothing surprised you, which parts felt most familiar?

DIGGING DEEPER

1. One of the girls gets to taste the honey harvested from the beehive in her auntie's yard. Have you ever tasted honey? Try making toast spread with butter and drizzled with honey to see what you think. Did you know that honey comes in different colors, textures, and flavors? These differences primarily depend on the type of nectar the bees gather. Try one or more of these activities: conduct a taste test using various honey sticks and decide which one you like most, visit a beekeeper to learn how honey is made, or make some milk and honey popsicles to enjoy.

2. What color would you use to describe your skin? Think of as many things as you can that are a similar color and express them in a fun way. Besides your magnificent skin, what other things do you love about yourself? What are some things that you find cool about other people you know?

3. The kids in this book saw rosebushes and rivers, mountains and forests, sandy beaches, busy markets, piles of autumn leaves, stormy clouds, and snowy nights. Which of these environments have you experienced? Draw a picture of yourself and others in one of these outdoor environments. Show your drawing to someone else and tell them all about it.

SECOND HELPINGS

» *Brown: The Many Shades of Love*
Written by Nancy Johnson James
Illustrated by Constance Moore

» *Skin Again*
Written by bell hooks
Illustrated by Chris Raschka

UPTOWN

Written and illustrated by Bryan Collier

"Jazz and Harlem are a perfect match—just like chicken and waffles."

The child narrator of this book takes readers on a personal tour of Harlem, New York, with brief stories accompanied by detailed collages and watercolors. The sights and sounds of the little boy's vibrant community come to life as he gives various definitive statements about Uptown and then explains why each idea rings true for him. Full of imagination and history, this book allows children to "travel" to a particular part of the most populous city in the United States by hitching a ride through the mind of one creative kid.

WHY I CHOSE THIS BOOK: With references to real people and places, this book serves as a modern introduction to Harlem, a part of Manhattan with great historical significance to Black American culture. The sparse, carefully chosen words and superb illustrations offer glimpses of brownstones that look like chocolate, the Apollo Theater, the importance of the local barbershop, photographs by James VanDerZee, the Boys Choir of Harlem, and more.

THOUGHT STARTERS

1. *Uptown* refers to a section of New York City that includes an area known as Harlem. On each page, a different characteristic of Uptown is described as a metaphor. The author writes, "Uptown is . . ." What's the name of your city or area? Come up with some statements that describe your city in the same format. For example, "Chicago is deep dish pizza" or "Chattanooga is lazy days on the river."
2. The boy in the story says that the brownstones where he lives look like they are made of chocolate. Is there something you see regularly in your home or town that reminds you of a type of food?
3. Name three or four things you learned from this book about Uptown or Harlem.

DIGGING DEEPER

1. Author and illustrator Bryan Collier used pictures of people and things he associates with his environment to create imagery for this book. Take, find, or draw pictures of places you see in your community. Cut them out and glue them together to create a community collage. Feel free to use paint, markers, or any other materials you have on hand.
2. In this book, the little boy attends a Boys Choir of Harlem concert. This was an internationally known singing group that performed many types of music, including gospel, jazz, hip-hop, classical, and R & B. The choir no longer exists, but you can ask a grown-up to play a video of them singing for you. Better yet, maybe you can see a different children's choir perform in your hometown.
3. The boy in this story refers to two foods that make a tasty combination when eaten together. Do you remember what they were? Ask an adult if you can visit a restaurant serving that dish, and if you don't have one nearby, work together to make the same thing at home. Yum!

SECOND HELPINGS

» *Harlem*
   Written by Walter Dean Myers
   Illustrated by Christopher Myers

» *Sugar Hill: Harlem's Historic Neighborhood*
Written by Carole Boston Weatherford
Illustrated by R. Gregory Christie

ALL BECAUSE YOU MATTER
Written by Tami Charles
Illustrated by Bryan Collier
*"Long before you took your place in this world,
you were dreamed of, like a knapsack full of wishes."*

This book reads like a love letter from parent to child that soothingly expresses the child's worth as someone who always has mattered and always will matter. Through the author's warm text alongside Collier's signature collage and watercolor images, we meet children from birth to adolescence who experience vibrant highs and discouraging lows as they're reminded that strength, power, and beauty lie within them.

WHY I CHOSE THIS BOOK: It offers a universal message of the hope, love, and dreams parents hold for their children. Many adults respond well to dynamic motivational speeches, but children rarely receive such direct messaging about who they are, where they've come from, and their value to their families and the world. This book, with English and Spanish words along with the Filipino expression for "I love you," is a remarkable ode to the fierce belonging of children in the spaces in which they're rooted. It specifically and directly addresses the value of books as mirrors, the pain of rejection, the fear of violence (very subtle), and the legacy of a people born of queens, chiefs, and legends.

THOUGHT STARTERS
1. Some kids in the book experience bullying or unwanted mean behavior. What can you do if someone bullies you or if you see someone else being bullied?
2. On page 25, the boy is shown with his eyes closed and lines running across his face. Why did the illustrator do that? What do you think those lines may

represent? (In an interview, the author said that the stripes represent the oceans and rivers that connect us, our past, and our ancestors.)[1]

3. The author asks this question: "Did you know that you are sun rays, calm, like ocean waves, tough, like *montañas*, magic, like stars in space?" (*Montañas* are mountains in Spanish.) Give examples of how people like you can be bright like the sun, calm, tough, and "magic."

DIGGING DEEPER

1. Throughout this book, the illustrator uses faces, colored images, and patterns cut in the shape of flower petals to adorn or decorate many of the pages. The petals shift and change to create new meanings throughout the story. Find things in your environment (scrapbook paper, newspaper, photographs, magazines, etc.) that you can cut into a shape of your choosing to create a collage. Make up a short tale to go along with your picture.

2. The words in this book are poetic. Pick your favorite page and memorize the words. Recite them back to people you know. It will help them to feel strong and loved!

3. Toward the end of the book, the mother, father, and child cup their hands together and hold some of the petals that have been bent at one end. The art of folding paper is called origami. Find or cut a square piece of paper and ask a grown-up to help you create an origami animal or shape from it.

SECOND HELPINGS

» *We Are Here*
    Written by Tami Charles
    Illustrated by Bryan Collier
» *I Am Every Good Thing*
    Written by Derrick Barnes
    Illustrated by Gordon C. James

OUR STORY STARTS IN AFRICA
Written by Patrice Lawrence
Illustrated by Jeanetta Gonzales

*"She loves feeling the warm Caribbean sun on her
face and drinking fresh coconut water for breakfast . . ."*

Paloma doesn't feel accepted by her cousins while visiting her extended family in the Caribbean, but Tante Janet is determined to give her a place to belong. She pulls Paloma in close and tells her the story of their people. The story sensitively connects generations of Black people across time, beginning with great kingdoms in Africa, continuing through colonization and enslavement, and ending in her backyard on a starry night in Trinidad. The back of the book provides clear answers to questions that young children may have after reading and offers suggestions for other books to read on related topics.

WHY I CHOSE THIS BOOK: I enjoy teaching history from a very young age, but I believe that the harshest details can be revealed over time. Many authors feel the same way and tend to shy away from sharing complicated history in early picture books. This book exemplifies how we can achieve both: sharing honest accounts while remaining age-appropriate. This is a sweet and simple introduction to how many Black people ended up in the Americas; it offers a basic understanding wrapped in a relatable family tale. The story within the story addresses some of the complicated feelings that occur among Black people raised in different parts of the African diaspora, and it gives a path for how some of those feelings can be resolved or used to gain understanding and build relationships. Illustrations of head wraps, kente cloth, Afro combs, cocoa, and more help bring subtle aspects of the culture to life.

THOUGHT STARTERS

1. Tante Janet tells Paloma stories about their family history. What types of stories are told in your home?

2. Paloma's cousins don't want to play with her because she speaks differently than them. What could her cousins have done differently to make Paloma feel welcome despite her differences?

3. What kind of comb do you use on your hair? What would it feel like to use a comb with fewer, bigger teeth spaced farther apart? What about one with many

smaller teeth placed closer together? Why do you think we have different types of combs?

DIGGING DEEPER

1. In the book, we learn that some African people told stories by painting them on jars. Try this art form by molding a bowl or jar from white air-dry clay. When it is completely dry, use acrylic paints to tell a story by painting pictures directly onto your piece. Another option is to visit a pottery painting studio if you have one near your home.

2. While Paloma's cousins play under the cacao tree, her aunt explains that its pods are like treasure chests because the seeds are used to make chocolate. Try making homemade hot chocolate by heating four cups of whole milk with ¼ cup each of unsweetened cocoa powder and sugar. Stir frequently until hot but not boiling. Add ½ cup of chocolate chips and stir until melted. Mix in a dash of vanilla extract and serve in a mug with or without mini marshmallows. While enjoying your yummy creation, watch a video about how chocolate is made.

3. Tante Janet tells Paloma about the Southern African Large Telescope (SALT) near Sutherland in South Africa as they stare at the night sky. Visit a planetarium to view a night sky projection in their dome-shaped theater. Ask a family member to take you outside on a clear night, lie on your back on a blanket, and do a little stargazing. What do you think you'll see?

SECOND HELPINGS

» *Free at Last: A Juneteenth Poem*
   Written by Sojourner Kincaid Rolle
   Illustrated by Alex Bostic
» *Build a House*
   Written by Rhiannon Giddens
   Illustrated by Monica Mikai

THE BAT BOY & HIS VIOLIN
Written by Gavin Curtis
Illustrated by E. B. Lewis

"I sashay my bow across the violin strings the way a
mosquito skims a summer pond."

....

Reginald is an accomplished musician who would love for his dad to enjoy and respect his violin playing, but Papa is distracted by his career woes. As manager of the worst team in the Negro National League, he's stressed about their losing streak. Papa asks his son to join the Dukes as a bat boy while hoping that the experience will lead his little boy to choose sports over the "fiddle." Reginald brings his instrument to the baseball field, and his classical music fills the dugout with beautiful sounds that motivate the players and turn Papa's heart toward his son.

WHY I CHOSE THIS BOOK: This honest portrayal of a father who doesn't always get things right but ultimately loves his son more than anything and is willing to change course for good is a healthy lesson for children to learn. The author demonstrates that sometimes parents are wrong and make mistakes before ending with a realistic display of unconditional love from father to son. Details about Negro Leagues baseball are nestled in this tale of family bonds, offering an opportunity to introduce young children to an important part of Black sports history.

THOUGHT STARTERS

1. Reginald makes several mistakes when he tries to handle typical ball-boy responsibilities for his dad's baseball team but makes very few mistakes while playing his violin. Why do you think he struggled with one task and not the other? What things come easily to you? What types of activities are more difficult for you?

2. How do you think it made Papa, Reginald, and the rest of the team feel when the hotels wouldn't allow them to stay there because of the color of their skin? If you owned a hotel, who would be allowed to stay at your place?

3. After the team enjoys their catfish and corn dinner, Reginald plays them a lullaby on his violin. A lullaby is a quiet song that helps people fall asleep. Do you know any lullabies? Ask an adult to teach you a lullaby or learn a new one together if they don't know any by heart.

DIGGING DEEPER

1. Have you ever heard anyone play the violin? What about other instruments like the piano or cello? Learn about the Kanneh-Mason siblings at Kanneh Masons.com. Watch a video of the family playing their instruments together. Which instrument do you like most? How does their music make you feel? If possible, attend an orchestra concert in your community or at one of your local schools.

2. When Mr. Forest, the shortstop, trips over the baseball bats, the crowd laughs at him when he falls. How do you think that made Mr. Forest feel? Imagine that you work at a baseball park. Make up a list of rules about how to treat the players (and each other) and pretend to share them with the whole stadium over the loudspeaker.

3. The Negro Leagues Baseball Museum in Kansas City, Missouri, is the only museum dedicated to celebrating the legacy of Black baseball players and the impacts they made on and off the field. You may get to visit the exhibits there someday. In the meantime, check out their virtual tour and fun videos at nlbm.com to learn more about the teams and their impact on American history.

SECOND HELPINGS

» *The Field*
   Written by Baptiste Paul
   Illustrated by Jacqueline Alcántara
» *I Got Next*
   Written and illustrated by Daria
   Peoples-Riley

SAVING THE DAY: GARRETT MORGAN'S LIFE-CHANGING INVENTION OF THE TRAFFIC SIGNAL

Written by Karyn Parsons
Illustrated by R. Gregory Christie

"All are given a gift. Something you cannot learn.
It's what you do with that gift that's your gift in return."

The rhyming text of this biographical story is sure to appeal to all kids, especially those who enjoy tinkering. Inventor Garrett Morgan didn't fit in with the other children in his family. Though he tried hard, he never seemed to excel at any of his peers' pastimes or household tasks. His parents recognized that he had a unique talent and chose to send him away for tutoring in the city to help maximize his potential. Over the years, he invented several valuable items, most notably the first three-way traffic signal.

WHY I CHOSE THIS BOOK: Little is known about many Black innovators, so books that bring their stories to light are always appealing. Children need to know that Black people always have created and continue to create revolutionary new ideas that change lives and transform entire industries. Morgan's life demonstrates the difficulties that sometimes accompany divergent thinking or creative genius. It also speaks to the power of perseverance and the results of working within your gifts and passions. In a unique twist, the parents demonstrate their love with a willingness to let Garrett spread his wings when their preference would have been to keep him near. Leaving home can be scary at any age, and this success story shows that family bonds can endure despite distance when various circumstances keep families apart.

THOUGHT STARTERS

1. Garrett learned that looking both ways is crucial before crossing a street. What are some other important safety rules that people should follow?
2. Garrett created the three-way traffic signal after witnessing a terrible accident that he felt could have been avoided with a better warning system. What invention would solve a problem you've seen in your home or community?
3. When he was by himself, Garrett would take long walks and think of new creations to make. What do you think about when you spend time alone?

DIGGING DEEPER

1. A *prototype* is an early sample of an invention made for testing or as a model for building or improving new designs. Think back to your invention ideas and draw or create a prototype from items you can find around your home.
2. Garrett Morgan was an entrepreneur who owned a sewing machine shop and a clothing store where he was a tailor or clothes maker. See if an adult can help you

practice hand-sewing a simple project. If you don't have a needle and thread, try designing clothes using markers to decorate a blank T-shirt. The design won't wash out if you use fabric markers, but they're not required.

3. Did you notice that the author wrote about Garrett Morgan's life using rhyming words? Think of a person who has done something important (It may even be you!) and come up with rhyming sentences or phrases about that person's life and contributions.

SECOND HELPINGS

» *Harlem Grown: How One Big Idea Transformed a Neighborhood*
   Written by Tony Hillery
   Illustrated by Jessie Hartland

» *Ice Cream Man: How Augustus Jackson Made a Sweet Treat Better*
   Written by Glenda Armand and Kim Freeman
   Illustrated by Keith Mallet

FLY

Written by Brittany J. Thurman
Illustrated by Anna Cunha

"Africa feels certain she can double Dutch until her shoes are in fast-forward, until her feet forget the ground, until she flies like the birds in the sky."

Africa surprises her family by signing up to participate in a double Dutch competition when she doesn't even know how to jump rope, but she's not a single bit deterred. As she spends her time learning various skills from friends, readers are left to wonder how she might pull off a competition without humiliating herself. Africa confidently steps up to the ropes armed with her new moves, and everything comes together beautifully.

WHY I CHOSE THIS BOOK: I appreciate every little touch in this book, from the contagious exuberance Africa exudes on every page to her Africa-shaped birthmark. She learns everything she needs to know for the double

Dutch competition from her friends as she dances, steps, cartwheels, sings, hand claps, and jives her way around with joy and a creative flair that highlights the carefree beauty of childhood.

Though it was widespread long before, double Dutch became a sidewalk staple among Black girls in New York City in the 1970s. Its popularity in the African American community extends well beyond NYC into other urban centers and rural areas alike, and it was formalized as an official sport in 1973. With accompanying songs and rhymes, making moves between two twirling ropes is an activity that continues to bring smiles to participants and those cheering them on from the sidelines. This book is a sweet acknowledgment of double Dutch wrapped in a story about the power of community and family legacy.

THOUGHT STARTERS

1. Africa has a birthmark in the shape of the continent by the same name, so it is easy to see where her name came from. What about your name? What does it mean, and where did it come from?

2. Africa's brother tells her that competitions allow you to "show the world what you're made of." If you could choose any competition in the world, real or imaginary, what would you like to compete in and why?

3. Africa's grandma was wonderful at double Dutch. What things have you seen older people do (or have heard about them doing) that you'd like to try?

DIGGING DEEPER

1. Double Dutch moves can be simple or complex and everything in between. Check out some videos of championship competitions to see the range of possibilities. If someone in your life can teach you how to double Dutch, ask them to show you the basics. Some communities even have experts who can teach you more tricks if you want to improve. If learning to jump with two ropes isn't an option right now, grab one rope, learn to jump well, and do simple tricks while you twirl for yourself. Have fun!

2. Africa's brother tells her she can't do something she's never done before. Was he right or wrong? How do you know? What's something you've never done before that you'd like to try? Ask a few friends, family, or community members to teach

you a skill that will help you accomplish your task. Take your time as you try to master your new activity.

3. Africa joins her friends Kay and Laura for a clapping game called Miss Mary Mack. If you already know the song, add some new verses to the original version. If you aren't familiar with the rhyme and clapping rhythm, grab a friend and ask someone to teach you. Many adults grew up playing hand games, so they may know this one, but if not, they can look it up for you.

SECOND HELPINGS

» *The Night Is Yours*
   Written by Abdul-Razak Zachariah
   Illustrated by Keturah A. Bobo
» *Playtime for Restless Rascals*
   Written by Nikki Grimes
   Illustrated by Elizabeth Zunon

THERE WAS A PARTY FOR LANGSTON

Written by Jason Reynolds
Illustrated by Jerome Pumphrey and Jarrett Pumphrey
*"Langston . . . could make the word AMERICA look
like two friends making pinky promises,
to be cool, to be true."*

Through the prism of a 1991 celebration held at the Schomburg Center for Research in Black Culture of the New York Public Library, this book tells the story of Langston Hughes and the African American authors he influenced. The story was shaped by a famous photo of poets Maya Angelou and Amiri Baraka dancing at the gathering, and the illustrators included other authors in an alphabetized bookshelf ranging from James Baldwin to Richard Wright with the likes of Ashley Bryan, Nikki Giovanni, and Alice Walker mixed in.

WHY I CHOSE THIS BOOK: This upbeat masterpiece introduces little ones to a beloved wordsmith and his jazzy style with celebratory verve. Through the creative use of letters, words, and stamps, the Pumphrey brothers outdo themselves by creatively rendering Reynolds's perfectly chosen soulful words. If only children could learn about and from all the great masters in this way.

THOUGHT STARTERS

1. Langston Hughes was a famous poet or "king of letters," as the author calls him, and he inspired many writers to follow in his footsteps. Who inspires you in the things you enjoy most? Why do you admire them?

2. The illustrators, two brothers, turn words into pictures and integrate them into the artwork throughout the book. If a poet wrote a book about you, what are five words you think the illustrators should incorporate into the images depicting your life?

3. If your friends were planning a big party to celebrate you, who would you want them to invite? What would you like to do at your party? What food should they serve? What kind of music would you want them to play?

DIGGING DEEPER

1. Langston means "tall man's town" or "long stone." What does your name mean? Create a short poem about your name and its meaning.

2. The Schomburg Center for Research in Black Culture is a research library of the New York Public Library, and information on people of African descent worldwide is stored there. Pick any topic you are interested in, go to your local library, and ask the children's librarian to help you learn how to conduct research. What did you learn about research? What did you learn about your topic?

3. Ask a grown-up to show you the photo of Maya Angelou and Amiri Baraka dancing at the real-life celebration depicted in the book. What does the picture make you think of? If you could ask Maya and Amiri one question about that special evening, what would it be?

SECOND HELPINGS

» *Something, Someday*
Written by Amanda Gorman
Illustrated by Christian Robinson
» *Thinker: My Puppy Poet and Me*
Written by Eloise Greenfield
Illustrated by Ehsan Abdollahi

EARLY ELEMENTARY (AGES 5–7)

SING A SONG: HOW "LIFT EVERY VOICE AND SING" INSPIRED GENERATIONS
Written by Kelly Starling Lyons
Illustrated by Keith Mallett

"Sing a song full of the hope that the present has brought us."

This book tells how five generations of a family passed on the lyrics to "Lift Every Voice and Sing" to their loved ones. Alongside the moving reverence for a song that carries so much meaning for Black people, children learn the significance of the lyrics and how they inspire and encourage people worldwide today. The illustrations were drawn freehand and painted digitally, resulting in bright colors tinged with dynamic use of light and an array of brown skin tones and natural hairstyles throughout. The entire song lyrics are conveniently included on the inside front cover, and the author's note shares her inspiration for the story.

WHY I CHOSE THIS BOOK: This is a song that I learned as a child from hearing it sung at so many events within the Black community. It is something that I've taught my children so they can join in the overwhelming sense of community and pride that swells in people's hearts when they gather to sing in fellowship. It is arguably *the* song of Black America. Others have proudly picked it up and carried it on in their hearts, and our children deserve to receive the gift birthed by the Johnson brothers and passed along by so many.

THOUGHT STARTERS

1. The beginning of this book takes place more than 120 years ago, in the year 1900. Look at the picture of the girl and her mom working in the kitchen. What clues remind you that the early scenes took place long ago?

2. "Lift Every Voice and Sing" is informally known as the Black National Anthem, and its message is particularly meaningful to African Americans. It also resonates with other people who relate to the lyrics and enjoy singing it alone or in solidarity with Black people. Describe something special to your family that others would also probably enjoy. Why do you think they would be interested in it?

3. "Lift Every Voice and Sing" is passed on by each generation within a family. What things have your parents or other adults in your family or community taught you?

DIGGING DEEPER

1. Listen to "Lift Every Voice and Sing" daily and challenge yourself to memorize it. Start by humming along like the girl in the book, then add as many words as possible. Then, you'll always be ready to join your voice with others when you attend an event where the song is sung.

2. James Weldon Johnson and his brother, John Rosamond Johnson, wrote the words and music for "Lift Every Voice and Sing" to commemorate President Abraham Lincoln's birthday. Think of someone with an upcoming birthday and create a poem or song for the celebration. Be sure to share it with them on their special day.

3. Artist Augusta Savage's signature sculpture was inspired by "Lift Every Voice and Sing." Known as *The Harp*, her sixteen-foot-tall piece featured young singers in long robes forming the strings of a harp. Ask an adult to show you a photo of this famous sculpture and use clay or Play-Doh to create your own sculpture based on a song you love. If you don't have something to sculpt with, you can draw a picture instead.

SECOND HELPINGS

» *We Shall Overcome*
   Illustrated by Bryan Collier

» *Standing in the Need of Prayer: A Modern Retelling of the Classic Spiritual*
Written by Carole Boston Weatherford
Illustrated by Frank Morrison

SWEET POTATO PIE

Written by Kathleen D. Lindsey
Illustrated by Charlotte Riley-Webb
"Mama always thought something sweet would help us solve our problems."

. . . .

A family of seven finds a deliciously creative way to raise money to save their farm during a drought. Despite their hard work, they could only get the sweet potatoes from their harvest, but Mama devised the perfect solution for resourcefully using what they had to make extra money. To bring her idea to fruition, the entire family must work together while overcoming losses and mishaps along the way. The acrylic illustrations offer lively, sweeping imagery that draws the eye to every part of the page. And like any good book about food and family, this one features a recipe for Mama's Sweet Potato Pie in the back, including instructions for baking an extra-flaky pie crust from scratch.

WHY I CHOSE THIS BOOK: There's so much to love about this book. I particularly appreciate the message of overcoming hard times by sticking together as a family. Mama's problem-solving and Papa's commitment to making it happen demonstrate the hardworking teamwork that characterizes the backbone of traditional Black families. Mama's graceful response to the children's mistakes is an excellent example of countering negative stereotypes of Black parents. Sweet potato pie is the star of this book, serving as a great reminder of its importance on a soul food menu.

THOUGHT STARTERS

1. How did you expect Mama to react when the children came in with less milk, eggs, and flour than they should have had? What do you think of her reaction? Can you think of a time when you've forgiven someone who did something that disappointed you or didn't meet your expectations?

2. Mama wins a blue ribbon for baking the best pie at the Harvest Celebration. What are you really good at? When can you practice or share your gifts and talents with others?

3. While the family returned to the wagon after the festival, Papa picked up a special surprise for Mama. Has anyone ever surprised you in some way? How did it make you feel? Think of a plan to make someone else's day by surprising them with something they'll enjoy.

DIGGING DEEPER

1. Try your hand at growing your own sweet potatoes. Stick a few toothpicks halfway down a sweet potato and place the potato in a jar of water, using the toothpicks to support it on the rim of the glass. Set it near a window and wait for the slips (rooted sprouts) to grow. When the slips are 6–10 inches long, gently separate them from the potato and plant them in a large pot of soil (or in the ground).

2. Candied yams are a classic soul food dish, but the name is misleading. Real yams have rough, textured brown skin and pale, starchy flesh. They're one of the most important food crops in Western Africa, but they can't be found in most American grocery stores. Our soul food dish is actually made with sweet potatoes cooked in a buttery, sugary syrup. Visit an African or Caribbean grocery store in your area (or look up photos online) and learn about the differences between yams and sweet potatoes.

3. Follow the recipe in the book to make a sweet potato pie to share with family and friends. On the last page, Mama, Papa, and the kids enjoy hot tea with their pie. Plan a little tea party and serve your favorite flavor of hot tea (or some old-fashioned Southern iced tea) to your guests.

SECOND HELPINGS

» *In My Momma's Kitchen*
    Written by Jerdine Nolen
    Illustrated by Colin Bootman
» *Rice & Rocks*
    Written by Sandra L. Richards
    Illustrated by Megan Kayleigh Sullivan

BINTOU'S BRAIDS

Written by Sylviane A. Diouf

Illustrated by Shane W. Evans

*"She says old people know so much because they have
lived such a long time and have learned
more than anybody else."*

. . . .

Filled with head nods to West African culture, this story about a little girl who wants the same hairstyle as the older girls and women in her village is something to which every child who wants to grow up quickly can relate. She feels her hair is short, fuzzy, plain, and silly, while the older women have beautiful long braids with gold coins and seashells. After Bintou does something brave, her mom says she can finally be rewarded with the braids she always wanted. However, wisdom from her grandmother leads to a new solution that preserves the childhood traditions of Bintou's family while honoring her desires. The story features playful oil paintings and includes a note from the author about her family roots in Senegal, discussion questions, writing prompts, and oral history exercises.

WHY I CHOSE THIS BOOK: Many mentions and illustrations of West African traditions are running in the background of this story. Given that many Black Americans can trace their roots to this area of the continent, I find it especially important for children to understand and appreciate the culture. One of the girls that Bintou admires is Terry, who is visiting from the U.S. She also has braids and shares that little girls in America sometimes put colorful barrettes on each braid. I like that this story includes an African American studying abroad in West Africa. It is rare to see a children's book showing Black Americans being interested and engaged in African culture. Finally, I found it refreshing that Bintou's standard of beauty was another traditional Black hairstyle.

THOUGHT STARTERS

1. What types of things about Bintou and her community are like you and your friends and family? Which things are different?
2. When Bintou is at the beach, she makes a brave split-second decision that helps

save her neighbors. Talk about a time when you or someone you know had to be brave.

3. Bintou needs to wait until she's older to get the hairstyle she longs for, but she can do other enjoyable things while she's young. What do you get to enjoy now at your age? What do you look forward to doing when you're older?

DIGGING DEEPER

1. After Bintou's family has the naming ceremony for her baby brother, she looks forward to eating lamb and rice, fish balls, sugary fritters, and papayas. Interview some of the adults in your life to find out which foods they remember enjoying during family celebrations when they were growing up.

2. Look up the country of Senegal on a world map and compare that to where you live. Notice the distance each place is from the equator and the nearest ocean or large body of water. Point to and name bordering countries or states for each.

3. Some women in Bintou's village wrap colorful fabric around their heads. Is there anyone in your life who wears head wraps? If so, ask her to teach you how it is done. If that's not an option, ask an adult to show you a video of Senegalese head wraps so you can learn more.

SECOND HELPINGS

» *Crown: An Ode to the Fresh Cut*
    Written by Derrick Barnes
    Illustrated by Gordon C. James
» *My Hair Is a Garden*
    Written and illustrated by Cozbi A. Cabrera

WHAT IS GIVEN FROM THE HEART
Written by Patricia C. McKissack
Illustrated by April Harrison
*"What is given from the heart reaches
the heart."*

In her last picture book before passing, Patricia McKissack gifted us this treasure about a young boy and his mother who experience hardship after losing their father and husband. Times are lean, so James Otis wonders what he can possibly donate to a family from church who lost everything in a fire. What he comes up with is proof that we all can experience the joy of giving, whether we have a little or a lot. The illustrations for this book were rendered in mixed media, including acrylics, collage, art pens, and found objects. I can't imagine more inspiring visual imagery accompanying one of the author's final projects.

WHY I PICKED THIS BOOK: While most of the books for this age group feature two-parent families, it is essential that loving single parents are reflected for children because they represent a significant portion of Black American households. This book also showcases the concept of communities rallying together to help those in need and the power of the Black church to meaningfully organize and engage the community. I couldn't resist the images of Black folks dressed up and walking to Olive Chapel, looking mighty fine in their church hats and Sunday best. Finally, the book respectfully and compassionately shows that financial poverty does not preclude good character, generosity, or kindness, and it does so without being preachy.

THOUGHT STARTERS

1. James Otis loses his father at the very beginning of the story. Have you ever lost someone or something you loved? How have you kept the memory of that person or experience alive?
2. What do you think a family who lost everything in a fire might need or want? What would you want someone to give you if your family lost all your belongings?
3. The book ends with Mama spinning joyfully in the snow. What do you like to do when you're bursting with joy?

DIGGING DEEPER

1. Work with your family to go through your toys and household goods to see what you can give away to bring a smile to another family in need. Continue to do this regularly as you cultivate a giving spirit.

2. James Otis wrote Sarah a book, and she loved it. Most people enjoy reading stories about themselves and others. Think of a great story to share with someone you care about. Ask an adult to type it out as you speak, and feel free to draw pictures that help tell the story. Add a cover and gift it to a special person.
3. The illustrator used mixed media to create the pictures in this book. That means she used more than one material to make the images you see. Re-create your favorite scene from the book using mixed media art. Anything you find interesting can be used, including paints, chalk pastels, photographs, magazine clippings, wrapping paper, old jewelry, yarn, buttons, etc.

SECOND HELPINGS

» *Uncle Jed's Barbershop*
   Written by Margaree King Mitchell
   Illustrated by James Ransome
» *Nothing Special*
   Written by Desiree Cooper
   Illustrated by Bec Sloane

BRONZEVILLE BOYS AND GIRLS
Written by Gwendolyn Brooks
Illustrated by Faith Ringgold
"Do you ever look in the looking-glass and see a stranger there?"

With verses by Gwendolyn Brooks and illustrations by Faith Ringgold, this treasure explores the thoughts and experiences of thirty-four children. The poems were initially published in 1956 and were inspired by Brooks's neighborhood in Chicago. Bronzeville was a mecca for civil rights, jazz, blues, and gospel music. Today, it is known for its African American cultural scene and rich history, including as the former home of activist Ida B. Wells and musician Louis Armstrong. The poems uniquely showcase the joys of childhood, and Ringgold's trademark art style brings excitement to every page.

WHY I CHOSE THIS BOOK: Admittedly, I'd clamor for any project that offers work from Brooks and Ringgold, but I specifically chose this book because of its honest and fresh view of how children see the world. I grew up outside Chicago, a major destination for Black people during the Great Migration. The connection is meaningful, as is the universal quality of the work. Though these kids were imagined in an urban setting, they could believably be found in any neighborhood, and their experiences remind us of the vibrancy of community, family, and friendship. Oh, and these kids are funny, too!

THOUGHT STARTERS

1. The children in this book live near each other in the Bronzeville neighborhood of Chicago, a big city. How do their lifestyle and environment or surroundings compare to yours?
2. Which child from the book is most like you and why?
3. Practice saying different words that rhyme. Try to make a short poem about your favorite thing to do for fun using some of those words.

DIGGING DEEPER

1. Look at the book's front cover and tell a short story about the people you see. Who are they? What are they doing? Where are they coming from, or where are they headed? What might they be thinking?
2. Select a poem from the book to memorize. Say it out loud each day in your best voice until you know the poem by heart. Then, recite it for an audience or teach it to someone you know.
3. The first version of this book had black-and-white pictures by another artist. This version features brightly colored illustrations by Faith Ringgold. Pick one of your favorite poems from the book and draw a new picture to go along with it. If you enjoy that process, continue to illustrate each poem in your personal style.

SECOND HELPINGS

» *The Undefeated*
   Written by Kwame Alexander
   Illustrated by Kadir Nelson
» *My Man Blue*
   Poems by Nikki Grimes
   Illustrated by Jerome Lagarrigue

MIRANDY AND BROTHER WIND

Written by Patricia C. McKissack

Illustrated by Jerry Pinkney

"Can't nobody put shackles on Brother Wind, chile.
He be special. He be free."

Mirandy wants to capture Brother Wind so he can do her bidding at the upcoming junior cakewalk. After unsuccessfully trying a handful of methods recommended by friends and family, she finally outsmarts the wind and traps him in the barn. She ends up dancing with her friend Ezel after another friend snubs him, but Brother Wind still helps her win in his special way.

WHY I CHOSE THIS BOOK: This story is full of action, and it calls on folklore, history, and fun to pull the plot along. I appreciate the ideas people give Mirandy about catching Brother Wind because they remind me of the folk remedies I heard from old folks while growing up. The central concept of the cakewalk is a creative way to introduce children to a real piece of African American history, and the language and imagery used throughout the book give a strong sense of rural Southern life. The watercolors are magnificent, and Pinkney's representation of Brother Wind is pure genius.

THOUGHT STARTERS

1. Mirandy tries to catch Brother Wind in several ways, but they all fail initially. She doesn't give up, though! Eventually, she corners him in the barn. Describe a time when you failed at a task but kept going and finally got it. Or is there a time that you wish that you'd kept trying when something wasn't working?

2. Mirandy quickly came to Ezel's defense and agreed to be his partner for the cakewalk when she heard Orlinda putting him down. What do you think about Mirandy's actions? Have you ever been in a situation where someone was being mistreated in front of you? What did you do? What would you do next time?

3. Illustrations are essential to a picture book because they convey information that isn't always included in the text. Look at each picture in this book and point out things you wouldn't have known if you only read the words without any illustrations. Examples from the first couple of pages could be the pictures showing us the outside and inside of Mirandy's house. What else can you find?

DIGGING DEEPER

1. Bake a cake from scratch. You can use the chocolate cake recipe on the book's inside front cover or select a different type of cake. When the cake is done baking and has cooled off, decorate it with icing and add any fancy touches that look good and taste delicious.

2. Read the author's note at the beginning of the book to learn the history of the cakewalk, and watch a video of people doing a traditional cakewalk. Once you've seen it, turn on some music with a good beat, grab your partner, and do your version of Mirandy and Ezel's dance when they "arched their backs, kicked up their heels, and reeled from side to side."

3. Make a wind chime so you'll hear whenever the wind blows by. Using materials you can find at home (beads, bottle caps, aluminum cans, buttons, old keys, etc.), tie or glue them to different lengths of string or twine. Tie the other end of each string to a stick and attach a single string to each end of the stick so you can hang your wind chime outside.

SECOND HELPINGS

» *Brothers of the Knight*
  Written by Debbie Allen
  Illustrated by Kadir Nelson
» *Hewitt Anderson's Great Big Life*
  Written by Jerdine Nolen
  Illustrated by Kadir Nelson

MAMA'S NIGHTINGALE: A STORY OF IMMIGRATION AND SEPARATION

Written by Edwidge Danticat
Illustrated by Leslie Staub
"Sometimes the stories are as sad as melted ice cream."

In this touching story, Saya's undocumented Haitian mother is sent to a U.S. detention center. While they're apart, Saya finds comfort in listening to her mother's outgoing greeting on the family's answering machine, but it accidentally gets erased. After a gut-wrenching family visit at the detention center, Mama sends Saya some bedtime stories that she has recorded on tape, and they comfort her in many ways. Saya ends up writing her own story and sending it to a newspaper with her father's help. Eventually, public opinion frees Saya's mother, and the family is reunited.

WHY I CHOSE THIS BOOK: The first time I read this book, I was filled with emotions I couldn't describe. The author's words and descriptions made me feel, for a moment, that I was Saya. I internalized her desperation and broken heart, and I could also imagine how her mama felt to have her daughter torn from her. This story will connect children to the people behind the immigration debate, and hopefully, they'll begin to understand just a bit of the complexity and impact on families. Another reason that I included this book is to show that there are immigrants and separation stories within the Black community because we don't hear their stories as often.

THOUGHT STARTERS

1. Saya's mama is an immigrant from another place who moves to a new country to live. Why might someone immigrate to the United States or elsewhere? What does it mean that Mama doesn't have "papers," and why won't Saya's papers work for her mom?

2. Describe Saya's experiences at Sunshine Correctional, the place where her mama is held. How do you think Saya feels, and how can you tell?

3. Read the author's note. She wrote this fictional book based on her own childhood experiences. What things in your life may you want to write about someday?

DIGGING DEEPER

1. Starting on the first page and continuing throughout the book, Saya's parents use words from a different language, Haitian Creole. It's an official language in Haiti and is spoken by millions of people worldwide, including some people living in the United States. We can tell from the story that Saya is bilingual; she can speak and understand two languages. Do you know more than one language? If so, write (or dictate) a letter to a friend or relative using words from both languages you know. If not, ask an adult to help you learn a few words in Haitian Creole you can use in your letter.

2. Why do you think the reporters want to print Saya's letter and interview her for the news? Does that help or hurt Mama's opportunity to come home? When you think about your family, community, or the world, what would you like to help improve? Record yourself explaining why you care and what you think should happen. Watch the video and continue practicing so you're prepared to use your voice when the time comes.

3. When Saya misses her mom very much, something comes in the mail that makes her feel better. Record a story for a family member or friend you miss and send it to them. Ask them, or another person, to send a recording back to you.

SECOND HELPINGS

» *A Walk in the Woods*
   Written by Nikki Grimes
   Illustrated by Jerry Pinkney and Brian Pinkney
» *Coming on Home Soon*
   Written by Jacqueline Woodson
   Illustrated by E. B. Lewis

THE PEOPLE REMEMBER

Written by Ibi Zoboi
Illustrated by Loveis Wise
*"The people's music and dance, art and stories, fashion
and poetry crossed boundaries and borders . . ."*

This book creatively uses the seven principles of Kwanzaa to tell the journey of African descendants in America. The lyrical narrative and bright illustrations make this an excellent look at Black American history for young children. It gives enough detail for early elementary kids to understand what happened while leaving them with a sense of joy and celebration rather than shame or desperation. The author's note and timeline of events at the back of the book offer additional context and valuable information about the author's background, celebrating Kwanzaa, and significant historical events. The back matter can be read a little at a time over multiple sittings.

WHY I CHOSE THIS BOOK: When reviewing history books for young children, I look for beautifully written stories with engaging artwork. I prioritize storytelling that balances the necessary and desirable truth-telling of the past with the equally essential celebration of our creativity, perseverance, innovation, and joy. And finally, I search for books that include the history of African kingdoms and communities before slavery, along with the achievements and accomplishments of Black people. This poetic book does all that while including language, symbols, and artifacts from African American culture—quilts, jumping the broom, playing the dozens, cakewalks, music, and more. This is one to read repeatedly over time as children will understand more and more of the references each year.

THOUGHT STARTERS

1. How do you feel inside when you read this book? Do you feel the same way on every page, or do your feelings change depending on the part of the poem or the pictures? Flip through and describe your emotions on a few of the pages.
2. On page 47 (with the picture of the breakdancers), it says, "... out of the heart comes the finest art." What do you think the author is trying to tell us about the music, dance, poetry, literature, and art that African Americans have created?
3. After reading this book, how would you describe the journey of African Americans? Use your own words to tell the story, starting in Africa and continuing until today.

DIGGING DEEPER

1. How does the celebration of Kwanzaa relate to your family's special celebrations? Look at each of the principles of Kwanzaa and give an example of how you see that show up in your life.
2. Pick one of the famous people named in the book and ask an adult to tell you about them, read another book about them, or watch a video about them or their work. Why do you think the author included this person in her poem?
3. Visit or call someone from an older generation. It can be a grandparent or someone else in that age group. Ask them to tell you stories from their family history, and then you share some stories you remember from your life.

SECOND HELPINGS

» *Your Legacy: A Bold Reclaiming of Our Enslaved History*
Written by Schele Williams
Illustrated by Tonya Engel

» *Opal Lee and What It Means to Be Free: The True Story of the Grandmother of Juneteenth*
Written by Alice Faye Duncan
Illustrated by Keturah A. Bobo

BLACK COWBOY, WILD HORSES

Written by Julius Lester
Illustrated by Jerry Pinkney
"Far, far away, at what looked to be the edge of the world, land and sky kissed."

....

Bob Lemmon was an African American cowboy who was once enslaved. In this story, he relies on his deep knowledge of the land and horses to track a herd of wild mustangs and bring them back to the corral, a feat that's usually impossible to accomplish alone. To do so, Bob demonstrates great patience, showing that he has embraced his natural talents and worked hard to perfect his skills.

WHY I CHOSE THIS BOOK: I included this vignette from Bob Lemmons's life because young readers are introduced to the beauty of nonfiction storytelling as they absorb the feeling and energy of the Old West. This is important because most children's books covering pioneer times never mention Black people. When I read this book to my children, my sons' eyes lit up, and they burst into imaginative play. It was the first time that they learned about the long and impressive history of Black cowboys, and they immediately saw themselves in the moment, riding alongside Lemmons and his horse, Warrior.

THOUGHT STARTERS

1. Bob Lemmons didn't know how to read or write because he grew up when teaching enslaved people to read was illegal, but he had other skills that helped him thrive. What's something you're naturally good at, and what would you like to learn how to do?
2. Lemmons created a plan to take over the herd of wild horses and patiently executed that plan. Describe a time when you patiently planned something. Be sure to tell the steps you took to bring your strategy to life. Tell what you would do differently next time if those steps didn't work.
3. Bob Lemmons had a special relationship with his horse. What type of animal would you like to build a friendship with and why?

DIGGING DEEPER

1. When Bob couldn't start a fire, he had to eat food from his saddlebag. Why do you think these particular foods were good for cowboys to carry with them? Gather a snack of nonperishable foods like dried fruit, beef jerky, and nuts, and see how you like it. What other foods can you eat on the go when you're unable to cook?
2. This book is filled with similes. A simile is figurative language that describes something by comparing it to something else with the words "like" or "as." For example, the first page says, "The sky was curved *as if* it were a lap on which the earth lay napping *like* a curled cat." Find other examples of similes while listening to the book again, and then make up a few of your own to describe common items in your home.
3. The author ends the book with Bob telling his horse, Warrior, "I know. Maybe someday." What do you think he means? What could have happened next? Tell your sequel or story extension to someone else who has read this story.

SECOND HELPINGS

» *I Have Heard of a Land*
    Written by Joyce Carol Thomas
    Illustrated by Floyd Cooper
» *Bad News for Outlaws: The Remarkable Life of Bass Reeves, Deputy U.S. Marshal*

Written by Vaunda Micheaux Nelson
Illustrated by R. Gregory Christie

THE POWER OF HER PEN: THE STORY OF GROUNDBREAKING JOURNALIST ETHEL L. PAYNE

Written by Lesa Cline-Ransome
Illustrated by John Parra

"I was beginning to have the seeds of rebellion churning up in me."

Ethel Payne was one of the first Black journalists in the White House briefing room, and her career exemplifies the power of the written word to bring about change in even the most challenging circumstances. Despite the hardships she endured, Ethel's gifts continually shone through, along with her commitment to spotlight the African American community's most pressing issues.

WHY I CHOSE THIS BOOK: I appreciate this book for teaching children (and me!) about someone who deserves more attention in our history books than she has been given. The author shares the hardships and racism Ethel faced but focuses more on how she moved through the world making space for her voice. I love it when books reference other important people and events because they plant seeds while familiarizing children with new concepts they can continue learning about. Examples from this book are mentions of auction blocks, sharecropping, Pullman porters, the *Chicago Defender*, the Great Depression, and the *Brown vs. the Board of Education* case.

THOUGHT STARTERS

1. What are some of the hard parts of Ethel's life described in the book? What difficult things have happened to you or someone you know?
2. Ethel left home to travel to Japan. What is the farthest you've ever been from home, and how was that city, state, or country similar and different from where you live?
3. Ethel asked various U.S. presidents tough questions on important topics. If you could speak with the president of our country today, what three questions would you ask?

DIGGING DEEPER

1. Ethel and her siblings enjoyed visiting the library, where she would flip through the pages and memorize passages from various books. Visit your local library and pick out a few interesting books to bring home. Look at the pictures, read or listen to the words in your books, and choose a short, enjoyable passage to memorize.

2. Ethel says, "You couldn't grow up in Chicago and be Black if you didn't know the *Chicago Defender.*" What do we learn about the *Chicago Defender* in this story? Pretend to be a newspaper reporter and make up a few headlines or story topics you'd like to report on. Why did you choose those?

3. Ethel was often the only Black woman in her environment. Have you ever been somewhere where everyone looked different than you or where everyone was different from you in some other way? How did that make you feel?

SECOND HELPINGS

» *Mae Makes a Way: The True Story of Mae Reeves, Hat & History Maker*
Written by Olugbemisola Rhuday-Perkovich
Illustrated by Andrea Pippins

» *Dream Builder: The Story of Architect Philip Freelon*
Written by Kelly Starling Lyons
Illustrated by Laura Freeman

DREAM STREET

Written by Tricia Elam Walker
Illustrated by Ekua Holmes
*"Every butterfly is different. Just like snowflakes
and people and dreams."*

· ·

This imaginative book is based on the Roxbury neighborhood in Boston, where the author and illustrator grew up together as cousins. It celebrates the power of community by highlighting the vibrant personalities on Dream Street along with their unique comings and goings. From Mr. Sidney, who sits on the stoop dressed "to the nines," to Ms. Sarah, the hat lady who whispers her stories when you come close, they create a safe place where children can live carefree experiences full of adventure and imagination.

WHY I CHOSE THIS BOOK: Dream Street is a familiar scene in many African American neighborhoods. I didn't experience this vibe in my hometown, but when we'd visit my grandparents in the summers, we'd "go walking" and encounter these same personalities and then some. This story's tone, language, and descriptions bring to life many elements of a lively Black community that children will either find familiar or entirely new. Either way, they'll walk away knowing that Dream Street is the place to be if you have big dreams and want the support of people who believe in you.

THOUGHT STARTERS

1. What makes Dream Street "the best street in the world"? Would you want to live there? Why or why not?
2. When the kids pass Mr. Sidney on page 6, he says, "Don't wait to have a great day. Create one!" What does he mean, and how can you create great days?
3. Ede and Tari, on page 16, are supposed to represent the author and illustrator, who are cousins in real life. They dreamed of someday writing a book together, and then they did it! What do you dream of doing one day? Is there someone in your life that you hope to do that with?

DIGGING DEEPER

1. Azaria is excellent at jumping rope (page 10). Double Dutch is a longtime favorite pastime in the Black community. Ask an adult to show you a video online if you've never seen it done. Then grab a couple of long ropes (we got ours from the local hardware store) and at least two friends and try it. It's not always easy at first, but stick with it because it can be loads of fun.
2. Interview a friend or family member and find out what's unique about where they live. Ask them to describe what they see when they look outside their window and walk around their neighborhood. What kinds of neighbors do they have? What do they enjoy most about where they live? If you're speaking with an adult, ask them to compare their current neighborhood to where they grew up.
3. Imagine that you live on Dream Street and the author wants to add you to the book. Draw a picture of yourself and write (or tell) what should be included on

your page. How should you be described? What is your personality? What might people see you do or hear you say?

SECOND HELPINGS

» *The World Belonged to Us*
  Written by Jacqueline Woodson
  Illustrated by Leo Espinosa
» *Sweet Music in Harlem*
  Written by Debbie A. Taylor
  Illustrated by Frank Morrison

HARLEM'S LITTLE BLACKBIRD: THE STORY OF FLORENCE MILLS

Written by Renée Watson

Illustrated by Christian Robinson

"If my voice is powerful enough to stop the rain, what else can it do?"

This is the story of singer, dancer, and activist Florence Mills, an acclaimed world-class performer from the 1920s. Known for her sweet voice and electrifying moves, Mills mesmerized audiences worldwide with her comedic timing and stunning vocals. The story begins in a "teeny-tiny, itsy-bitsy house" where Florence lives with her parents and siblings and ends with her untimely illness and premature death from tuberculosis. In between, the author shares as much about Mill's commitment to standing up for the rights of African Americans as she does about her talent. Despite her fame, Mills consistently sought opportunities to promote other Black entertainers and used her notoriety to call attention to issues impacting the rights and livelihoods of her community.

WHY I CHOSE THIS BOOK: Florence Mills was a sensation in her time, with more than 150,000 mourners attending her funeral. I love how she remained tethered to the African American community, even turning down lucrative offers when she felt she could help Black people more if her talents were used elsewhere. I think that's a mighty lesson for kids to learn. This book gingerly introduces the idea of segregation while delivering a clear message that children can and should follow their dreams even in the face of injustice, setbacks, or obstacles. Song lyrics to spirituals and Mills's favorite song (which was a beautiful cry for equal rights) are artistically sprinkled into Robinson's bright, retro illustrations, shedding light on what most inspired Mills and how she, in turn, encouraged others.

THOUGHT STARTERS

1. How do you think Florence felt when people wouldn't let her family and friends in the theater or didn't want to hear her sing because of her skin color? What would you say if you could talk to the people who mistreated her?

2. Florence turned down a dream job to "use her voice for more than entertainment." If someone handed you a microphone and you could teach the world about anything you'd like, what would you share and why?

3. Florence was known as "The Queen of Happiness," and she left such an impression that some of her fellow musicians wrote songs dedicated to her after she passed away. (Listen to Duke Ellington's *Black Beauty*, which he dedicated to her memory.) What are some ways that you can show people that you think they're great? How would you like others to show their appreciation for you?

DIGGING DEEPER

1. On page 2, we can read some of the lyrics to a spiritual that Florence's mom used to comfort her during thunderstorms. African American spirituals (also known as Negro spirituals) are a form of American folk songs created by enslaved Black people to express their faith, sorrows, and hopes. Listen to "It Is Well With My Soul" online. (Search for performances by Anthony Evans or Wintley Phipps.) Why do you think Florence's mom picked this song to help Florence through hard times? Think of five things you can do to help someone you love feel better if they're having a hard day or when they're sad or scared. Pick one to do this week!

2. Sadly, her voice was never recorded, but you can listen to someone else singing Florence's favorite song, "I'm a Little Blackbird." As you listen, consider what the song might be about and make up a little dance to go with it.

3. Florence was very generous, always showing kindness to friends and strangers while freely sharing her resources (time, money, energy, etc.). What are some

examples of her generosity in the book? Think of something you give, do, or make that you can share with someone else without expecting anything in return. When you share your resource(s), let the recipient know that Florence Mills inspired you.

SECOND HELPINGS
» *RESPECT: Aretha Franklin, the Queen of Soul*
  Written by Carole Boston Weatherford
  Illustrated by Frank Morrison
» *Nina: A Story of Nina Simone*
  Written by Traci N. Todd
  Illustrated by Christian Robinson

JOHN HENRY
Written by Julius Lester
Illustrated by Jerry Pinkney
"The sun yawned, washed its face, flossed and brushed its teeth, and hurried up over the horizon."

This is a one-of-a-kind retelling of an age-old American folktale featuring young John Henry, who is born with mighty strength. After leaving home to find his way in the world, he winds up in the contest of his life: testing his natural strength and speed against a steam-powered drilling machine. The story of John Henry celebrates his victory against seemingly unsurmountable odds while leaving us to wrestle with the fact that his strength and determination are also what ultimately killed him.

WHY I CHOSE THIS BOOK: This tale has been told in many ways, but *this* version stands out from all the rest. It's an irresistible read-aloud that leaves listeners sitting on the edge of their seats as they ride an emotional roller coaster with one of America's biggest folktale heroes. Learning about John Henry allows children to see a Black man saving the day in an imaginative story—a rare find. This story has humor, depth, and nuance that isn't always found in books for young children.

THOUGHT STARTERS

1. *John Henry* is a tall tale based on a man who may have really existed. A tall tale is a folklore story with unbelievable or exaggerated elements told as if they were real. What hints does the narrator (storyteller) give on the first page that tell us this is not an entirely true story?

2. Tall tales usually have a humorous or funny aspect. What parts of this story do you find funny? What other emotions do you experience while reading this book?

3. Flip through the book and find your favorite picture. Narrate (tell back) what was happening in this part of the story.

DIGGING DEEPER

1. What qualities do you admire in John Henry? What do you think he should have done differently? Write or dictate a letter to John Henry letting him know what you think about his life and decisions.

2. What if John Henry reappeared today in your town? Make up a new folktale about his modern-day adventures. What problem would he solve and how? How would your neighbors and community members react? Be sure to give your story a strong beginning, an exciting middle, and a satisfying ending.

3. Tall tale heroes are larger than life. It's almost as if they have superpowers that allow them to do things that no one else can do. Draw a picture of yourself as a tall tale character. What would you be able to do that no one else can do, and how would you use your super talent?

SECOND HELPINGS

» *Thunder Rose*
   Written by Jerdine Nolen
   Illustrated by Kadir Nelson
» *The Little Mermaid*
   Written and illustrated by Jerry Pinkney

THE PEOPLE COULD FLY: THE PICTURE BOOK

Written by Virginia Hamilton
Illustrated by Leo and Diane Dillon

"And they flew like blackbirds over the fields. Black,
shiny wings flappin against the blue up there."

Originally part of the twenty-four stories in Virginia Hamilton's *The People Could Fly: American Black Folktales*, this tale was pulled out as its own picture book after Hamilton's death. It's one of her most well-known works, illustrated by Leo and Diane Dillon, making it a classic in more ways than one. *The People Could Fly* is a mythical story based on folklore references to Black people flying, often related to escaping slavery, as passed on through oral tradition. This magnificently stunning fantasy tells of the pain and terror of heartless enslavers and their overseers while offering an uplifting response from those who could fly away with the help of the old man Toby.

WHY I CHOSE THIS BOOK: For the African people who were captured into slavery and brought to America, folktales like *The People Could Fly* helped them dream and imagine a time of freedom. Though they were physically imprisoned, no one could take away their dreams. I adore this story because it acknowledges the truth and existence of trial and pain but screams FREEDOM at every turn. It also gives attention and redemption to the enslaved who couldn't escape as they become the keepers of our people's stories. The illustrations are evocative and will remain with you forever. Children who experience this book can instantaneously point out the Dillons' artwork in other books because they form a fast relationship with their signature style here.

THOUGHT STARTERS

1. The people shed their wings after being captured but kept their ability to fly. What do you think that means? Why did they lose one but keep the other?
2. If you could fly like Toby, where would you go, and how would that change your life?
3. Why do the people describe the so-called Master as a "hard lump of clay"?

DIGGING DEEPER

1. People can't fly, but this story and the illustrations make us feel like they can. If you were going to make up your own fantasy story, what imaginative and

wondrous things would you include? What would the people in your tale be able to do? Draw a cover that will entice potential readers to read your book.

2. Toby didn't have time to teach the remaining people how to fly, so he had to leave them behind. Though this is a make-believe story, the idea of enslaved people having to leave family and friends behind when they sought freedom is real. Have you ever had to make a difficult choice or decision? What happened, and how did you handle the situation? Think of another story you've read or heard where someone had to make a hard choice. How did their choice compare to the one that Toby had to make?

3. In stories, wings are often symbolic of freedom. Using things available in your environment (indoors or outdoors), create a pair of wings for yourself.

SECOND HELPINGS

» *The Bell Rang*
   Written and illustrated by James E. Ransome
» *Big Jabe*
   Written by Jerdine Nolen
   Illustrated by Kadir Nelson

GRANDPA'S FACE
Written by Eloise Greenfield
Illustrated by Floyd Cooper
*"Tamika knew she was safe then, safe enough to
hug Grandpa and kiss the sturdy brown of his face."*

In this heartwarming story, little Tamika adores her grandfather. They enjoy spending time together doing all sorts of things until the day Tamika sees Grandpa making an angry face that she fears he may use with her someday. Eventually, Grandpa understands what's on Tamika's mind and lovingly puts her greatest fears to rest.

WHY I CHOSE THIS BOOK: The innocent, pure love that the little girl has for her grandfather won me over. I remember how I adored my grandpas, and they still hold places atop the highest of pedestals to me. Elders, especially grandparents, are honored within the African American community, and the tenderness demonstrated in this story helps spotlight the preciousness of that bond. This is also the first picture book illustrated by Floyd Cooper, making it a notable contribution to children's literature.

THOUGHT STARTERS

1. Imagine you were Tamika. How would you feel about Grandpa's various facial expressions? What would you do when you saw Grandpa's angry face?
2. Have you ever gotten in trouble for your behavior when you were keeping your feelings inside? How did you feel after you shared what was on your mind?
3. How do you show love to your family members and friends? How do they show love to you?

DIGGING DEEPER

1. Sharing our feelings with safe people who care about us is crucial. Pretend you're Tamika and write (or tell) a letter to Grandpa letting him know how you feel. Or write a letter expressing your feelings to someone in your life.
2. We can learn so much from older people. Interview a grandparent or family friend. Ask them to tell you about some of the things that they enjoy doing. Also, ask them how they handle situations when they need to have a difficult conversation with someone they love.
3. Get a partner. Make different facial expressions and ask your partner to guess your feelings. For each expression you make, develop a short story explaining why your pretend character feels that way.

SECOND HELPINGS

» *The Patchwork Quilt*
    Written by Valerie Flournoy
    Illustrated by Jerry Pinkney
» *Grandma's Records*
    Written and illustrated by Eric Velasquez

SULWE
Written by Lupita Nyong'o

Illustrated by Vashti Harrison

"Brightness isn't just for daylight. Light comes in all colors.
And some light can only be seen in the dark."

. . . .

This elegant fantasy story tackles the problem of colorism and recognizing true beauty within the context of family and friendship. Sulwe has skin the color of midnight and is the darkest person in her family and at school. She wishes to be lighter like her mom and popular sister, but nothing seems to help until a magical experience opens her eyes to how perfect she is.

WHY I CHOSE THIS BOOK: Nearly every Black person has experienced or witnessed discrimination based on skin color. Colorism within the Black community most often (though not always) results in darker-skinned people being treated inferiorly, and it can lead to severe emotional distress. In my family's experience, the negative psychological consequences of colorism have impacted both the lighter and darker sisters, and I think this topic deserves much more attention than it typically receives in children's books. I hope that reading this story will open opportunities to discuss the origins of self-hatred, how to recognize it, and what to do when children are praised or disdained due to the ills of colorism.

THOUGHT STARTERS

1. Sulwe's mom says natural beauty begins with "how you see yourself, not how others see you." Do you believe this is true? What does real beauty mean to you?

2. How does the author describe each member of Sulwe's family? How would you describe each member of your family, including yourself? How are you all similar, and what makes you each different?

3. Sulwe dreams of having lighter skin because she thinks it will help her make real friends like her sister. Why do you think Sulwe believes she must have lighter skin to make friends? What advice would you give to Sulwe?

DIGGING DEEPER

1. Record a video of yourself making a commercial that teaches children about colorism (treating someone differently because of their darker or lighter shade of brown skin) and why it's harmful to our community.

2. What does Sulwe learn from the story of Night and Day? How does the story relate to Sulwe? Make up another story that you could use to help Sulwe understand her value.

3. Think of ten things that you love about yourself. Ask an adult to help you write each thing on a separate sticky note. Place the sticky notes on your bathroom mirror or in your bedroom where you can see them daily to remind you of how special you are.

SECOND HELPINGS

- » *Nana Akua Goes to School*
  Written by Tricia Elam Walker
  Illustrated by April Harrison
- » *Wings*
  Written and illustrated by Christopher Myers

IT JES' HAPPENED: WHEN BILL TRAYLOR STARTED TO DRAW
Written by Don Tate
Illustrated by R. Gregory Christie
"Bill saved up memories of these times deep inside himself."

Bill Traylor was born enslaved on a cotton plantation in rural Alabama. After the Civil War, his parents stayed on as sharecroppers, and eventually, he ran a farm of his own. In his eighties, he found his way to Montgomery and started drawing on cardboard or discarded paper. This biographical book tells of his life and how he became a self-taught artist with work shown in galleries and museums.

WHY I CHOSE THIS BOOK: As an artist who didn't begin drawing until very late in life, I find Traylor's story inspiring. It reminds us that we can create and grow, even if no one is watching. I also think it's important for children to contemplate the definition of art. Who gets to decide what is and isn't art, and whose opinion matters? Too often, art created by Black people is set aside as "merely" folk art or cultural art but not "real" art.

THOUGHT STARTERS

1. How would you describe Bill Traylor to someone who has never heard of him? What kind of person was he? Is he someone we should look up to? Why or why not?
2. Bill Traylor started drawing when he felt lonely, and his art made him feel better. What do you like to do when you feel lonely? How does doing that help you to feel better?
3. Would you recommend It Jes' Happened to your friends? Do you think they would enjoy hearing the story? Why or why not?

DIGGING DEEPER

1. Throughout his life, Bill Traylor "saved up memories . . . deep inside himself." Make a picture book with photos or your artwork that shows some of the special memories you have of friends and family you'd like to save deep inside yourself.
2. Ask an adult to show you some of Bill Traylor's original artwork online or in an art museum. How would you describe his art style? Create a poster advertising a Bill Traylor art show. Include plenty of details that will interest people in attending the show.
3. Bill Traylor didn't begin drawing art based on his memories until he was eighty-five. Interview an older family member or someone in your community and ask them what dreams they would still like to pursue. What excites them? What type of music, art, or other creative projects speak to them?

SECOND HELPINGS

» Radiant Child: The Story of Young Artist Jean-Michel Basquiat
   Written and illustrated by Javaka Steptoe
» Stitchin' and Pullin' a Gee's Bend Quilt
   Written by Patricia C. McKissack
   Illustrated by Cozbi A. Cabrera

CHEF EDNA: QUEEN OF SOUTHERN COOKING, EDNA LEWIS
Written by Melvina Noel
Illustrated by Cozbi A. Cabrera

> *"Simple, pure ingredients, plus lots of love, a dash*
> *of smile, the taste of home."*

"*Godmother* of Southern cooking . . . *Queen* of Southern cooking . . . *Grande dame* of Southern cooking." No matter how you put it, Edna Lewis is known to all as one of the most influential names in the culinary world. Her second book, *The Taste of Country Cooking*, is said to have set the standard for genuine Southern cooking by turning it into a respected cuisine, and her unique blend of recipes and personal history made it a classic. Known for promoting fresh, local, seasonal food, Lewis became an admired chef with a knack for applying her signature style to any food.

WHY I CHOSE THIS BOOK: When I think of soul food, I think of Edna Lewis. This is despite her publicly distancing herself from it in interviews. I can't speak for her, but I think she was separating the idea of making do with what you have from scratch-cooking with carefully selected seasonal ingredients. Today, we recognize that authentic soul food can come from both intentions. I collect cookbooks, and hers is one of my all-time favorites, not only for the excellent recipes but also for the storytelling. I find myself lost in her descriptions of "all the traditional holiday cakes: caramel and coconut layer cakes, pound cake, and my mother's rich, dark, flavorful fruitcake . . . plates of fudge and peanut brittle and crocks filled with crisp sugar cookies . . . mince pies, and fruit pies made with the canned fruit of summer."

In the introduction to her most popular cookbook, she explains that her hometown in Virginia was called Freetown because the earliest residents, including her grandfather, had formerly been enslaved and wanted to be known as Free People. I find that these types of details from her family history and lush descriptions of foods that African Americans have long perfected in country homes make Lewis the perfect chef, teacher, and author for children to become acquainted with.

THOUGHT STARTERS

1. Edna Lewis learned many of her cooking skills from family members while growing up in Freetown, Virginia. What would you like your family to teach you that you can pass on to your children and others when you're an adult?

2. This book is filled with beautifully detailed drawings. Which picture is your favorite? Study it carefully. Close the book and describe everything that you can about the image. Think of each part of the page. Now, turn to that picture again and see how much of it you remembered. Why do you like this picture best?

3. Which of the foods in this book have you tasted? Which ones have you never heard of? Ask an adult to help you look up the ones that are new to you online. Check out photos and learn how the food is typically prepared in Southern-style dishes.

DIGGING DEEPER

1. Host a Southern dinner party. Choose several dishes mentioned in the book, look up the recipes in one of Edna's cookbooks (check your library!), and prepare a yummy feast for family and friends.

2. Edna Lewis was known for cooking fresh, local, seasonal food. Visit your local farmer's market and note which fruits and vegetables are being grown in your area. If this isn't possible, look up the information online and create a chart that will remind you and your family which foods to shop for during different times of the year.

3. Make your own cookbook. Collect recipes for your favorite dishes from family members, friends, cookbooks, or online. Take or draw pictures for each one and bind them together in a simple book. If you can, make copies to share with others.

SECOND HELPINGS

» *George Crum and the Saratoga Chip*
   Written by Gaylia Taylor
   Illustrated by Frank Morrison
» *Freedom Soup*
   Written by Tami Charles
   Illustrated by Jacqueline Alcántara

TROMBONE SHORTY
Written by Troy "Trombone Shorty" Andrews
Illustrated by Bryan Collier

*"I listened to all these sounds and mixed them together,
just like how we make our food."*

In this boisterous biographical book, Troy Andrews tells of his musical child-hood in the Tremé neighborhood of New Orleans. Andrews is a Grammy-nominated musician who tours the world with his band, Trombone Shorty & Orleans Avenue. His story makes for an uplifting ode to community, family, music, and the power of opportunity. Andrews describes how he made his instruments from found materials because he desperately wanted to be like the musicians he saw around his city. One day, he finally gets an instrument of his own and never looks back.

WHY I CHOSE THIS BOOK: Besides the head nods to the rich culture of New Orleans and jazz music, I love that this book demonstrates how Andrews rises but always looks back and pulls others up with him. That's something that the Black community relies heavily on, and children need to learn early on that success isn't measured in dollars, titles, and accolades but rather in how they share, give back, and help others.

THOUGHT STARTERS

1. What lessons can you learn from Trombone Shorty's life?
2. How would you feel if someone you admire called you up on stage to speak or perform? Who would you want to call you up, and what would you do on stage?
3. Trombone Shorty is Troy Andrews's nickname. Do you have a nickname? If so, how did you get it, and what does it mean? If not, what would be a great nickname for you and why?

DIGGING DEEPER

1. Make a musical instrument using a cardboard paper towel tube stuffed with bent-up pipe cleaners and filled with ½ cup of rice or ¼ cup of dried beans. Cover both ends of the tube with a piece of a brown paper bag held by rubber bands, and feel free to decorate the outside. Turn your musical "rainstick" instrument upside down to hear the sounds created by the movement of the rice or beans.
2. Ask an adult to play one of Trombone Shorty's songs online. While you listen to

the music, draw what you hear and how it makes you feel. Do you hear small, quiet circles or huge, loud waves? Does the music remind you of blues and purples or reds and oranges? Let your imagination lead you.

3. Trombone Shorty compares making music to making gumbo, a traditional soup in Louisiana. It's a truly unique dish that everyone should have the chance to try! Ask an adult if you can visit a restaurant or friend's house serving gumbo or follow a recipe to make your own.

SECOND HELPINGS

» *Little Melba and Her Big Trombone*
Written by Katheryn Russell-Brown
Illustrated by Frank Morrison

» *Duke Ellington: The Piano Prince and His Orchestra*
Written by Andrea Davis Pinkney
Illustrated by Brian Pinkney

GOING DOWN HOME WITH DADDY

Written by Kelly Starling Lyons
Illustrated by Daniel Minter

"Daddy hums as he packs our car with suitcases and a cooler full of snacks. He says there's nothing like going down home."

Family reunions are a hugely important tradition within the African American community. This book highlights all the beauty (and fun!) to be had at large multigenerational gatherings as one family celebrates their history of loving relationships. Lil Alan gets to go down home to Granny's for the reunion, and he must decide how to pay a special tribute to his loved ones.

WHY I CHOSE THIS BOOK: I grew up attending family reunions, and I have decades of priceless memories that my kids are now collecting each time we attend. Spending time with elders and their offspring is an experience that can't be replicated, and it's an integral part of the Black experience that children can grow from. Minter's acrylic wash illustrations in this book blend

African patterns with American landscapes and portraits to represent the duality of our ancestry.

THOUGHT STARTERS

1. What does "going down home" mean to Lil Alan and his family? Do you and your family take memorable trips to visit family? If so, where do you go? What do you usually do while you're there?
2. What's one of your favorite family memories? What makes it so special to you?
3. What are the three items Lil Alan presents to his granny? What does each item symbolize? What things would you choose to represent your family?

DIGGING DEEPER

1. Most family reunions have a reunion committee. This group of family members works together to plan aspects of the gathering, including the lodging, menu, and activities. Imagine that you're on a family reunion committee. Where would it be held and why? What activities would you want to plan for the kids in the family? Which foods would be included on your menu?
2. Ask an older family member to help you create a family tree. Try to go back at least two generations and add photos, if possible. If this isn't possible or doesn't sound fun for your family, interview someone else and help create their family tree. Consider presenting it to them as a special gift.
3. At many family reunions, everyone wears matching T-shirts to celebrate and make the group photo more festive. Use a plain T-shirt and fabric markers (or a piece of paper and colored pencils) to create an original T-shirt design representing your family. You can also use a digital design app like Canva if you can access it.

SECOND HELPINGS

» *Ellen's Broom*
 Written by Kelly Starling Lyons
 Illustrated by Daniel Minter
» *My Rows and Piles of Coins*
 Written by Tololwa M. Mollel
 Illustrated by E. B. Lewis

THE NO. 1 CAR SPOTTER

Written by Atinuke

Illustrated by Warwick Johnson Cadwell

*"In the days when this village was full of men we
would have cut a tree, planed the wood and fixed the cart.
It is the village that has become useless. Not the man!"*

This lighthearted chapter book is about a fictional boy named Oluwalase Babatunde Benson, who lives in a rural African village. He's known as the No. 1 car spotter because he can identify every vehicle that travels past his village, even when they're far off in the distance. Oluwalase is a resourceful problem solver who is always ready to lend a helping hand to his family and others. In this first book in the series, his ingenious idea helps his village get goods to market after their cart breaks. The author includes intergenerational connections as No. 1 spends plenty of time under the iroko tree with his grandfather and helps his sick grandmother get the care she needs. The heartfelt story also highlights cooperative living and strategic thinking as No. 1 finds clever solutions to problems that initially seem impossible.

WHY I CHOSE THIS BOOK: I generally prefer books that center on a single African country rather than referring to the entire continent, but Atinuke's books are an exception. In an interview, the Nigerian author explained that she wants readers to understand that her characters could exist in many African countries because the plots set amid loving nuclear and extended families and friends are not unique to just one area. An intelligent Black boy experiences the relatable stories of mishaps and adventures in a safe and caring community. I appreciate the contemporary African setting and the positive messages throughout the storyline. Though it's clear that the families in his village don't have many material possessions, this is not a story of financial poverty. Instead, the focus is on the richness of relationships and how they overcome obstacles together. These stories are funny (there's no way to read them without regularly cracking a smile!), but they introduce children to important issues along the way.

THOUGHT STARTERS

1. How is No. 1's life like yours? In which ways is it different?
2. Car spotting is No. 1's favorite hobby. What kinds of things do you enjoy doing in your free time? Is there anyone in your life who likes to do those things with you?
3. Many of the characters in No. 1's village are named after common words like Sunshine, Tuesday, and Emergency. Others are named after well-known American brands like Nike and Coca-Cola. If you could pick a fun nickname based on a word or brand you know, what would it be and why?

DIGGING DEEPER

1. No. 1's family and friends know about big cities with skyscrapers, running water, and electricity, but they "only talk about such things" in his village. Based on the clues throughout the book, draw a map of what you think No. 1's village looks like.
2. Mama Coca-Cola sells *akara* by the roadside. *Akara* is a Nigerian deep-fried bean cake made from black-eyed peas and a handful of simple ingredients. Ask an adult to help you look up a recipe for *akara* and make some for your family or friends.
3. The wheelbarrows made a considerable difference in No. 1's village in more ways than one. They even enabled Papa to start a new business. Think of a business you could start with a donation of just one item and then record a video pitching your idea to others.

SECOND HELPINGS

» *Anna Hibiscus*
   Written by Atinuke
   Illustrated by Lauren Tobia
» *Too Small Tola*
   Written by Atinuke
   Illustrated by Onyinye Iwu

ALVIN AILEY
Written by Andrea Davis Pinkney
Illustrated by Brian Pinkney

"Alvin's tempo worked from his belly to his elbows,
then oozed through his thighs and feet."

....

This biography from the Pinkney husband and wife duo gives a behind-the-scenes look at the making of a star. It begins with Alvin Ailey's childhood and carries through to his successful career in dance. The book's final pages highlight the performance of Revelations, considered a choreographic masterpiece and one of the most popular and most performed ballets in the world. The story brings the man behind the famed dance company to life through pictures and text. It serves as an example of the innovation and creativity that pulses through African American arts.

WHY I CHOSE THIS BOOK: The first time I saw the Alvin Ailey American Dance Theater perform, my jaw dropped. I had never seen anything like it before, and my children had the same reaction years later when I took them for the first time. They literally couldn't stop talking about it. Granted, this was long after Alvin Ailey had passed away, but our awe at his legacy inspired us to learn as much as we could about the man behind the dance company. Our research led to this book, which fueled a connection with his work and what it still means to creatives, performing artists, and audiences today.

THOUGHT STARTERS

1. Alvin Ailey's mentor encouraged him to use his rich cultural heritage to make unforgettable dances. What makes you unique? What natural qualities, abilities, and talents can you share with others?

2. Listen to "Rocka My Soul in the Bosom of Abraham" online. This song and its inspired dance are described on page 24 of the book. What music inspires you to dance your heart out and why?

3. If you could speak to Mr. Ailey or someone who knew him, what three questions would you ask about his life or work?

DIGGING DEEPER

1. Alvin Ailey expressed various feelings and emotions through his dances. Turn on some music and create a dance that shows your feelings. To see what it is like to be a choreographer, try to teach the dance to someone else.

2. Attend an Alvin Ailey Dance Theater performance or watch a video online. Describe what you see. How are the movements similar to or different from those of dancers you've seen before? Create a list of words that come to mind when you watch this type of dancing.

3. The Alvin Ailey Dance Theater is the company Mr. Ailey started, and it is part of his legacy. What kind of company or business would you like to start? What's the name of it? What will you sell or do? Who will work with you? Where will it be? Once you have your idea down, draw a picture of a book cover featuring your company's story.

SECOND HELPINGS

» *Pigskins to Paintbrushes: The Story of Football-Playing Artist Ernie Barnes*
Written and illustrated by Don Tate
» *Game Changers: The Story of Venus and Serena Williams*
Written by Lesa Cline-Ransome
Illustrated by James E. Ransome

MY DADDY, DR. MARTIN LUTHER KING, JR.

Written by Martin Luther King III
Illustrated by AG Ford
*"That night, as my brother and I watched our gifts burn,
we believed we were destroying all the hate in the world."*

· ·

This important book, written by the son of Dr. Martin Luther King, Jr., exposes children to King's work through intimate storytelling. The text doesn't shy away from the realities of his life and death, but it nestles the trials within the safe space of family life, making it easier for children to process the injustices King fought against. By recalling the difficulties of watching his dad jailed and wondering if he would be home for Christmas, the author reminds readers that before MLK, Jr., was an American hero, he was a proud dad committed to improving the lives of children who deserved more, including his own.

WHY I CHOSE THIS BOOK: There are many books on MLK, Jr., to choose from, but I selected this one because it's told from his son's insider perspective and illuminates the personal toll of King's public activism. By learning of King's life through the lens of a little boy telling a story about his daddy, children can engage with King's work while getting to know him first as a man rather than only a larger-than-life civil rights activist. I also appreciate the opportunity to introduce kids to a first-person memoir, a form of writing that gives access to the author's intimate thoughts. Though children will encounter King's life story and messages many times across their formative years, a review of African American culture and history is incomplete without honoring his impact and sacrifice.

THOUGHT STARTERS

1. In which ways did Marty feel different from other children? Have you ever felt different than your friends or other people around you? How did that make you feel? What can you do to help someone else feel accepted?

2. In the book, King said, "We must meet violence with nonviolence. We must meet hate with love." What do you think he meant? Why do you think he didn't want to fight against injustice physically?

3. If King were alive today, do you think he would approve of how the people you know treat one another? Why or why not? He wanted to make the world a better place. What can you do to help make that dream come true?

DIGGING DEEPER

1. Ask an adult to help you find someone who was a teenager or adult when MLK, Jr., was living. Interview the person and ask them what it was like to read about, listen to, or watch King while he was alive and how they felt when they found out that he was killed.

2. Some people mistakenly think King's commitment to nonviolence meant he never fought back, but this isn't true. King would travel to different cities and help people who were being mistreated at work or in their communities, and he fought back by protesting while calling out and resisting unfair laws. This resistance often landed him in jail, yet he didn't let that stop him. When people protest, they often carry signs that help others understand why they're protesting. Use a poster board or a piece of paper and create a protest sign supporting a cause you care about or calling out something you believe to be unfair. Tape or

glue the sign to a ruler or stick and use it to teach others about the importance and power of peaceful protest.

3. Ask an adult to play Stevie Wonder's version of "Happy Birthday" for you. This song has been nicknamed "the Black birthday song," and it's often sung after or instead of the traditional birthday song at parties honoring Black people. Many don't realize that Stevie Wonder first wrote this song in honor of MLK, Jr., as he worked alongside many others to get King's birthday recognized as a national holiday. Create a list of ideas for kids who want to celebrate the next MLK Day (the third Monday in January each year). Share your thoughts with your family and friends.

SECOND HELPINGS

» *Malcolm Little: The Boy Who Grew Up to Become Malcolm X*
  Written by Ilyasah Shabazz
  Illustrated by AG Ford
» *Moses: When Harriet Tubman Led Her People to Freedom*
  Written by Carole Boston Weatherford
  Illustrated by Kadir Nelson

TO BOLDLY GO: HOW NICHELLE NICHOLS AND *STAR TREK* HELPED ADVANCE CIVIL RIGHTS
Written by Angela Dalton
Illustrated by Lauren Semmer
"After Star Trek *showed the possibilities of peace among life-forms during prime-time hours, the nightly news showed the real-life suffering the marchers endured because of racism."*

In this biography of actress Nichelle Nichols, stories about her experience on the television show *Star Trek* show readers how her role as Uhura impacted the Black community. As one of Captain James T. Kirk's crew members, her character challenged the prevailing thoughts of the time: Black actresses could only play the role of servants. While she was breaking barriers on screen, Nichelle was left to deal with the effects of racism and racialized conflict across America, including in her own life. Ultimately, after a real-life visit with Dr. Martin Luther King, Jr., Nichelle began to understand how meaningful her work and sacrifices were for her community.

WHY I CHOSE THIS BOOK: This book sends the message that any space you operate in presents an opportunity to do your best and make a difference, even when obstacles stand in your way. The author acknowledges that Nichelle quit her job when things weren't fair, and that's real. Sometimes racism and other challenges feel overwhelming, and we crave respite. But then, the story shows the power of friendship, mentorship, and community. Knowing she wasn't alone in her struggles helped Nichelle endure challenging circumstances, especially those she couldn't change. These are all important themes that appear frequently in African Americans' lives.

THOUGHT STARTERS

1. A "Trekker" or "Trekkie" is the name given to people who are huge fans of the old television show *Star Trek*. What are you a big fan of, and what do you think people like yourself should be called?
2. Why do you think speaking with Dr. Martin Luther King, Jr., made Nichelle change her mind about her job?
3. How did Nichelle use her fame to help people of color and women enter the NASA space program? What can you do to make a difference in an organization you care about?

DIGGING DEEPER

1. Watch a video clip of Nichelle as Uhura on an episode of *Star Trek*. Use what you can find around the house to create your own spacecraft communications officer costume. How does yours compare to Uhura's? What would you change about hers to make it more realistic?
2. Check out a photo of how Nichelle Nichols looked before she passed away in 2022 to see how long it had been since she was on *Star Trek*. What are some things that you do now that you hope people will still remember or talk about when you're old?
3. If possible, visit a television studio for a behind-the-scenes tour or an aviation and space museum to see how massive spacecraft and aircraft can be. If a visit isn't possible, check out the Smithsonian National Air and Space Museum

website and search for "Star Trek Starship" to see pictures of the actual mini model the television studio used to make viewers feel like there was a full-size spacecraft while filming the show.

SECOND HELPINGS

» *Curve & Flow: The Elegant Vision of L.A. Architect Paul R. Williams*
    Written by Andrea J. Loney
    Illustrated by Keith Mallett
» *Gordon Parks: How the Photographer Captured Black and White America*
    Written by Carole Boston Weatherford
    Illustrated by Jamey Christoph

LATE ELEMENTARY (AGES 8–10)

BUZZING WITH QUESTIONS: THE INQUISITIVE MIND OF CHARLES HENRY TURNER

Written by Janice N. Harrington

Illustrated by Theodore Taylor III

"Questions that itched like mosquito bites, questions that tickled like spider webs, questions you just couldn't shoo away!"

Charles Henry Turner was a curious and determined boy who grew up to become a leading-edge researcher of animal behavior, a highly regarded entomologist, and one of the premier scientists of his time. This book captures his enduring determination and passion for plants, animals, and insects while acknowledging the racial barriers he encountered.

WHY I CHOSE THIS BOOK: I find this story to be a fascinating introduction to the life of a great scientist. The inspiring biography mentions the difficult circumstances under which Turner lived without focusing on his trauma. A key takeaway is that remaining curious and fascinated about the world makes us more observant and available to do good work. Kids will enjoy learning about his observations on spiders, bees, ants, moths, doodlebugs, and more before perusing the photos, quotes, timeline, author's note, and bibliography in the back.

THOUGHT STARTERS

1. How would you describe Charles Henry Turner to someone who has never heard of him? Do you think he's someone to be admired? Why or why not?

2. Charles spent much time observing insect behaviors. If you were to spend hours watching a living thing move or go about its work, which insect or animal would you choose? What questions would you have about that animal's behavior before the observation?

3. Describe some of the difficulties that Charles faced in his life. How do you think those experiences made him feel? What impact do you think they had on his life choices?

DIGGING DEEPER

1. Use cardboard or foamboard to build a small maze. Place a crawling insect (cockroach, ant, beetle, etc.) inside and see if it can reach the end. Try introducing different foods within the maze to see what attracts the insect most. Capture your observations in a notebook and include your hypothesis (an educated guess about what will happen), methods (how you conducted the experiment), and results.

2. Charles discovered a new crustacean and named it after his former teacher. Imagine that you've found a new insect in a nearby park. What does it look like? How does it move? Does it make any sounds? What does it eat? Draw a picture of your newly discovered imaginary organism, give it a name, and make a video of yourself presenting it as a scientific discovery on a make-believe television show.

3. Besides his work as a scientist, Charles poured into his community by raising money for needy families and helping to provide affordable meals to children who didn't have enough to eat. Think about the needs in your community, and work with a trusted adult to develop a plan for how you can help meet those needs.

SECOND HELPINGS

» *Hidden Figures: The True Story of Four Black Women and the Space Race*
   Written by Margot Lee Shetterly with Winifred Conkling
   Illustrated by Laura Freeman

» *The Vast Wonder of the World: Biologist Ernest Everett Just*
   Written by Mélina Mangal
   Illustrated by Luisa Uribe

SATCHEL PAIGE
Written by Lesa Cline-Ransome
Illustrated by James E. Ransome
"After just a few games Satch became so sure of his pitching he'd bet anyone who'd listen he could knock ten bottles off a wall or throw ten straight pitches over a hankie."

• •

Satchel Paige was the first Black American to pitch in a major-league World Series and the first to be inducted into the Baseball Hall of Fame. This story tells of his childhood, including how he got the nickname "Satchel." It also details his meteoric career, during which he developed and named his pitches, like the "bee ball," which would "always *be* where I want it to be." After sailing through the Negro Leagues and starting a family, Satchel accepted an offer to pitch in the big leagues before winding down one of the most brilliant careers in baseball history.

WHY I CHOSE THIS BOOK: Satchel Paige was a Black American hero and a stellar sportsman, and this book teaches children how he made his mark. To this day, Paige holds the record for the oldest player to play in a major league game at age fifty-nine. Long after his decades-long career ended, he's still remembered as one of the most dynamic pitchers to ever take the mound, yet because of racism, he was never able to demonstrate his full potential. This book highlights his successes, but it doesn't gloss over the racist treatment he faced in his life. It inspires kids to dream big even if everyone doesn't have their best interests in mind.

THOUGHT STARTERS
1. How did Leroy Paige get the name Satchel? If you were to give nicknames to everyone in your family or to your closest friends, what would you name them and why?

2. Satchel would always smile as he released the ball. Why do you think he did that? What's something that the people who know you best would say that you always do?

3. How were the Negro Leagues different than the white major-league teams? Why do you think the Negro players continued to play if traveling posed so many difficulties? Think of a time when you persisted in doing something you found challenging. What kept you going?

DIGGING DEEPER

1. Satchel is known for his unique pitching style and gives his throws personal names like "hesitation" and the "trouble ball." Give some of the tasks in your life special names and explain what they mean.

2. Watch a clip of Satchel pitching online. Why do you think people enjoyed watching him so much? Pretend to be a sports announcer and narrate what's happening for people who can only hear the game over the radio.

3. Cheers from the crowd boosted Satchel's confidence in his skills. Interview three people you know and ask them what kinds of things have boosted their confidence in the past.

SECOND HELPINGS

» *Traveling Shoes: The Story of Willye White, US Olympian and Long Jump Champion*
 Written by Alice Faye Duncan
 Illustrated by Keith Mallett
» *Major Taylor: World Cycling Champion*
 Written by Charles R. Smith, Jr.
 Illustrated by Leo Espinosa

GLADIOLA GARDEN
Written by Effie Lee Newsome
Illustrated by Lois Mailou Jones
"In red and orange, cream and rose, the happy gladiola grows."

One of the first volumes of children's poetry published by a Black author, this book is filled with sweet verses about children and their meanderings through fields and forests alongside the crickets and toads. Though rooted in nature, some poems describe the intrigue of a puppet with an oversized head, a bright green parrot by the bakery door, and the allure of little shops that sell lollipops. The black-and-white drawings on nearly every page help bring the poems to life for young and old alike.

WHY I CHOSE THIS BOOK: Originally released in 1944, this book has been republished by Living Book Press, and I wrote this in the foreword of the new edition: "When I began to introduce my children to poetry as a daily practice within our homeschool, I was struck by the homogeneity of the sweet images included within the pages of our favorite poetry books. As I read more, I heard familiar refrains and verses that strike the many shared emotions of humanity—joy, fear, love, discomfort, and belonging. But none celebrated the unique experiences of Black children . . . Feeling certain that poetry reflecting my children and their attachment to the natural world was somewhere to be found, I began a hopeful search, telling myself that diligent effort would perhaps pay out in the end." This book by Harlem Renaissance writer Effie Lee Newsome is a gift to every child.

THOUGHT STARTERS

1. Which poem is your favorite and why?
2. In "Passage" on page 25, the girls pass through their grandmother's door throughout the year and see different things at various times. What can be found outside your home during each season of the year?
3. Sometimes, the plants and animals we observe in nature can remind us of specific people or things. Read "Lombardy Poplar Princess" on page 128 again. What does the tree remind her of, and why? Think of something you've seen in nature that reminds you of a completely different thing and share the idea with a friend.

DIGGING DEEPER

1. "In the Grass," on page 9, describes all kinds of insects the child sees while lying on the ground. Go outside in your yard or a park and see how many insects you can find. Did you see any of the ones named in the poem?

2. Plan a tea party for a few family members or friends and serve hot tea and cookies. Pass *Gladiola Garden* around the table as each guest reads poems aloud for the group. Kick things off with "Sassafras Tea" on page 37 and "Cooky Jar Ball" on page 92.

3. Read "The Pantry's View" on page 26. In an unexpected twist, the pantry speaks to the child in this poem. Choose an object in your home and write a poem or short story about what it would say to you if it could speak.

SECOND HELPINGS

» *Soul Looks Back in Wonder*
   Written by various authors
   Illustrated and edited by Tom Feelings
» *The Women Who Caught the Babies: A Story of African American Midwives*
   Written by Eloise Greenfield
   Illustrated by Daniel Minter

LET IT SHINE: STORIES OF BLACK WOMEN FREEDOM FIGHTERS

Written by Andrea Davis Pinkney

Illustrated by Stephen Alcorn

"If you hold your hand closed, nothing good can come in. The open hand is blessed, for it gives in abundance, even as it receives."—Biddy Mason

The ten dynamic women celebrated in this book consistently used their voices to speak the truth in the name of freedom. The pages are filled with detailed biographies and splendid portraits of Sojourner Truth, Biddy Mason, Harriet Tubman, Ida B. Wells-Barnett, Mary McLeod Bethune, Ella Josephine Baker, Dorothy Irene Height, Rosa Parks, Fannie Lou Hamer, and Shirley Chisholm. Each woman demonstrated incredible courage and resilience when met with opposition and indifference, and their lesser-heard stories will inspire readers to new heights.

WHY I CHOSE THIS BOOK: So many stories of people fighting for freedom before, during, and after the Civil Rights Movement are focused on men and the incredible work they did to usher in seasons of change. Those stories are fascinating and critically important, but Black women have always been in the thick of things, making waves and changing hearts alongside and apart from the men. Their stories need to be told, too, and this book shares them in an engaging way. Even the author's introduction adds much as she tells of a childhood steeped in her parents' Black empowerment work and gives readers insight into why the book and the women it features are so meaningful.

THOUGHT STARTERS

1. Which woman's story did you enjoy most and why?
2. If these women were still living and you could speak with one of them, what are three questions you would ask her?
3. Why do you think these women aren't more famous? How can you help their stories become more well known?

DIGGING DEEPER

1. Many of the women in this book founded or cofounded organizations that helped progress their mission while expanding their positive influence. Research a few of these organizations and learn about their purpose and critical actions. What kind of organization would you start to help address a current societal problem? Describe the name and plans for fulfilling your mission.
2. Stellar oratory or public speaking skills is something that most of these women had in common. The ability to command the attention of a crowd, communicate your point effectively, and persuade many to join your cause is a gift. Effective public speaking comes naturally to some people, but everyone can improve their skills in this area. What is a problem that you think more people should know about? Prepare and record a 3–5 minute speech convincing an audience (real or pretend) to join in your cause.
3. The author uses quotes to bring the people and their ideas to life. Find a creative way to share these quotes with others. Examples: Use calligraphy to write them on beautiful paper. Create a video of images while using the quotes as a voice-over. Draw, paint, or digitally render new portraits of the women and include the quotes somewhere in the picture.

SECOND HELPINGS

» *Rosa*

   Written by Nikki Giovanni

   Illustrated by Bryan Collier

» *Through My Eyes*

   Written by Ruby Bridges

THE 1619 PROJECT: BORN ON THE WATER

Written by Nikole Hannah-Jones and Renée Watson

Illustrated by Nikkolas Smith

"They say our people were born on the water, but our people had a home, a place, a land before they were sold."

. . . .

This powerful book is filled with stunning illustrations that help carry the story from beginning to end. A teacher asks her students to trace their roots and draw a flag representing their ancestral land, leaving one student bewildered and ashamed because she doesn't know much about her family's history. Her grandmother takes that opportunity to gather the family and tell the story of Black Americans that started long before slavery, when we had our own words "for love, for friend, for family." Ultimately, the girl embraces the legacy of her ancestors and claims the freedom to proudly belong right where she is.

WHY I CHOSE THIS BOOK: The authors give a concise but exquisite overview of the story connecting Black Americans to Africa and the United States, beginning with the rich cultural life in West Africa before the Middle Passage. They don't hold back on the realities of slavery, but they unfold an appropriate amount of detail for children who are getting older and need to learn more about the story. The lyrical text and deeply emotional imagery offer incredible depth to the story as each poem builds upon the others to weave a complex story.

THOUGHT STARTERS

1. Describe life in the Kingdom of Ndongo.
2. What do you think kept enslaved people from giving up?
3. Why do you think the girl feels better at the end of the book even though parts of the story her grandmother told were sad?

DIGGING DEEPER

1. The illustrator helps us see things in this book that we may not necessarily learn through the words alone. Find examples where pictures help communicate meaning beyond the authors' words.
2. This story is told through a series of poems. Choose a significant event or special day and write a poem about it. If you'd like, draw a picture that gives your readers more information than you've communicated through words alone.
3. In the poem "Legacy," the authors share that Black Americans are teachers, librarians, scholars, authors, healers, pastors, activists, doctors, counselors, songwriters, musicians, inventors, athletes, nurses, cooks, pilots, architects, farmers, housekeepers, singers, artists, dancers, poets, mathematicians, and scientists. Wow, that's a lot! List as many Black people as you can think of that fall into these categories. They can be famous people or adults that you encounter or know in your everyday life. Feel free to ask friends and family for ideas, use other books, or conduct research on the Internet (with permission) to get help with your list.

SECOND HELPINGS

» *That Flag*
   Written by Tameka Fryer Brown
   Illustrated by Nikkolas Smith
» *Unspeakable: The Tulsa Race Massacre*
   Written by Carole Boston Weatherford
   Illustrated by Floyd Cooper

CORETTA'S JOURNEY:
THE LIFE AND TIMES OF CORETTA SCOTT KING

Written by Alice Faye Duncan

Illustrated by R. Gregory Christie

"When hard times unloaded like a ton of bricks, she did not flail her arms or wail for pity. Placid waters possessed her inner constitution."

Using a mix of prose and poetry (acrostics, free verse, haiku, and tanka poems), this book tells the little-known story of a committed activist, including who she was long before meeting her famous husband and becoming his partner in every sense of the word. Starting with her childhood in Heiberger, Alabama, the author introduces readers to a spunky young girl, a class valedictorian, a wise college student, an aspiring opera singer, a lover of peace, a hater of racism and poverty, a mother, a wife, and a freedom fighter.

WHY I CHOSE THIS BOOK: Many kids are familiar with Coretta Scott King as MLK's wife, but there's very little they can tell you about her personal story and vibrant life. They don't know how she grew up, the type of person she was, her talents and dreams, or the visionary work she did before and during her marriage. And they especially don't know of her accomplishments after her husband's death. This book fills in these unknowns through sharp storytelling and soft, beautiful mixed-media watercolor.

THOUGHT STARTERS

1. On page 11, young Coretta is sitting in a tree, gazing at the stars, wondering who she'll grow up to be. What do you want to be when you grow up? What kinds of things are you doing now that will help you with your future dreams and aspirations?

2. When they met, Martin used four words to describe what he admired about Coretta: "character, intelligence, personality, and beauty." What four adjectives would someone use to describe you and why?

3. Mrs. King believed in nonviolence, but that didn't mean she sat back and did nothing in the face of injustice. What nonviolent things can you do when you know someone is being bullied or mistreated?

DIGGING DEEPER

1. On pages 15, 31, and 39, the author uses acrostics to discuss Mrs. King's life. In an acrostic poem, the first letter of each new line spells out a word. Write an acrostic about Coretta using the letters of her first name.

2. After her husband died, Mrs. King devoted herself to caring for her four children and forming the King Center in Atlanta to teach nonviolence as a path to peaceful living. Visit the King Center website (www.thekingcenter.org/visit) to see the Coretta Scott King Peace and Meditation Garden featuring the Coretta Scott King Monument. If your community was going to install a monument honoring Coretta Scott King, what would it look like? Draw a picture or write a poem of what you're imagining and explain your design to a friend or family member.

3. Coretta worked diligently to honor Dr. King with a federal holiday. Come up with a list of ways you and others in your community can celebrate the Kings on that day and keep the spirit of their work alive all year long.

SECOND HELPINGS

» *Memphis, Martin, and the Mountaintop: The Sanitation Strike of 1968*
   Written by Alice Faye Duncan
   Illustrated by R. Gregory Christie
» *How Do You Spell Unfair? MacNolia Cox and the National Spelling Bee*
   Written by Carole Boston Weatherford
   Illustrated by Frank Morrison

THE ROOTS OF RAP:
16 BARS ON THE 4 PILLARS OF HIP-HOP
Written by Carole Boston Weatherford
Illustrated by Frank Morrison
"From Atlanta to Zanzibar, youth spit freestyle freedom sounds."

• •

Through spot-on, energetic illustrations and rhyming text, this book speaks to the influence of ever-popular rap and hip-hop and how other forms of music and creative expression have contributed to or been birthed from the art form and its rich culture. The backmatter includes an author's note, illustrator's note, glossary of hip-hop terminology, and a Hip-Hop Who's Who with twenty iconic musical masters.

WHY I CHOSE THIS BOOK: With a foreword from Swizz Beatz, and head nods to Langston Hughes, James Brown, DJ Kool Herc, the Sugarhill Gang, Biggie, Tupac, Queen Latifah, and more, this book provides an entertaining introduction to the roots of rap and history of hip-hop. This type of knowledge has historically only been picked up around-the-way from music-loving relatives, friends, the radio, and television, but now kids can take note of this rich musical history in a perfectly illustrated book, too.

THOUGHT STARTERS

1. How would you describe hip-hop to someone who is unfamiliar with it?
2. DJs often use music and a mic to give shout-outs and create a welcoming atmosphere at events. Their unique touches and attention to detail make partygoers feel special. What can people do to make you feel special? How can you help others feel special when you're playing together or doing something you love?
3. The author reminds us that hip-hop can be heard worldwide. Why do you think it appeals to such a diverse audience?

DIGGING DEEPER

1. The opening pages feature Langston Hughes and Paul Laurence Dunbar, two famous poets. Why do you think the author brings them up in a book about rap and hip-hop? Read the end of the author's note for a hint. Then, check out a few poems by Hughes and Dunbar and see if you can find a connection between poetry and rap.
2. Have you ever seen someone breaking or breakdancing? You can sometimes see street performers doing this type of hip-hop dance in urban settings. If you regularly run across these dancers, take a few moments to stop and watch their moves. Otherwise, ask an adult to help you find a breakdance battle video online. What do you think? How does this type of dancing make you feel?
3. Organize a rap battle with your family or friends, but instead of boasting or insulting one another, try to see who can spontaneously come up with the best verses that lift and inspire your competition. Watch the "Compliment Rap Battle" from *Trolls: The Beat Goes On* for fun examples. You can find the clip on the @DreamworksTVWorld YouTube channel.

SECOND HELPINGS

- » *Hip Hop Speaks to Children: A Celebration of Poetry with a Beat*
  Edited by Nikki Giovanni
  Illustrated by various artists
- » *Song for Jimi: The Story of Guitar Legend Jimi Hendrix*
  Written by Charles R. Smith Jr.
  Illustrated by Edel Rodriguez

FAITH RINGGOLD:
NARRATING THE WORLD IN PATTERN AND COLOR
Written by Sharna Jackson
Illustrated by Andrea Pippins
*"My stories and illustrations are a tribute
to the endless beauty and creativity of children."*

Spanning ninety years, this colorful book covers the life of artist and activist Faith Ringgold. Starting with the many hours she spent bedridden with asthma as a child, continuing through college, traveling abroad, and transitioning to quilting, the story culminates with retirement and time spent creating in her home studio. Faith's connection to her culture and work as an activist on several issues impacting Black people and women are highlighted through the author's words and many vibrant illustrations.

WHY I CHOSE THIS BOOK: While teaching children about Black creators of the past is vital, it's just as imperative that they connect with contemporary artists whose work reflects today's cultural landscape. Faith Ringgold was a committed and multitalented creator who paved the way for new, unique styles of quilted portraiture from modern artists like Bisa Butler while setting a standard of using her voice and artistic talents to change the world.

THOUGHT STARTERS

1. Faith Ringgold said that children are "the greatest, most consistently innovative artists of all." What do you think she meant?

2. Faith Ringgold is best known for her painted story quilts, combining painting, quilted fabric, and storytelling. Look at Faith's "Street Story Quilt" in the key artworks section near the back of the book. What makes this piece different than other art you've seen? What tiny details do you notice?

3. After sharing about Faith's first trip to Europe, the author asks this question: If you could go on vacation anywhere in the world, where would you go, and what would you draw? What is your answer?

DIGGING DEEPER

1. This book's endpapers (first and last sheets of paper) reflect patterns and colors found on the story pages. Use colored pencils, paints, or digital designs to create new endpapers for this book. Explain the meaning behind what you created.

2. Cut a piece of paper into a square and draw or paint a scene that could become part of a larger quilt. What topic, event, or idea did you choose to represent and why?

3. Faith was an activist who participated in many protests as she worked to make life better for herself and others. Create a poster that communicates a solution to a problem you feel passionate about. Show it to three other people and ask them to share their thoughts on your chosen topic.

SECOND HELPINGS

» *If a Bus Could Talk: The Story of Rosa Parks*
  Written and illustrated by Faith Ringgold
» *Aunt Harriet's Underground Railroad in the Sky*
  Written and illustrated by Faith Ringgold

HER STORIES:
AFRICAN AMERICAN FOLKTALES,
FAIRY TALES, AND TRUE TALES
Told by Virginia Hamilton
Illustrated by Leo & Diane Dillon

"A moment before my mother made up the story, our house felt as if it had gathered itself in. It braced itself; it shook and trembled, and so did I."

Her Stories is an incredibly unique compilation of well-researched folklore from the oral African American tradition. Featuring girls and women as fairies, mermaids, witches, and animals, the stories elicit a range of moods from fun and lighthearted to creepy and serene. The author remained faithful to the style of stories from the sea islands of Georgia, the Carolinas, and Florida, the Creole ancestries of Louisiana, and other regions from which these stories were birthed. While the book primarily focuses on imaginary fairy tales, supernatural stories, and legends, three true stories are also featured.

WHY I CHOSE THIS BOOK: This classic collection of folktales and fairy tales is an intriguing addition to any home or school library. As the author points out in her opening note, magical, funny, and strange stories about women are relatively rare in African American folklore, as most stories revolve around the experiences and antics of men. The bright, full-color illustrations adorning every vignette are an excellent addition to this extraordinary book. *Please note: This book contains magical folklore, and some of the supernatural stories, images, and unexpected deaths may be disturbing for sensitive readers.*

THOUGHT STARTERS

1. Folktales are stories passed down through generations, mainly by word-of-mouth. This includes fairy tales, tall tales, trickster tales, myths, and legends. Which of the folktales in this book is your favorite and why? Which one did you least enjoy and why?

2. How can stories serve as sources of hope in difficult times and situations? Which of the tales in *Her Stories* could be used to encourage someone during a difficult time?

3. The names of each illustration are listed in the table of contents. What new names would you give if asked to rename one picture from each section?

DIGGING DEEPER

1. Choose one of the stories in this book and create a video of you retelling it in your own words. Feel free to add twists, turns, and personality to the story, but include the original main points so the plot remains recognizable.

2. Now, create an entirely original story that explains some modern phenomena or describes an aspect of your family's history in a strange or delightful way.

3. The illustrators, Leo and Diane Dillon, created the pictures in this book and many others by working together. Find a partner willing to pursue a project with you and work together to develop a piece of art in any medium (painting, sculpture, recycled art, etc.). What are the pros and cons of working together? Would you like to create with a partner again, or do you prefer to work alone?

SECOND HELPINGS

» *Mufaro's Beautiful Daughters: An African Tale*
Written and illustrated by John Steptoe
» *The Dancing Granny*
Retold and illustrated by Ashley Bryan

MAYA'S SONG

Written by Renée Watson
Illustrated by Bryan Collier

"Sometimes words itch the tongue, beg to come out,
rise but then get swallowed by fear, by shame."

In this gorgeous tribute to Maya Angelou, Renée Watson chronicles the poet, activist, and storyteller's life through a series of elegantly written, original, free-verse poems. It's a beautiful introduction to one of our most celebrated authors, and between Watson's words and Collier's watercolor and collage, each page is dripping with emotion. The poetic narrative parallels Angelou's storytelling in her autobiography *I Know Why the Caged Bird Sings*, making her story accessible to younger readers with a gentle introduction to some of its most difficult subjects.

WHY I CHOSE THIS BOOK: As a young woman, I had the honor of visiting Maya Angelou's home for a holiday dinner, and it stands alone as one of my life's most enduring memories. I was so nervous leading up to the moment, but when I walked through the door, all the anxiety melted away as I was whisked into a picture-perfect land of friends, family, food, laughter, and music (Ashford & Simpson were casually standing there singing!). This book is reminiscent of that night. It has profoundly moving descriptions of her life, the family that loved her, and the "framily" she claimed as her own. It's a story every child should experience.

THOUGHT STARTERS

1. Miss Annie's store was a special place for young Maya. What do you think she enjoyed about her grandmother's shop? Tell about a place in your community (other than your home) where you feel welcomed, safe, and happy.

2. Maya enjoyed hearing and reading the words of famous Black poets and writers like Paul Laurence Dunbar and Langston Hughes. Who are some of your favorite authors? Why do you like to read their writing?

3. While living in Accra, Ghana, Maya learned, "Home was anyplace her voice could be heard. Home was anyplace there was love." What do you think that means? What other ways would you describe the feeling of being at home or belonging somewhere?

DIGGING DEEPER

1. When the audience gave Maya a standing ovation, she realized that even though her voice sounded different than everyone else's, she had her way of communicating, and it was enough. Write a poem (rhyming or not) about what makes you different and why you are enough.

2. Maya fell in love with Ghanaian culture while learning the language, cooking the local food, engaging in the community, and making new friends. Follow in Maya's footsteps by choosing an African country to fully embrace. Learn ten words in a local language, find and prepare two or three of their recipes, attend an event or watch a movie or documentary, and find someone from that culture to interview and get to know (look to neighbors, local businesses, universities, or even online). If you're uncertain about which country to choose, Ghana, Nigeria, Ethiopia, Somalia, Eritrea, and Kenya are possible choices where you'll likely find plenty of resources and people from those countries living in the United States.

3. Maya was the first Black person and first woman to recite a poem at a presidential inauguration. Since then, Elizabeth Alexander and Amanda Gorman have done the same. Read their poems "On the Pulse of the Morning," "Praise Song for the Day," and "The Hill We Climb." How does each poem make you feel? Watch a video of each woman reading her piece at an inauguration. What are the key messages from each poem?

SECOND HELPINGS

» *Jump at the Sun: The True Life Tale of Unstoppable Storycatcher Zora Neale Hurston*
  Written by Alicia D. Williams
  Illustrated by Jacqueline Alcántara
» *On Her Wings: The Story of Toni Morrison*
  Written by Jerdine Nolen
  Illustrated by James E. Ransome

FREDERICK DOUGLASS: THE LION WHO WROTE HISTORY

Written by Walter Dean Myers
Illustrated by Floyd Cooper

"This is the story of how one man's careful decisions and many accomplishments not only made his own life better but in many ways changed the history of America."

. . . .

This eloquent account of the life of Frederick Douglass begins with his birth in 1818 to an enslaved mother and his subsequent journey to free himself from slavery and embark on a lifelong career of abolitionist work. Drawing from Frederick's autobiographies, the author provides just enough detail to demonstrate Frederick's indomitable spirit without overwhelming young readers. At the same time, the oil and eraser-rendered paintings give a strong sense of time and place. Text from the document signed by Hugh Auld officially freeing Frederick Douglass is included in the back of the book.

WHY I CHOSE THIS BOOK: Some children may be familiar with Frederick Douglass's name, but after reading this book, they'll truly understand why he's one of America's most honored historical figures. A core idea presented in the story is that slavery and the inability to read were inextricably linked. This lays a foundation for why reading and access to quality books and education have often been at the heart of Black Americans' fight for freedom.

THOUGHT STARTERS

1. Give examples of when Frederick Douglass exhibited great courage. When have you had to be brave and strong?

2. The author writes, "Free black sailors had always been a problem for slaveholders." Why were they such a problem, and how did meeting them impact Frederick Douglass? In what other ways was Douglass encouraged or helped by others? Give a few examples of how you can use your resources (talent, time, money) to help someone else.

3. Frederick died when he was seventy-seven years old. What questions would you like to ask him if he were still living?

DIGGING DEEPER

1. Frederick Douglass said, "Once you learn to read, you will be forever free." What does that mean? Create a reading campaign that encourages others to value books and reading. Make a video commercial, marketing poster, or promotional bookmark that creatively advertises your program with the campaign name, logo, and primary communication points.

2. Frederick was a powerfully engaging and persuasive speaker who used his voice to fight against the evils of slavery and for the equality of all people. He convinced others to do the right thing by how and what he spoke. Pick a topic you're passionate about and deliver a short speech to someone you know. If you prefer, look up the words to one of Frederick's speeches and recite that one instead. What did you find most challenging about giving your speech? What was the most enjoyable part?

3. Cedar Hill, where Frederick spent the last seventeen years of his life, is a national historic site you can visit in person or online. Watch a video about the home, see pictures, and take a virtual tour on the National Park Service's website.[1]

SECOND HELPINGS

» *Dear Benjamin Banneker*
    Written by Andrea Davis Pinkney
    Illustrated by Brian Pinkney
» *Preaching to the Chickens: The Story of Young John Lewis*

A CHILD'S INTRODUCTION TO AFRICAN AMERICAN HISTORY: THE EXPERIENCES, PEOPLE, AND EVENTS THAT SHAPED OUR COUNTRY

Written by Jabari Asim

Illustrated by Lynn Gaines

"I did take the blows [of life], but I took them with my chin up, in dignity, because I so profoundly love and respect humanity."—Josephine Baker

· ·

This comprehensive guide includes but goes well beyond the Black American history typically shared with younger children. Slavery and civil rights are not ignored, but the author shares so much more: the abolitionist movement, the Harlem Renaissance, artists, scientists, athletes, writers, musicians, and other aspects of history children can learn and grow from. The core text is sprinkled with highlighted profiles of heroines, trailblazers, and influential leaders through the centuries. Every page has gorgeous illustrations that bring people and places to life.

WHY I CHOSE THIS BOOK: This isn't a book that most kids will sit down and read (or listen to) from cover to cover. Instead, it's a treasure of Black American history to be enjoyed, perused, and referenced over time. It's like a literary and visual encyclopedia of Black people, events, and achievements from the Middle Passage to today—the type of book you want to invest in to keep in your home for all times. With a list of African American history museums and places of interest and a three-panel, removable timeline in the back, this book is a necessary contribution to every home and classroom.

THOUGHT STARTERS

1. Open the book to any random page and read about the person or people on both pages. What do you have in common with any of them? What are some significant differences between their lives and yours?

2. This time, flip through and find a picture you like. Who's pictured? What did they do? Do you know anyone else (famous or not, alive or deceased) who has done something similar?

3. Read "Olympic Medals, Raised Fists" on page 55. What do you think about how the athletes chose to protest? Do you think the punishment they received was fair? Why or why not?

DIGGING DEEPER

1. Which topic or person in this book would you enjoy learning more about? Ask an adult to help you find additional information and books about them. Try to become an expert on that person's life.

2. Check out pages 74–78. Ask a grown-up to play music and video clips of the musicians for you. Whose music do you like most? Come up with a song in the same style as that performer. Give your piece a title and put together a few matching dance moves.

3. On page 29, in the section titled "Something for the Kids," the author teaches about *The Brownies' Book*, the first magazine created for Black children. Create a digital magazine cover (or a hand-drawn or painted version) for the type of kids' magazine you'd like to make. Think of a title, a theme, and who or what would be on the cover of your first issue. What kinds of articles would kids find inside? Be sure to include details on the cover that will entice children to open it up and subscribe.

SECOND HELPINGS

» *African Icons: Ten People Who Shaped History*
   Written by Tracey Baptiste
   Illustrated by Hillary D. Wilson

» *Brave. Black. First.: 50+ African American Women Who Changed the World*
   Written by Cheryl Willis Hudson
   Illustrated by Erin K. Robinson

TALKIN' ABOUT BESSIE: THE STORY OF AVIATOR ELIZABETH COLEMAN

Written by Nikki Grimes

Illustrated by E. B. Lewis

"To rest, even for a moment, weightless and silent, on a cushion of cloud, near enough the sun to scoop up a handful of yellow was a privilege more than worth the price of pain."

. . . .

This is a fictional account of the real-life Bessie Coleman, the world's first licensed Black female pilot. Told in twenty poetic eulogies with dramatized perspectives based on real people, the story is presented as if they're speaking at her funeral after she died in a plane crash in 1934. Through soft, realistic paintings of events from Bessie's life and miniature portraits of each "speaker," the illustrator conveys warmth and emotion on each page.

WHY I CHOSE THIS BOOK: The style and form of the book provide a fine example of creative writing. The author perfectly blends historical facts and real-life characters with fictional thoughts and words to bring across the spirit of Bessie Coleman's life. Grimes's approach is brilliant. Bessie was daring and intelligent, believing in herself when no one else did. What a fresh and inspiring story!

THOUGHT STARTERS

1. Based on the poems in the book, how would you describe Bessie to someone who has never heard of her?
2. Choose which poem is your favorite and tell why.
3. If someone were going to write a story about your life as told by those who know you best, whom should they ask to contribute to the story, and what kinds of things do you think they would say about you?

DIGGING DEEPER

1. Watch the short Bessie Coleman video from Unladylike2020 on the PBS Learning Media website.[2] What's something interesting about the book they should add to the video? What did you learn from the video that you didn't know after reading the book?

2. Gather a few friends for a paper airplane contest. Have each person create a design and compete to see which travels the farthest. Try to determine why the winning design succeeded and then generate another round of planes using the new knowledge that you've gained.

3. Act out your favorite poem from the book by pretending to be the person telling the story about Bessie.

SECOND HELPINGS

» *Njinga of Ndongo and Matamba*
   Written by Ekiuwa Aire
   Illustrated by Natalia Popova
» *Jesse Owens: Fastest Man Alive*
   Written by Carole Boston Weatherford
   Illustrated by Eric Velasquez

THE BOOK ITCH: FREEDOM, TRUTH & HARLEM'S GREATEST BOOKSTORE

Written by Vaunda Micheaux Nelson
Illustrated by R. Gregory Christie
*"This house is packed with all the facts
about all the Blacks all over the world."*

Lewis Michaux, Sr., started the National Memorial African Bookstore in Harlem in the 1930s. This book is told from the perspective of his son, Lewis Michaux, Jr., as he witnesses the stimulating conversation and literary ideas that poured forth from what became a cultural landmark and the most extensive bookstore by and about Black people in the nation.

WHY I CHOSE THIS BOOK: Located at the busy intersection of 125th Street and Seventh Avenue, Michaux's (as it was affectionately called) catered to the likes of famous leaders and creators such as Muhammad Ali, Nikki Giovanni, James Baldwin, Louis Armstrong, and Malcolm X, who sometimes spoke on a platform outside the store. The elder Lewis's niece wrote this book, and her interest in the subject shines through with many personal quotes punctuating a story that gives an unapologetic voice to the importance of Black history, community, and spaces of deep, heartfelt belonging.

THOUGHT STARTERS

1. Lewis, Jr.'s dad liked to play with words and rhymes by making up little sayings to help get his point across. What common phrases or expressions have you heard people use, and what do they mean?
2. Lewis's dad said, "Not every book is true, but the more you read, the easier it is to figure out for yourself what is true." What do you think he meant? Why was it so important to him that people could come and read in his store, even without buying the book?
3. If you could open any store in your community, what would you name it? What would you sell and why?

DIGGING DEEPER

1. Come up with a list of 5–7 books you think would belong in Michaux's store if it were still open today, and tell why you chose them.
2. Michaux was passionate about reading and sharing Black history with as many people as possible. What do you love to read about? Which books would you want to bring with you if you had to spend an entire week alone on a deserted island?
3. Organize a children's book drive in your area. Find a local organization that would benefit from receiving gently used copies of children's books. Ask them what kinds of books they need most, as many have shortages of books featuring Black children and families. Ask for contributions from friends, neighbors, community members, bookstores, libraries, etc. Collect the books and drop off your donation at the appointed time.

SECOND HELPINGS

» *Champion: The Story of Muhammad Ali*
    Written by Jim Haskins
    Illustrated by Eric Velasquez
» *Malcolm X: A Fire Burning Brightly*
    Written by Walter Dean Myers
    Illustrated by Leonard Jenkins

BLACK-EYED PEAS AND HOGHEAD CHEESE: A STORY OF FOOD, FAMILY, AND FREEDOM

Written by Glenda Armand
Illustrated by Steffi Walthall

"Every meal Grandma cooks comes with a story."

· ·

Nine-year-old Frances happily spends the day in the kitchen with her grandmother while visiting family in Louisiana. Grandma shares the stories behind many foods they prepare for their traditional New Year's meal, including plenty of Black history. With lots of love and a sprinkling of Creole words, she tells about black-eyed peas, pralines, hoghead cheese, jambalaya, gumbo, pigs' feet, turnip greens, sweet potatoes, and more. In the end, Frances, Grandma, and the extended family give thanks and share a fine feast around the dining room table.

WHY I CHOSE THIS BOOK: I picked this one entirely because of the food, glorious food! That and the informative sidebars—that build upon things mentioned during the story. It's the type of detail commonly shared at the end of a book, but I like how it's dispersed throughout because it ensures that kids fully understand what's being shared in the moment. No one can read this book without getting hungry, so the yummy recipe for Fay's Fabulous Pralines in the back is perfect.

THOUGHT STARTERS

1. Why do you think many Black American families still enjoy the dishes their ancestors created or ate while enslaved?
2. Look at the family's New Year's Day menu on page 26. Which of these foods were you already familiar with before reading this book? Which ones are new to you?
3. Enslaved people had reasons to celebrate even on the darkest days. What are some ways people show joy during hard times today?

DIGGING DEEPER

1. Find a recipe for one of the dishes mentioned that you've never tried, or use the pralines recipe in the back, and work with an adult to make it for family or friends.

2. Enslaved people added variety to their diet by fishing, hunting, gardening, and gathering nuts and berries in their limited time. Pick one of these activities and devise a plan for trying it with a trusted adult.

3. At the beginning of each new year, many adults set intentions or make plans for things they'd like to do, experience, or become over the next twelve months. These are often called New Year's resolutions. Come up with a list of resolutions you'd love to pursue during the remainder of this year or starting in January.

SECOND HELPINGS

» *Black Music Is*
    Written by Marcus Amaker
    Illustrated by Nathan Durfee
» *Discovering African American Art for Children (Come Look with Me)*
    Written by James Haywood Rolling, Jr.

GOING PLACES: VICTOR HUGO GREEN AND HIS GLORIOUS BOOK

Written by Tonya Bolden
Illustrated by Eric Velasquez
"Victor Hugo Green seemed to walk about with sunshine inside."

During the Great Depression, Black families took advantage of buying less expensive cars as new highways made travel more accessible. However, they still had the added burden of encountering dangerous circumstances while traveling through certain areas. Black newspapers tried to share tips on safe lodging and places to eat, but Victor Hugo Green was the first to conduct research and pull the information into a single volume called *The Green Book*. This story explains how and why he created the book while shedding light on the significance of his contribution to Black Americans.

WHY I CHOSE THIS BOOK: Victor Hugo Green provides an empowering example of how ordinary people without fame or fortune can make a powerful impact on their community by simply doing what needs to be done. Primary source documents are incorporated throughout the book, giving an excellent introduction to using maps, newspaper articles, old advertisements, and more to learn about historical times. The illustrations are absolutely on point, but I expected nothing less from Velasquez because he always delivers.

THOUGHT STARTERS

1. What traditions does your family have when you travel?
2. What is a sundown town, and do you think they still exist? How do you know?
3. Some people have compared *The Green Book* to a modern underground railroad. Why would they make that comparison, and what do you think about it?

DIGGING DEEPER

1. Visit the New York Public Library's website, Navigating *The Green Book*, to map an imaginary trip using information from various editions of the book.[3]
2. Interview a Black adult who lived during segregation and ask them about life when they traveled around town or out of state.
3. Check the digital collections of the New York Public Library's website to find multiple copies of *The Green Book* through the years.[4] Pick an edition and look at the index to see the page for your state. Would a Black traveler have had a safe place to eat, sleep, or use the restroom near your hometown? Does the answer surprise you?

SECOND HELPINGS

» *Just Jerry: How Drawing Shaped My Life*
   Written and illustrated by Jerry Pinkney
» *Delivering Justice: W.W. Law and the Fight for Civil Rights*
   Written by Jim Haskins
   Illustrated by Benny Andrews

CLUBHOUSE MYSTERIES: THE BURIED BONES MYSTERY
Written by Sharon M. Draper
*"Talk to the old people . . . They know more than you think.
It's just, no one asks them."*

This first book in the series of Clubhouse Mysteries introduces readers to best friends Ziggy, Jerome, Rico, and Rashawn, who spend the summer hanging out in their new clubhouse, collecting treasures, and having fun until they discover a box of bones and must contend with old Mr. Greene and his mysterious behavior.

WHY I CHOSE THIS BOOK: The Black Dinosaurs, as the boys call themselves, set up a clubhouse in Ziggy's backyard "which was almost like a real jungle. The grass was never cut. It was a place where flowers, weeds, rabbits, and ten-year-old boys could grow wild." I adore this description because it sounds like our backyard and reminds me of the childhood innocence and joy found in this fun-filled early chapter book. And with plenty of Black history subtly woven into the entire series, there's no shortage of adventures to keep kids busy reading and learning with a smile.

THOUGHT STARTERS

1. How are the families of the four boys alike? How are they different?
2. Why does Mr. Greene start crying? Have you ever seen an adult cry? How did that make you feel?
3. What did the boys learn about remembering the past?

DIGGING DEEPER

1. Jerome's gift to the crew was a kalimba. He told his friends that a kalimba was an instrument played in Africa. Have you ever had the opportunity to play one? Search on YouTube for the Kinobe Kalimba Performance.[5] What does the sound remind you of? How does the music make you feel?
2. Mr. Greene sang the lyrics to an African American folk song or spiritual: "I know it, I know it, Indeed I know it, Brother, I know it, yeah—Them bones gonna rise again!" Listen to someone (preferably George Goodman) singing "Dem Bones Gonna Rise Again" online. What do you think the song is about, and why did Mr. Greene choose to sing it?
3. What would you call it if you were going to create a club with three of your friends? Where would you meet? What kinds of things would you do when you got together? Create an invitation for your club idea—just for fun or to give to the friends you'd like to join.

SECOND HELPINGS

» *Donavan's Word Jar*
   Written by Monalisa DeGross
   Illustrated by Cheryl Hanna

» *Tippy Lemmey*
   Written by Patricia C. McKissack
   Illustrated by Susan Keeter

WAYS TO MAKE SUNSHINE

Written by Renée Watson
Illustrated by Nina Mata

"Dad is always telling me our people come from royalty, that my ancestors lived in Africa and were kings and queens and inventors and hard workers. Mom tells me their strength is running through my veins."

Ryan Hart is experiencing a lot of difficult changes, but she's weathering them well with the support of her family and friends. Her dad lost his job, so the family must downsize to a smaller home and reduce spending. In the closet of her new bedroom, she discovers a canister with several trinkets inside, and her curiosity leads her down the path of discovery.

WHY I CHOSE THIS BOOK: It has just the right combination of light kid fun balanced with weightier real-life issues to keep readers interested in Ryan Hart's life. There are plenty of cultural references naturally woven in, but the story is not about being Black as much as it is about growing up and navigating the world with kindness and curiosity while Black. This approach is a refreshing addition to my recommendations that address culture and ethnicity more directly. This is a series children can continue to enjoy along with the author's other book for this age group, *Some Places More Than Others*.

THOUGHT STARTERS

1. Ryan's dad always tells her to "be who we named you to be." What does he mean?

2. Ryan has "adventurous taste buds," but her brother, Brandon, does not. What

about you? Are you an adventurous eater, or do you play it safe? What are some of your favorite foods? What's your favorite flavor of ice cream?

3. Her mom says, "Ryan, we'll all still be together. This is just a house. We are the ones who make it home. Home is wherever we go." How can she say that? What makes someplace feel like home?

DIGGING DEEPER

1. Work with your friends and family to put together toiletries, coats, or blankets for people in your community who may have a sense of home in their hearts but are without consistent or safe housing.

2. When Ryan's grandma comes over to do her hair, she says, "Child, there is no mistaking it. You are a Black girl and you have Black hair." What do you think she means? How can styling someone's hair be an act of love? Ryan thinks she looks prettier when her hair is straight, but her grandma corrects her because that's not true. What does her grandma say makes her beautiful? Watch the Sony Pictures Animation short film *Hair Love* online. In it, a father is intimidated by all his daughter's thick, curly hair until he tenderly embraces the process.

3. Ryan wants to be on the Rose Festival Court when she's in high school. She hopes to meet the mayor and tell him about her idea for the community. What was her idea? What would you like to change or do in your community? Pretend that you're meeting your mayor tomorrow. Write down the main points of any changes you'd like to suggest, and practice delivering them confidently in the mirror.

SECOND HELPINGS

» *Just Right Jillian*
   Written by Nicole D. Collier
» *The Sweetest Sound*
   Written by Sherri Winston

THE LAST LAST-DAY-OF-SUMMER
Written by Lamar Giles
Illustrated by Dapo Adeola

*"She stood at the stove with her back to them like she always
did when making her banging macaroni and cheese, and also-banging
-but-in-a-lesser-way collard greens."*

....

When cousins Otto and Sheed accidentally freeze time on the last day of summer, they have to figure out how to make things right again, so they set out on a wild adventure to save Logan County from robots, a giant platypus, and the mysterious stranger who makes everything more suspicious. This is Book One in the Legendary Alston Boys Adventures series. The other titles are *Last Chance for Logan County* and *The Last Mirror on the Left*.

WHY I CHOSE THIS BOOK: This science fiction, fantasy, adventure book could have been about any kids, but these kids happen to be Black, and I love that. Their culture is not ignored, but no racial strife or drama exists. My family listened to it on audiobook during a long car ride, and it was a hit with everyone.

THOUGHT STARTERS

1. Though they're cousins and best friends, Otto and Sheed differ in many ways. What are some significant differences between the two boys, and how do they overcome them?

2. Describe the boys' relationship with their grandmother. Are you close to your grandparents? If so, what kinds of things do you enjoy doing with them? If you don't see yours much or they have passed away, who are some adults you enjoy spending time with and what do you do together?

3. The characters talk a lot about missed opportunities. What do you think this means? Can you think of a missed opportunity in your life?

DIGGING DEEPER

1. The boys use various "maneuvers" in the book. What kinds of wisdom have you used to help in a sticky situation? What new maneuvers would you suggest if asked to help write another book in this series? Send the author, Lamar Giles, a letter with your ideas on this or anything else you'd like to share with him.

2. If you could do anything or go anywhere, how would you like to spend your last day of summer? Poll your friends to see what they'd choose and share your

ideas. Do your plans have anything in common? What did you learn about your friends from their responses?

3. Would you rather go back or forward in time? What would you do once you arrived? Using cardboard and any other materials you can access, use your imagination to create a time machine prototype.

SECOND HELPINGS

» *Dragons in a Bag*
    Written by Zetta Elliott
    Illustrated by Geneva B
» *Epic Ellisons: Cosmos Camp*
    Written by Lamar Giles
    Illustrated by Morgan Bissant

BIRD IN A BOX

Written by Andrea Davis Pinkney
Illustrated by Sean Qualls
"There's no more yesterday.
There isn't even tomorrow. All I have is now."

Revolving around the lives of three twelve-year-olds—Hibernia, Willy, and Otis—this coming-of-age book tells how their lives converge and blossom under their shared love for heavyweight boxing champion Joe Louis. Terrible loss and heartache color each child's story, but they find hope and comfort in each other and the excitement of Joe Louis's meteoric rise, all playing out over the real-life radio broadcasts incorporated into the story.

WHY I CHOSE THIS BOOK: I always appreciate an excellent historical fiction novel, and in this one, fact and fiction are blended so seamlessly that many readers will need to read the back matter to determine what's real and what is artfully imagined by Pinkney. It takes place in the 1930s amid the Great Depression and deals with death, abandonment, and life in an orphanage—all heavy topics that could weigh a story down, but that is not the case with this book. It's balanced and beautiful.

THOUGHT STARTERS

1. Why are Joe Louis's boxing matches so important to the Black community?
2. Describe each child and what they're struggling to overcome. If you were a character in a book, how would the author describe you? What are some of your biggest strengths and struggles?
3. What is the Great Depression? How did living during that time impact the lives of Hibernia, Willy, and Otis?

DIGGING DEEPER

1. In the 1930s, radio shows were the most popular form of family entertainment. Everyone would gather around the radio to hear their favorite shows or acts performed. Turn on your favorite show but turn your back to the TV or screen so you can only listen to what's happening without any visuals. How was that experience? What would TV shows need to do differently if they became audio-only?
2. What do you know about Joe Louis? Look up an interview of him online to see what he looked like and how he sounded when he spoke with the media. Pretend to be a sports reporter and think of one question you would ask him if you got the chance.
3. What will happen to Hibernia, Willy, and Otis after the story ends? Take a few minutes to think through your plot and then write or record your idea for a sequel to the book.

SECOND HELPINGS

» *The Magic in Changing Your Stars*
   Written by Leah Henderson
» *Cookies & Milk*
   Written by Shawn Amos
   Illustrated by Robert Paul Jr.

FORTY ACRES AND MAYBE A MULE
Written by Harriette Gillem Robinet

"Inside him blossomed the freedom that had been growing. It seemed to burst his chest. He promised himself to never let it go."

At the end of the Civil War, two formerly enslaved brothers set out in search of a Freedman's Bureau where they hope to claim the "forty acres and a mule" they've heard the government is distributing to freed families. They connect with others looking to start a new life during the journey. They become a chosen family, living and thriving together on rich farmland until they experience backlash from a former enslaver, and they're forced to redefine freedom.

WHY I CHOSE THIS BOOK: The story offers a rare glimpse into the period of Reconstruction, something that is rarely addressed in any books, especially those for this age group. The idea of claimed family or chosen kinship that was and is such an essential part of African American culture comes through loudly and clearly in this story.

THOUGHT STARTERS

1. Formerly enslaved people were freed but not given any help to start new lives (or what they were given was taken away). What problems do you think this caused, and how could it have been handled differently? Do we see any manifestations of the government's decision today? If so, what are they?

2. Though most weren't biologically related, the people who came to Green Glory-land formed a family. Why do you think it was so easy for them to embrace one another?

3. What hardships did Gideon and Pascal endure after being freed from enslavement? What are some of the ways that they claimed joy?

DIGGING DEEPER

1. Trees play a significant role throughout the story. There was the whipping tree, the Ghost Tree, and the apple tree that Gideon and Gladness received. Visit an orchard to go apple picking if you have the chance. If not, observe some of the trees outside your home. Then, construct a tree from memory using sculpting clay, papier-mâché, or items found outdoors.

2. The schoolteacher, Miss Anderson, changes her mind about what her students should be learning by the end of the book. How was schooling with her different than what you experience? Create an ideal school schedule listing the subjects or activities you think are most important for someone your age.

3. To keep Green Gloryland running smoothly, each person had to do what needed to be done. Look around your home today and find some way that you can help your household and then do the task without being asked.

SECOND HELPINGS
» *Loretta Little Looks Back: Three Voices Go Tell It*
Written by Andrea Davi Pinkney
Illustrated by Brian Pinkney
» *Stella by Starlight*
Written by Sharon M. Draper

WHEN WINTER ROBESON CAME
Written by Brenda Woods
*"Instantly, Winter and I became a duo; our ballad, a duet.
But it wasn't long before the tempo of our song changed."*

Set in 1965 California, this verse novel follows two cousins—Eden (12) and Winter (13)—as they search for Winter's missing dad just as trouble starts brewing in their southern Los Angeles neighborhood. The author deftly tackles tough topics like the Watts race riots while offering warm views of family life and friendship with a heaping dose of hope.

WHY I CHOSE THIS BOOK: There's much to love about this book. Woods takes what could easily be a depressing historical novel and turns it into an engaging and uplifting story with historically accurate difficulties. African American culture and life in the mid-1960s come through loud and clear for the reader, and the verse format makes the writing accessible to a wide range of readers without oversimplifying the text. Eden's love for music is woven into the story naturally, adding nuance and interest to an already perfect plot.

THOUGHT STARTERS
1. What are some differences that Winter notices between Mississippi and California? Have you ever visited somewhere that felt very different than where you live? What was different, and how did you feel while there?

2. What would change about this book if it took place today?

3. What surprised you most about "Winter Robeson's Lifetime List of Things to Do?" What kinds of things would be on your list?

DIGGING DEEPER

1. What were some causes of the unrest in Watts, and how did they contribute to the riots? What topics cause unrest or disagreements in your home or community? Think of three ideas for how families can help improve communication at home or in tense situations in their community.

2. Make a list of five questions you would ask various characters in the book if they were real people and you could meet them. Then, go through and answer the questions as if you were that character. What would they think? How would they feel? Use evidence from the book to support your assumptions.

3. Were you surprised by the ending? Make a video of yourself describing an alternate ending if you got to rewrite the last part of the book.

SECOND HELPINGS

» *Ninth Ward*
   Written by Jewell Parker Rhodes
» *Saint Louis Armstrong Beach*
   Written by Brenda Woods

ONE CRAZY SUMMER

Written by Rita Williams-Garcia

"We're trying to break yokes. You're trying to make one for yourself. If you knew what I know, seen what I've seen, you wouldn't be so quick to pull the plow."

This is the first book in a trilogy about the Gaither sisters. Eleven-year-old Delphine has been caring for herself and her younger sisters, Vonetta and Fern, since their mom abandoned them years ago. This summer, their dad and Big Ma send them to spend time with their mom, whom they call Cecile. But rather than taking them to Disneyland, Cecile sends them to a summer camp run by the Black Panthers, opening the door for the girls to learn about themselves, their mother, and the world.

WHY I CHOSE THIS BOOK: This period, the late 1960s, seen through the eyes of a vulnerable child who is wise beyond her years, makes for a compelling read. Delphine and her sisters give voice to children growing up without the motherly affection they crave. The Black Panthers rarely appear in books for this age group, so this also serves as a rare opportunity for kids to learn about their historical significance.

THOUGHT STARTERS

1. How does the girls' life in Brooklyn differ from Cecile's in Oakland?
2. Why do the Black Panthers refer to Cecile by another name? Why did she choose that name?
3. What type of experience do the girls expect to have with their mother? How would you describe their actual experience? How do the girls feel about Cecile at the end?

DIGGING DEEPER

1. Pretend to be Delphine and write a letter to your dad and Big Ma about your experiences in California and how you're feeling about everything.
2. Who's your favorite character in the book, or who do you relate to the most? Write a poem incorporating that character's personality and voice without revealing their name. Read it to a friend who has also read this book and see if they can guess who your poem is about.
3. After hearing Cecile's story, we understand more of why she's the way she is toward her daughters. Interview an adult and ask them to share some defining moments of their childhood and adulthood.

SECOND HELPINGS

» *Zoe in Wonderland*
   Written by Brenda Woods
» *Love Like Sky*
   Written by Leslie C. Youngblood

FINDING LANGSTON

Written by Lesa Cline-Ransome

*"I never told no one, but I loved being alone with Mama.
Wouldn't want it no other way . . . Mama made it seem like
I was all she ever wanted."*

. . . .

After his mother's death, an eleven-year-old boy and his dad moved from their small Alabama farm to a dreary apartment in Chicago. His dad works long hours, and Langston is left to contend with bullies and loneliness in a new city that feels too far from home. Eventually, he finds solace at the local public library that isn't segregated like the one back home, and he digs deeply into the work of a poet who shares his name, Langston.

WHY I CHOSE THIS BOOK: At just over one hundred pages, this slender introduction to the Finding Langston trilogy is an unassuming option for reluctant readers whose attention will be captured from beginning to end. The references to Langston Hughes and other Black poets, the complexities of loss and grief, bullying, friendship, family, and a relentless pursuit of words and books all come together to make this a memorable read.

THOUGHT STARTERS

1. What does Langston miss most about Alabama? What about Chicago makes him feel like he doesn't belong? How could you help a new kid feel welcome in your town or neighborhood?

2. Were you already familiar with the poet Langston Hughes before reading this book, or is this your first time "meeting" him? Based on the parts of his poetry shared in this book, do you admire Hughes's work? What do you like or dislike about his poetry?

3. In the end, Langston realizes that his mama has helped him claim a sense of belonging. How did that happen?

DIGGING DEEPER

1. Once he discovers it, Langston goes to the George Cleveland Hall Branch of the Chicago Public Library every day after school. Visit your local library branch

and ask the children's librarian for some poetry book recommendations featuring Black poets.

2. If your library has it, check out the book *Langston Hughes: Poetry for Young People*, edited by David Roessel and Arnold Rampersad and illustrated by Benny Andrews. Read five or six poems that interest you most and choose one to memorize and perform in front of friends and family. If your library doesn't have the book, ask an adult to help you find suitable poems online.

3. Bullies target Langston throughout the book. What are some things you can do if you're ever bullied? What if you witness someone else being bullied? Write a script for a TV commercial sponsored by an anti-bullying organization. Provide good information for someone being bullied or help for those who are doing the bullying.

SECOND HELPINGS
» *Garvey's Choice*
   Written by Nikki Grimes
» *Isaiah Dunn Is My Hero*
   Written by Kelly J. Baptist

BUD, NOT BUDDY
Written by Christopher Paul Curtis
"There comes a time when you're losing a fight that it just doesn't make sense to keep fighting. It's not that you're being a quitter, it's just that you've got the sense to know when enough is enough."

It's 1936, and ten-year-old Bud is convinced that he can find his dad based on clues that his mom left behind when she unexpectedly died. He's shuffled between cruel foster homes until he runs away to find Herman E. Calloway and his famous band, the Dusky Devastators of the Depression. What ensues is an adventure in which Bud finds acceptance and belonging in some of the least expected people and places.

WHY I CHOSE THIS BOOK: A full range of emotions can be found within the pages of this book. Tragedy and trial give way to expectancy and joy, and the ending is imperfect yet satisfying, which is often the case in life. Bud is a character you can't help cheering for as his journey draws the reader further in. Jazz music and Black life during the Great Depression are highlights that bring added relevance to the story.

THOUGHT STARTERS

1. Why is Bud so convinced that Herman Calloway is his father? What type of relationship do you think Bud will have with him?
2. Why does Mr. Calloway always have a white man in the band? What does this suggest about how Black people were treated then?
3. Bud encounters mean people in some of his foster homes, but several people also show him kindness. How do they help Bud, and why do you think they offer a helping hand?

DIGGING DEEPER

1. *Bud, Not Buddy* is considered historical fiction. What does this mean? If you could choose the period of your next historical fiction book, what year would you want it to take place and why?
2. Use the computer or a paper and pen to imagine and re-create one of the band's flyers that Bud keeps in his suitcase.
3. This book has been made into a movie and a play. With the help of an adult, search online for a clip of one version. Based on your reading, do the costumes and set or environment look as you imagined?

SECOND HELPINGS

» *Clayton Byrd Goes Underground*
    Written by Rita Williams-Garcia
    Illustrated by Frank Morrison
» *Catching a Story Fish*
    Written by Janice N. Harrington

NIC BLAKE AND THE REMARKABLES: THE MANIFESTOR PROPHECY

Written by Angie Thomas

"Goodness, girl, be smart, not brave!"

In this first book of a thrilling fantasy trilogy, readers take a wild ride filled with top-notch world-building as Nic Blake harnesses her magical powers as a Manifestor, one of the most potent Remarkables. Along with her two friends, Nic sets out on an adventure filled with unpredictable twists and turns as she searches for answers to save her family and the world.

WHY I CHOSE THIS BOOK: It serves as an excellent entry into the world of Afrofuturism, and the author raises the bar in this category by infusing the story with Black history and folklore from the African diaspora. Nic loves to read, and she discovers that her favorite series isn't entirely made up. The book, her history, and her life are filled with intrigue, suspense, humor, and more. This story is everything I want in a fantasy book for this age group . . . and then some.

THOUGHT STARTERS

1. What are the most extraordinary things about the Remarkables? What are some things they struggle with or find challenging?
2. What do you think is the best piece of Giftech in the book? How would the story change if it didn't exist? What other technological advancements or magic would you add to the mix if you were the author?
3. Nic experiences many changes throughout the book. How is she different in the end than she is in the beginning?

DIGGING DEEPER

1. The author uses a lot of words from other languages. Look up some of these words and see if you can determine why she chose them.
2. If you aren't familiar with it, read the story "The People Could Fly" by Virginia Hamilton. What similarities do you see between that folktale and this book?
3. Use your imagination to come up with a new category of Remarkables. Who

would they be? What powers would they be granted? What color Glow would they have? Write a new chapter and draw a picture featuring your new Remarkable.

SECOND HELPINGS

» *Onyeka and the Academy of the Sun*
   Written by Tolá Okogwu
» *Future Hero: Race to Fire Mountain*
   Written by Remi Blackwood
   Illustrated by Alicia Robinson

9

MIDDLE SCHOOL (AGES 11–14)

VOICE OF FREEDOM: FANNIE LOU HAMER, SPIRIT OF THE CIVIL RIGHTS MOVEMENT

Written by Carole Boston Weatherford

Illustrated by Ekua Holmes

"The truest thing that we have in this country at this time is little children . . . If they think you've made a mistake, kids speak out."—Fannie Lou Hamer

This is the moving story of civil rights champion Fannie Lou Hamer, told through a series of poems accompanied by collage illustrations. Born in the Mississippi Delta "where the soil was as rich as black folks was poor," Hamer was the twentieth child of a sharecropping family. These experiences grew Hamer's resolve to represent the voice and interests of Black people in their fight for civil, voting, and economic rights.

WHY I CHOSE THIS BOOK: It can be easy for kids to think that the injustices they learn about in history books were all a "really long time ago," but that's simply not true. Hamer died the year I was born, and when I look at what she went through and how bravely she fought not only to survive but to pave an easier road for me and my children, I feel more motivated than ever to share her story. She endured pervasive racism, including a hysterectomy for which she did not consent, repeatedly being denied the right to vote, and a brutal beating after being arrested for eating at a segregated lunch counter.

These are difficult things for children (and even adults) to hear, but the stories must be told. This book offers a beautifully redemptive view of one woman's life; every reader will walk away changed.

THOUGHT STARTERS

1. What type of childhood did Fannie Lou Hamer have in Sunflower County, Mississippi? Describe the environment in which she grew up and her relationship with her family. Is there anything about her life that feels familiar to you?

2. Which stories from Hamer's adult life most resonated with you and why? How long ago did these stories take place? Who do you know that was alive at the same time as Hamer?

3. On her fund-raising tour, Hamer called racism "America's problem." What do you think she meant by that? Is that still true today, or is it no longer relevant? How do you know?

DIGGING DEEPER

1. Carefully study the collage by Ekua Holmes on pages 8 and 9. Describe what's happening in the scene. What elements or images do you see beyond the people (examples: sheet music, patterned paper, a map)? Choose a moment in time from your life and create a collage that brings the memory to life using some of the same types of elements seen here.

2. Hamer and many others were denied the right to vote due to discriminatory literacy tests and other unfair practices designed to exclude Black people from the voting process. The Voting Rights Act of 1965 is a landmark federal law prohibiting racial discrimination in voting. What are today's voting requirements in the United States? How are they enforced? What percentage of Americans voted in the last election? What about Black Americans? Create a campaign to encourage more people to register to vote. You can use video, print, audio, or any other format.

3. She passed away in 1977, but imagine you had the opportunity to meet Fannie Lou Hamer. Write a letter detailing what you admire about her, how your life is different today because of the work she and others like her did, and what you think would concern her today.

SECOND HELPINGS

» *You Can Fly: The Tuskegee Airmen*

Written by Carole Boston Weatherford
Illustrated by Jeffery Boston Weatherford
» *Schomburg: The Man Who Built a Library*
Written by Carole Boston Weatherford
Illustrated by Eric Velasquez

WORDS WITH WINGS: A TREASURY OF AFRICAN-AMERICAN POETRY AND ART

Selected by Belinda Rochelle
Written and illustrated by various artists
"They speak of isolation and community, joy and sorrow,
the ways people heal or harm one another—but seldom of despair:
African American artists know they cannot afford to give up."

. . . .

This incredible collection floods the senses with hope, determination, and wonder. It features twenty beautiful works of art accompanied by poems from poets and artists like Alice Walker, Langston Hughes, Horace Pippin, and Augusta Savage. The creators explore various topics influencing Black American culture through words and images, and the brief biographical sketches in the back help give context to each page.

WHY I CHOSE THIS BOOK: This melding of visual art and poetry is a masterpiece, and I'm delighted with every opportunity to share the lovely pairings with children. Each writer has a different style, and the accompanying illustrations communicate through various lenses, but the entire collection comes together like a symphony. We need our children to absorb and appreciate these words and images of Black America.

THOUGHT STARTERS

1. Which poem and picture pairing go best together and why? Flip to the back of the book and read about the poet and artist for that pairing. Are they still living? Did they live at the same time? What stands out most to you about their lives?

2. In "How Poems Are Made," Alice Walker says poems are the "tears that season the smile." What do you think she means by this?
3. Revisit "Night" by E. Ethelbert Miller. What makes this poem similar to and different from others you've read? What do you think the poet is trying to convey about the woman described? What type of person do you think she is, and how do you imagine he feels about her? How do *you* feel about her?

DIGGING DEEPER

1. Listen to Afaa Michael Weaver read Paul Laurence Dunbar's "Little Brown Baby" on the Library of Congress webpage (Poetry of America, www.loc.gov).[1] How would you describe the language Dunbar used in this poem? How important is it for Black writers to express themselves this way? Is it appropriate, or should he have written his thoughts differently? Why or why not?
2. Look closely at the painting *Can Fire in the Park* by Beauford Delaney. During the Great Depression, impoverished people gathered around a can fire became a familiar image. Create a picture in the medium of your choice that indirectly highlights a societal issue of today.
3. Reread Rita Dove's "Fifth Grade Autobiography." Find a family photograph you're in, or select another interesting photo online if you don't have one, and write a poem describing what you see and what you know or imagine about the people in the picture, including yourself if relevant.

SECOND HELPINGS

» *Blues Journey*
    Written by Walter Dean Myers
    Illustrated by Christopher Myers
» *Legacy: Women Poets of the Harlem Renaissance*
    Edited and written by Nikki Grimes
    Illustrated by various artists

KIN: ROOTED IN HOPE
Written by Carole Boston Weatherford

Illustrated by Jeffery Boston Weatherford
"If I had a childhood, it was before I could remember."

. . . .

Through a series of poems and scratchboard illustrations, the Weatherfords (mother and son) skillfully summon the voices of their ancestors, crafting a compelling story that is both raw and transformative. The rhythmic poems and artistic storytelling combine disquieting details drawn from extensively researched historical records and genealogical exploration. Inspired by Alex Haley's *Roots*, this is a fresh, creative telling of the story of enslaved people, told with clarity and reshaped for a new generation of readers.

WHY I CHOSE THIS BOOK: This book is rooted in the Weatherfords' family tree, but it includes voices from Frederick Douglass, Harriet Tubman, the plantation house, and even the land. It provides a poignant exploration of African American cultural heritage and offers a profoundly relatable experience for innumerable Black families. The poems and art confront hard truths that older children need to know and understand, but they're rendered so beautifully that they give a fresh perspective to the traditional slavery narrative.

THOUGHT STARTERS
1. While reading this book, what did you learn about slavery that you didn't already know? How do you feel about this new insight? What relationships do you see between people's lives in the years covered in the book and your life today?
2. Reread "Fruits of Whose Labor?" on page 112. In this poem, the author wonders whether her kin ever tasted lemon, her favorite flavor. What do you wonder about your ancestors? If you had only one hour to visit with them, what would you want to know and why?
3. Enslaved people often resisted in various ways, such as tainting the food they were forced to prepare or intentionally breaking tools. What are some examples of resistance described in the book? Can you think of any ways that people are resisting unfair treatment today?

DIGGING DEEPER

1. *Kin* refers to family members and those with whom you share a familial connection. However, due to the cruel practices of slavery, enslaved individuals were frequently torn apart from their loved ones, resulting in the formation of new family units forged through shared experiences and survival. Find examples of "chosen" families in the book. Are there examples of this in your family? Interview older relatives and ask about people with whom you don't share a bloodline but are still considered family.

2. The author had to conduct a lot of research before writing this book, and her passion shines through. Choose a historical topic that interests you and begin to research it. Consider asking a librarian to help you select the best resources for learning more about your chosen area. Once you've gained a good understanding of your person, place, or experience, write a poem to creatively share what you know with others.

3. How did the scratchboard illustrations impact your reading of this story? Choose your favorite image and remake it in your artistic style.

SECOND HELPINGS

» *Freedom Over Me*
   Written and illustrated by Ashley Bryan
» *Carver: A Life in Poems*
   Written by Marilyn Nelson

HEART AND SOUL:
THE STORY OF AMERICA AND AFRICAN AMERICANS

Written and illustrated by Kadir Nelson

"It had taken hundreds of years, millions of lives, marches, martyrs, protests, wars, and much more for America to come closer than ever before to becoming what it was meant to be."

This highly engaging account of Black American history is told by an unnamed elderly narrator whose ancestors were brought to the United States as enslaved persons. It highlights the trials and triumphs of African Americans from enslavement through the Civil Rights Movement while effortlessly blending the narrator's fictional story with historical facts. The illustrations are stunning, and each invokes deeply emotional experiences ranging from intense tragedy and suffering to undeniable courage and determination. The storytelling masterfully highlights major stops from the 1600s to modern times.

WHY I CHOSE THIS BOOK: Many children will have encountered some of these stories before middle school, so I didn't place this book here as an introduction but rather a capstone retelling of what they've learned or should know by this age. The nonfiction text is steeped in Black history but compellingly reads like a novel in some ways. Nelson's honest yet hopeful storytelling and piercing images will capture the hearts and minds of many while cementing the timeline, ideas, and people that frame the African American story. It's a treasure that belongs in every home as it begs to be revisited.

THOUGHT STARTERS

1. On page 21, Kadir Nelson writes, "It would be a long while before we figured out that we could not win our freedom with our fists or guns. We would have to find another way." What are some of the ways that enslaved people tried to fight back, and how successful were they? What approach do you think the author is alluding to?

2. Reconstruction ended with the Compromise of 1877, and Jim Crow laws effectually created slavery with a new name. Why did Reconstruction fail, and how did Jim Crow reverse the progress made?

3. At the end of the book, the narrator calls the Civil Rights Act of 1964 a "glorious victory" and the "beginning of a new struggle for every American." How were both true? Is the struggle over or still happening? Why do you think so?

DIGGING DEEPER

1. Which topics shared in this book do you wish you could learn more about? What other people or events could be added to "the story of America and African Americans?" Research your proposed topic and write another chapter to this book in the same narrator's voice (revisit the Prologue to hear her voice clearly) or in another storytelling style. Illustrate your chapter if you enjoy drawing or

painting. Otherwise, identify a piece of art that you think complements your chapter.

2. Choose an illustration that speaks to you and write a letter from the person in the portrait to a group of students studying history today. What would the person want to convey about their life? Be sure to research the era in which they lived so you can include details beyond what's provided in the book. Introduce their experiences and lifestyle, tell how they spend their time, and describe their hopes and fears. Use your imagination to fill in the unknown, but root the letter in historical fact.

3. Which of the inventions in chapter 10 did you find most surprising or intriguing? Find out more about the inventor. Then, develop your own design to address a problem you see in homes, businesses, or communities today. Write detailed notes on the how and why of your invention. Sketch and label a picture or make a prototype if feasible.

SECOND HELPINGS

» *Pathfinders: The Journeys of Sixteen Extraordinary Black Souls*
  Written by Tonya Bolden
» *Dark Sky Rising: Reconstruction and the Dawn of Jim Crow*
  Written by Henry Louis Gates, Jr., with Tonya Bolden

DEFIANT: GROWING UP IN THE JIM CROW SOUTH

Written by Wade Hudson

"We all knew that if Madear told us to stop the game and go home, we had to do it. Almost all respected adults in our community had that kind of authority over us. You listened to older folks. You had better."

A memoir highlighting the experiences of a young man coming of age amid the turmoil of segregation and social unrest in America, this book gives voice to the freedom fighters whose stories have never been heard. As the author outlines his beginnings in Mansfield, Louisiana, and ties them to his college life and well beyond, readers gain a distinct sense of time and place while enjoying the real-life story of an ordinary person who chose (and still chooses) to live a full life in service to his people.

WHY I CHOSE THIS BOOK: The first-person biographical story offers insight into the Civil Rights Movement beyond the stories of Dr. Martin Luther King, Jr., and Rosa Parks. Their stories are critically important, but children need to know that many other people were involved, working in various capacities to bring the humanity of Black Americans to the forefront of our nation's consciousness. Hudson shares his experiences with a new perspective and accessible storytelling that will touch the hearts and open the minds of older children.

THOUGHT STARTERS

1. In what kind of family and community did the author grow up? What was his childhood like? What are some things that you have in common with him? What are some things about your life that are entirely different than his?

2. What surprised you most about Hudson's life? What did you learn from his experiences?

3. If you could ask the author three questions, what would you ask? If he asked you to share some highlights from your life, what would you share with him?

DIGGING DEEPER

1. Interview someone in your family or community who grew up during segregation. Tell them about some of the author's experiences and ask them to share their memories and reflections on that time. How was their experience similar to or different than Wade Hudson's?

2. Wade often played football on their neighbor's large lawn with his brother and friends. He explained that Mr. and Mrs. Blow built a lovely brick house in the Black neighborhood because "Black folks couldn't live in those White-only suburbs" where that type of home would usually be found. Search online for "Willie Mays denied housing" to learn how racism in segregated neighborhoods even impacted famous people. Ask a few adults whether they see any lingering effects from these practices in your town today. Do you agree with what they've said? Why or why not?

3. Hudson references *Ebony* and *Jet* magazines in his book while discussing the news coverage of Black athletes. Research the history of both publications and imagine starting your own magazine featuring people and topics relevant to your family, friends, or community. Write an article introducing the magazine to new readers and create the cover of your first issue.

SECOND HELPINGS
» *This Promise of Change: One Girl's Story in the Fight for School Equality*
    Written by Jo Ann Allen Boyce and Debbie Levy
» *Evicted! The Struggle for the Right to Vote*
    Written by Alice Faye Duncan
    Illustrated by Charly Palmer

WE ARE THE SHIP: THE STORY OF NEGRO LEAGUE BASEBALL
Written and illustrated by Kadir Nelson
"Armed with only their intellectual and athletic talents,
and the sheer will to play the game that they loved so dearly,
this group of men assumed control of their destiny."

Starting with its launch in the 1920s and carrying through Jackie Robinson breaking the color barrier into Major League Baseball in 1947, this book pays tribute to unsung heroes while unfolding the history of Negro Leagues Baseball. Using the first-person insider voice of a fictional "everyman" player, Nelson weaves an emotional story of tragedy and triumph. Peppered with awe-inspiring artwork, including a remarkable foldout spread, this book highlights a part of sports history rarely given its due.

WHY I CHOSE THIS BOOK: This is a story of passion and hope, and Kadir Nelson is the consummate storyteller. He takes an important topic that could be difficult to write about without boring anyone who is not a die-hard baseball fan and makes it intriguing and relevant to all. The story of Negro Leagues Baseball is a fascinating one that stands alone as a record of sportsmanship amid racial discrimination, but it also represents the story of Black Americans in a broader sense. The idea that Black people have always found (and will continue to find) creative ways to circumvent hatred is one that all children should understand.

THOUGHT STARTERS

1. Rube Foster, the founder of the Negro National League, said, "We are the ship; all else the sea." What do you think he meant, and why do you think the author chose part of that quote as the book's title? If you had to rename the book, what would you call it?

2. Think back to the third inning (or chapter). What was life in the Negro Leagues like for the players? What do you think kept them going? How do you think their lives were different than Black professional athletes today?

3. What caused the end of the Negro Leagues? If you were living during the 1940s, would you have celebrated Jackie Robinson and other players integrating the major leagues, mourned the loss of the Negro Leagues, or both? What makes you feel that way?

DIGGING DEEPER

1. Select your favorite painting from the book and write a poem about the person in the picture or re-create the image in your chosen art medium. Or both!

2. Create a magazine ad or promotional video that encourages people to visit the Negro Leagues Baseball Museum in Kansas City, Missouri. Gather details from the website, online sources, interviews, and personal experience if you've had the chance to visit.

3. Why do you think the author chose to use a fictional character as the story's narrator? Think of a historical event you're familiar with and pretend to be an author living during that time. Write a short story about the event using the same storytelling technique as Kadir Nelson.

SECOND HELPINGS

» *Warrior on the Mound*
   Written by Sandra W. Headen
» *12 Rounds to Glory: The Story of Muhammad Ali*

Written by Charles R. Smith, Jr.
Illustrated by Bryan Collier

AMARI AND THE NIGHT BROTHERS

Written by B. B. Alston
Illustrated by Godwin Akpan
*"You're not going to change the world unless
you hang with people who want to change the world too."*

* *

This magical fantasy book (the first in a series) follows thirteen-year-old Amari from her rich private school to a secret supernatural world where she learns she's an illegal magician. Labeled and rejected in both worlds, she learns to harness her powers, lean into friendship, and not let anything distract her from her ultimate goal: finding her missing brother, Quinton, before it's too late.

WHY I CHOSE THIS BOOK: Fantasy books with Black female protagonists have been nearly nonexistent for this age group, but things are beginning to change. This book represents the best of everything that causes children to get completely lost in a book: engaging world-building, mythical creatures, inexplicable mysteries, familiar cultural elements, and a dose of relevant social commentary. It celebrates Black characters in spaces where they don't typically exist without sugarcoating real issues that remain in the known world by mirroring them in the supernatural world. This book is fun! And the cherry on top is that children will walk away understanding how fear and unfamiliarity can cause irrational and hurtful actions.

THOUGHT STARTERS

1. After Amari gets scolded at school, she says that people with money "can do whatever they want with no consequences while the rest of us have to watch our every step." Why did she feel that way? Do you think this is true? Give some examples to support your answer.

2. Which department in the Bureau of Supernatural Affairs would you want to be in and why?

3. Amari compares the racism she experiences at school to the prejudice against magicians in the supernatural world. What are some of the similarities and differences?

DIGGING DEEPER

1. Consider the department you chose above and draw a full-color diagram depicting what you think it would look like based on details shared in the book and what you imagine would be needed based on the activities taking place.

2. If you were a character in this story, which of your talents or strengths would your supernatural ability arise from? Describe your role in the story. Who would you be? What's your backstory? How does Amari influence you? Dress up like your character and make a training video introducing yourself and the Bureau to newcomers.

3. What does it take to develop a compelling fantasy world? Create your own world, and be sure to include all those elements. Make a map that gives a strong sense of the environment as a physical space. What kind of magical system operates there? How did the system or its leaders arise? How is it controlled? Who are the major players in this world? What is their history? Take notes detailing every aspect of your world, describe it to someone else, and answer any questions they have about how your world works.

SECOND HELPINGS

» *The Marvellers*
   Written by Dhonielle Clayton
   Illustrated by Khadijah Khatib
» *Zahrah the Windseeker*
   Written by Nnedi Okorafor-Mbachu

TRISTAN STRONG PUNCHES A HOLE IN THE SKY
Written by Kwame Mbalia
"Those who help you may not be on your side,
and those who oppose you can be your greatest allies."

Tristan Strong, a likable thirteen-year-old, reluctantly heads out to spend a month at his grandparents' farm to grieve the loss of his best friend in an accident. The first night, a little sticky creature tries to steal Tristan's treasured journal, the only thing he has left of his friend Eddie. While struggling to get his journal back, Tristan accidentally falls into the strange realm of MidPass, an island of folk legends where he learns to harness his storytelling power to help his allies fight a war against evil forces.

WHY I CHOSE THIS BOOK: This fantasy adventure novel is rooted in West African mythology and African American folklore, including the trickster Anansi, John Henry, Brer Rabbit, and High John the Conqueror, all of whom play central roles in the storyline. This twist adds another layer to an already rich story filled with well-placed symbolism and metaphors for the legacy of the transatlantic slave trade and beyond. It's not a requirement for enjoying the book, but children will get much more from it if they read or hear some of the individual folktales before experiencing them woven together in this masterful work.

THOUGHT STARTERS

1. Before reading this book, had you ever heard about John Henry, Brer Rabbit, Anansi, or the other folklore characters? If so, what did you find helpful to know about them beforehand? If not, which ones are you most interested in learning more about now?

2. Tristan shares that his Nana used to say, "Everybody has a story. Listen to it, and they'll be friendly. Engage with it, and they'll be your friend." What do you think that means? Have you ever experienced a situation that leads you to believe Nana is right?

3. Other than Tristan, which character from this story would you like to meet in person and why?

DIGGING DEEPER

1. Eddie's journal is Tristan's most treasured belonging, and his quest to get the journal back results in mayhem and adventure. Why were the journal's stories so important? Why is it essential for us to tell our stories? Gather art materials and decorate a journal where you can keep your stories and memories along with the stories of others.

2. Tristan is an Anansesem, a powerful storyteller who can bend his environment to re-create the stories he tells. What makes a great storyteller, and how did Tristan demonstrate those characteristics? Look up a traditional folktale about Anansi or another character featured in *Tristan Strong*, read it carefully, and retell it to someone else using your best storytelling techniques. Be creative! Consider playing music in the background, using props, or changing voices dramatically to capture your audience's attention.

3. Tristan received various Adinkra charms throughout his journey. These West African symbols represent proverbs or central ideas and can be found in fabrics, jewelry, pottery, and other places. Look up some symbols' meanings at adinkra symbols.org, or elsewhere, and choose one that speaks to you. Create an artistic interpretation of that symbol using your favorite art form. Examples include painting, clay modeling, video, digital illustration, fashion design, dance, etc.

SECOND HELPINGS

» *Last Gate of the Emperor*
   Written by Kwame Mbalia and Prince Joel Makonnen
» *Ikenga*
   Written by Nnedi Okorafor

MIDNIGHT WITHOUT A MOON

Written by Linda Williams Jackson
*"That sun beat down on me like I owed
it money from six years back."*

In this coming-of-age novel, thirteen-year-old Rose longs to move up north and away from the harassment, violence, and injustices that Black people in 1950s Mississippi face daily. The fictional characters pay homage to real-life heartbreak when Emmett Till is lynched for allegedly flirting with a white woman. This tragedy spurs Rose and parts of her community to action even as she wrestles with personal suffering amid her own family.

WHY I CHOSE THIS BOOK: The author offers a bird's-eye view of a pivotal historical moment. She doesn't hold back critical details, but she keeps the reader's age in mind when unfolding all that happened during this tumultuous time. The expert weaving of fact and fiction softens the blow of an otherwise devastating and traumatic piece of our past that galvanized the Civil Rights Movement. Kids need to know Till's story to keep his memory alive, and this is a well-played approach to telling it. Faith also plays a big part in Rose's life, and this book gives context to the role of the Black church during this period.

THOUGHT STARTERS

1. When Ma Pearl described Rose's skin color as darker than midnight without a moon, it was not meant as a compliment. Rose says, "I was as black as a cup of Maxwell House without a hint of milk," and she tried to use bleaching creams to lighten her skin. Prejudice or discrimination against someone with darker or lighter skin is called *colorism*, and it occurs frequently within and without the Black community. How do you think colorism impacts Rose in this book? Have you ever witnessed or experienced colorism? How did it make you feel? What might you say to someone who comments negatively about another person's skin?

2. Even though slavery ended ninety years before this story takes place, what effects do we see in Rose's life and community? What effects do you see in your personal life? What about our country today? How has America changed, and how is it still the same?

3. What are some ways that Rose showed courage throughout the book? Tell about a time when you had to be courageous. What happened, and how did you react? Would you do anything differently next time?

DIGGING DEEPER

1. Emmett Till's murder and the outcome of the court case inspired many people to join in the fight for civil rights for Black people in America. Pretend you were a journalist back then and write an article telling the world what happened and why it matters.

2. Hallelujah says, "Dreams have more meaning when you have to fight for them." Do you think that's true? Why or why not? Write down your dreams for your future and share them with two or three others. Ask them to share their biggest dreams with you, too.

3. This book takes place during the Great Migration when many Black people moved from the American South to northern states, seeking better economic opportunities, more freedoms, and a reprieve from some of the abuse they regularly faced. Watch a video about the Great Migration to learn more about this critical historical time. Search for *Great Migration: Crash Course Black American History #24* as one option.[2]

SECOND HELPINGS
» *Choosing Brave: How Mamie Till-Mobley and Emmett Till Sparked the Civil Rights Movement*
  Written by Angela Joy
  Illustrated by Janelle Washington
» *A Wreath for Emmett Till*
  Written by Marilyn Nelson
  Illustrated by Philippe Lardy

ROOT MAGIC

Written by Eden Royce

*"A wide-brimmed hat covered her black hair,
which she had pressed straight with a hot comb
off the stove that morning."*

In this magical novel written by a member of the Gullah Geechee Nation, girl/boy twins Jez and Jay learn to use their family's ancestral magic in a swirling tale about friendship, family, traditions, folklore, and . . . monsters! This story takes place in South Carolina's Gullah region in the 1960s. The twins have just lost their grandmother, who was the glue holding the family together. Now, they learn the family ways from their uncle to help protect their loved ones from a local deputy who has it out for them.

WHY I CHOSE THIS BOOK: Kids who enjoy reading about magic, boo-hags, and folklore (like my youngest daughter) will love this book, and there are far too few options in this category to satisfy their appetites. Along with the obvious cultural connections, *Root Magic* touches on racism, classism, friendship, and the balance between independence and family relationships. The book artfully informs readers of the tension in the Black community over rootwork, and it's an excellent mirror for children from families like the Turners and a window for those interested in learning about a unique culture within some Black Southern communities.

THOUGHT STARTERS

1. Why is it important for families to pass along knowledge?
2. Jez observes a contradiction: while some schoolmates ridicule rootwork, their parents regularly visit her family's shop seeking healing remedies and spells. It's puzzling to see individuals benefiting from a cultural practice yet showing disdain for it. Can you recall other instances where people benefit from something they criticize or mock?
3. Jez's mom says that a person is an artist if they use their mind and hands to create. What do you think about this? Based on this definition, are you an artist? How so, or why not?

DIGGING DEEPER

1. Are you aware of any herbs growing in your yard or near your home that can be used for medicinal purposes? If so, create a little book with sketches of the useful plants and note how they can be safely used at home. Be sure to always check with an adult before using any herbal remedies.
2. At the beginning of the book, Jez and Jay experience a significant loss when their grandma passes away. Have you ever lost someone that you loved? How did and does that loss make you feel? What are some ways that we can keep the memory of loved ones alive?
3. Though she gave an excellent introduction, there is much more to Gullah culture than what the author could fit into this book. Do some research about the Gullah Geechee Nation and the history and customs of its people. And if you live near or get the chance to visit the barrier islands off the southeast coast of the U.S. (North Carolina, South Carolina, Georgia, or Florida), be sure to explore one of the museums dedicated to preserving their cultural traditions, including oral traditions, folklore, storytelling, artisan crafts, and foods.

SECOND HELPINGS
» *The Jumbies*
   Written by Tracey Baptiste
» *A Comb of Wishes*
   Written by Lisa Stringfellow

THE FORGOTTEN GIRL

Written by India Hill Brown

"The snow fell heavier, no longer looking like frosting.
The white branches were now skeletal hands,
waving them backward. Iris could almost feel it,
a pull trying to keep them there."

One snowy night, best friends Iris and Daniel sneak out to play in the woods behind their homes, where they uncover an abandoned cemetery. When Iris makes a snow angel, she realizes she's right on top of the grave of a twelve-year-old girl named Avery. The kids rush home, but Avery's ghost continues to haunt Iris, wanting her to help right past wrongs.

WHY I CHOSE THIS BOOK: Many kids love a good ghost story, and this one is intriguing enough to hold their interest without being overly spooky. The history of segregated cemeteries—where Black people were kept separate even in death—is explored in a fresh and inviting way, as is the racism that accompanied the time. Historic preservation is presented as being important, and the children in the story have the agency to impact change. The values of friendship, family, and storytelling also play key roles.

THOUGHT STARTERS

1. Do you think cemeteries and the bodies buried there matter? Do we have any responsibility to preserve or maintain them? Why or why not?
2. What are the similarities and differences between the racism that Avery encountered and what Iris encounters? Have you ever experienced or witnessed racism? How did it make you feel?
3. Older people often have much wisdom and information to share with younger

generations, and the kids learn a lot about Avery from Suga. What lessons have you learned from your grandparents or other elders? .

DIGGING DEEPER

1. Research the history of segregated cemeteries and determine whether there are any Black cemeteries or burial grounds in your area. If possible, get a tour and discover the untold stories held there. Consider reading *The Secret of Gumbo Grove* by Eleanora Tate for another story about a girl on a search to learn the truth about those buried in a cemetery.

2. Re-create your version of the book cover for *The Forgotten Girl*. Start with a photograph of yourself or someone else and add snowy branches and other details along with a title and your name as the author. You can create the art digitally or print the photo and use paint, collage, or other means to create the cover.

3. Ghostlore has often been used by African American storytellers to subtly address complex societal conditions. Read a few stories from *The Dark-Thirty: Southern Tales of the Supernatural* by Patricia C. McKissack (or a novel like *The House of Dies Drear* by Virginia Hamilton) and compare them to *The Forgotten Girl*. What do they have in common? What are the significant differences?

SECOND HELPINGS

» *Ophie's Ghost*
   Written by Justina Ireland
» *When Life Gives You Mangoes*
   Written by Kereen Getten

THE KAYA GIRL

Written by Mamle Wolo
Illustrations by Bright Ackwerh
*"A wise person once told me that looking
and seeing were not the same thing."*

. . . .

While working in renowned Makola Market in Accra, Ghana, Abena, a wealthy doctor's daughter, and a Muslim migrant girl named Faiza meet and form a powerful bond. Their friendship exposes social and class tensions that open Abena's eyes to her privileged life while illuminating Faiza's journey. Though they meet as teens, the book jumps ahead to their adult relationship, bringing a fulfilling and redemptive close to a heartwarming story.

WHY I CHOSE THIS BOOK: This book highlights local cultural practices through engaging dialogue and perfectly detailed descriptions. Readers gain a realistic view of how stigmas can hinder or splinter relationships as the story explores the socioeconomic variability across Black global communities. The teeming vibrance of market life provides an intriguing background for experiencing life alongside the teens while offering a story that demonstrates the power of friendship and counters deeply seated stereotypes. And though it deals with hardship, *The Kaya Girl* doesn't swim in it. Instead, it's a fun book with interesting characters that readers will enjoy.

THOUGHT STARTERS

1. Do you relate most with Abena's or Faiza's story, and why? In which ways are their experiences mirrored in your life? How is your life entirely different than theirs?
2. What was most surprising about life in Accra, Ghana? How do the environment and people described in the book differ from what you expected?
3. Friendship requires forgiveness. Tell of a time that you've forgiven a friend or when you've been forgiven by someone you care about.

DIGGING DEEPER

1. *Kayayoo* is a Ghanaian word for a female porter or a woman who carries goods (typically on her head) for a fee. Research other informal ways that women often earn an income in Ghana.
2. Ghanaian artist Bright Ackwerh created the cover art for this book. Using the medium of your choice, re-create your version of his cover or create an entirely new one based on your own idea.
3. Identify 3–5 small, locally owned businesses in your area, and list how you and your family can intentionally support them on an ongoing basis.

SECOND HELPINGS

» *The Red Pencil*
  Written by Andrea Davis Pinkney
  Illustrated by Shane W. Evans
» *The Boy Who Harnessed the Wind (Young Reader's Edition)*
  Written by William Kamkwamba and Bryan Mealer
  Illustrated by Anna Hymas

CROSSING THE STREAM

Written by Elizabeth-Irene Baitie

*"High up is a place of fear for the chicken.
And yet for the falcon, high up is where
it finds freedom to live true to itself."*

· ·

Twelve-year-old Ato and his two best friends work hard to win a trip to Nnoma, a Ghanaian bird island sanctuary that Ato's late father helped create. Things go well at first, but something suspicious begins negatively impacting their area's land, vegetation, and animals. The kids are the only ones who suspect foul play, and this is the story of how they help solve the mystery and save the day.

WHY I CHOSE THIS BOOK: I greatly appreciate this book for giving an insider's view of contemporary life in Ghana without telling the story through a lens of unredeemed trauma. When children read about Africa, often the only story they hear is one of deprivation and devastation. This book includes realistic depictions of poverty and hardship but doesn't leave the reader feeling like that's all there is to Ghana. The main characters are resourceful, innovative, and ready to change the world.

THOUGHT STARTERS

1. Why did so many people fall prey to Prophet Yakayaka? What can help prevent people from mindlessly following leaders who abuse their power?
2. Ato says he doesn't want to use fear to get others to do what he desires. Do you

agree or disagree? What are some ways that people can negotiate or be heard without using fear or manipulation?

3. What did you think Nana was going to bury in her yard? Were you surprised by what she did at the end of the book? Is there anything else you think she could have done instead to bring closure?

DIGGING DEEPER

1. This book exposes the tension between environmentalism and development or the usage of natural resources versus economic prosperity. Sustainable development balances economic development, environmental protection, and social well-being. What are some sustainability activities that young people can pursue? Pick one or two that are important to you and get started on them.

2. Visiting Nnoma, the bird sanctuary, is Ato's greatest dream, and he references birds throughout the book. He compares Leslie to a parakeet and Dzifa to a magpie. He draws a picture of a cassowary and adopts the hunting skills of a peregrine falcon, his favorite bird, when exposing wrongdoings. If you were a bird, which bird would you be and why? What about your closest friends or family members? What kinds of birds would they be? Draw a picture or write a poem that best represents one of your chosen birds.

3. The title *Crossing the Stream* refers to the Forbidden Stream separating Tamarind Ridge, Nana's higher-income neighborhood, from the Zongo, an area that lacks suitable housing and basic conveniences. Do you have a river, railroad, street, or other line of demarcation in your town that similarly separates neighborhoods? Research how that socioeconomic separation began. If you can't find details, research gentrification to learn more about one possible cause.

SECOND HELPINGS

» *One Shadow on the Wall*
Written by Leah Henderson
» *The Door of No Return*
Written by Kwame Alexander

THE GLORY FIELD

Written by Walter Dean Myers

"She was free. It was a scary free, and it was a
hungry free and a tired free, but it was free."

....

This must-read novel tells the story of five generations of the Lewis family beginning in Africa in 1753 with the capture and enslavement of eleven-year-old Muhammad Bilal. It reveals how his descendants pursued self-emancipation from a South Carolina plantation before settling into life in the North. In 1964, another descendant struggles with the tension between acting against injustice on behalf of his community and looking the other way for personal gain. The book ends in 1994 as one young man discovers the power of family while helping his drug-addicted cousin travel from New York to their family reunion in South Carolina to spend time with the family elders on the land that has held them together for so long.

WHY I CHOSE THIS BOOK: Because of the wide span of years covered, *The Glory Field* serves as a one-stop shop for Black American history and culture through the generations. Not only does the format give a view into many centuries of Black life, but the stories situate the history in engaging plots and circumstances. The book is also an excellent springboard for future reading; it could spark interest in particular decades with children intrigued by one section or another. It doesn't detract from the reading, but the word "heifer" is used in a derogatory manner by some characters, so you may want to explain that usage to kids since they may not have heard it before. Also, the last vignette includes a character who is addicted to drugs, but his family rallies around him and offers him hope.

THOUGHT STARTERS

1. Through this storyline, we can see how decisions and circumstances influence families over time. How has your life today been influenced by your ancestors or family members before you?

2. When asked if she knows where Joshua is headed after he leaves the plantation, Saran says he's probably headed north because "Every black person who ain't

dead sooner or later gets them a freedom dream." What did she mean? Do you think her statement was true? Why or why not?

3. The stories in the book emphasize family, freedom, and hope. What are some examples the author gives of each, and how do these themes appear in your life?

DIGGING DEEPER

1. The book spans from 1753 to 1994. Think about life before Muhammad was kidnapped in Africa or after the family reunion at Curry Island and write a pre-quel or sequel chapter for this book.

2. Luvenia Lewis has a rent party to raise money. Research the history of rent parties and create a list of other creative things people have done to survive tough times. What about today? What would you recommend to someone who needs money to live but struggles to find enough work?

3. To get a visual idea of the shackles passed down to Malcolm at the end of the book, search for "shackles" on the Smithsonian National Museum of African American History & Culture website. If you could have just one artifact from your home or family to keep and pass down to future generations, what would it be and why? Ask this same question to three adults and see if any of their responses surprise you.

SECOND HELPINGS

» *Roll of Thunder, Hear My Cry*
   Written by Mildred D. Taylor
» *Never Caught, the Story of Ona Judge: George and Martha Washington's Courageous Slave Who Dared to Run Away (Young Readers Edition)*
   Written by Erica Armstrong Dunbar and Kathleen Van Cleve

FREEWATER

Written by Amina Luqman-Dawson

"With a dream of adventure and a flick of her wrist, she released the sling and watched the stone soar high in the air, catch the moonlight, and disappear into the cauldron of fog below."

With a beautifully fleshed-out story of resistance and self-emancipation, this book tells how twelve-year-old Homer and his little sister, Ada, get separated from their mom and find their way to a secret community of formerly enslaved people and their freeborn children deep in the Great Dismal Swamp. In the society of Freewater, the children find security and comfort until the existence of their secret society is threatened. The characters are fictional, but the plot is based on historical accounts of people living in swamps after fleeing slavery.

WHY I CHOSE THIS BOOK: In *A Place to Belong*, I write, "Rooted in reality but not hemmed in by factual occurrence, historical fiction often brings humanity to the triumph and credibly redeems tragedy," and this is why I love using historical fiction to teach children about the past, particularly times or topics that can be difficult to hear or process. *Freewater* is a fascinating story of resistance with rich characters set against a strikingly vivid outdoor setting, and even at four hundred pages, it holds the reader's riveted attention.

THOUGHT STARTERS

1. Everyone in Freewater gets to choose a new name. What was your favorite character's name? If you lived there, what name would you choose and why?
2. How were Sanzi and Juna's lives and perspectives different from those of the children who had been enslaved? What other differences may exist between people who have always been free and those who have not?
3. What type of relationship do the people of Freewater have with the land on which they live? What kind of relationship do you have with nature and your outdoor environment? How or why do you think that relationship developed?

DIGGING DEEPER

1. The author was inspired by research on maroon communities of enslaved people who resisted by escaping captivity and finding sanctuary in the swamps of the American South. Research other ways enslaved people fought back. Are any of the methods new to you?
2. Homer memorized the steps to Freewater for his mam: "Forest, river, vines and bush, watch for the sinkhole, more vines and bush, green water, tree boat, lily pads, secret water door, tree hideout." Draw a detailed map or picture of what

you think Freewater looked like based on this and other descriptions found in the book.

3. In an interview with We Need Diverse Books, the author says, "In creating Freewater, I could center the voices of enslaved Black folks over their victimization within the system of slavery. Freewater does have elements of pain and suffering; however, they aren't centered." Give examples from the book that demonstrate this truth.

SECOND HELPINGS
» *Elijah of Buxton*
    Written by Christopher Paul Curtis
» *The Watsons Go to Birmingham—1963*
    Written by Christopher Paul Curtis

PIECING ME TOGETHER
Written by Renée Watson
*"Those girls are not the opposite of me. We are perpendicular.
We may be on different paths, yes. But there's a place where we touch,
where we connect and are just the same."*

Sixteen-year-old Jade wants to experience a vibrant life beyond the confines of her "bad" neighborhood, but as one of the only Black kids in her private high school, she's regularly forced to confront issues of race, class, and body image. She resents being identified as something for people to fix and has a complicated relationship with the mentor assigned to her through a new program. Jade processes the world around her through collage; ultimately, her art gives her the voice she's been struggling to harness.

WHY I CHOSE THIS BOOK: This book confronts issues that many young Black women today deal with, and teens need to bear witness to the pain and confusion caused by stereotypes, racial profiling, fat shaming, and more. I appreciate that Jade is encouraged to advocate for herself and use her voice to meet her needs. Art plays a powerful role in Jade's story, becoming a worthy example of how photography, collage, poetry, and other creative expressions can be therapeutic and celebratory. Recommended for the older end of this age range.

THOUGHT STARTERS

1. At the beginning of the book, Jade says, "Girls like me, with coal skin and hula-hoop hips, whose mommas barely make enough money to keep food in the house, have to take opportunities every chance we get." What does this tell us about Jade and her thoughts about herself and her circumstances? How is your identity similar to or different than Jade's?

2. What do you think about her father's advice for Black families to remove their photos and artwork so potential buyers won't know the homeowners are Black? Maxine's parents coach her to tone down her Blackness. What does that mean? What are they afraid of? Have you ever seen someone experience consequences for being "too Black?"

3. Jade is mistreated at the mall and is sure that it's because she's Black, but Sam tries to explain it away. Why do they see things so differently? Do you think situations like these happen in real life? Why or why not?

DIGGING DEEPER

1. How does Jade use collage to make sense of her circumstances? Using any materials that speak to you, create a collage representing who you want to become.

2. Reread Lee Lee's poem in chapter 75. What stands out most to you? How do you see yourself? How do others see you? Write a poem about who you are.

3. Research York's story online (or read *The Journey of York: The Unsung Hero of the Lewis and Clark Expedition* by Hasan Davis). Why do you think Jade references York throughout the book?

SECOND HELPINGS

» *Genesis Begins Again*
    Written by Alicia D. Williams
» *The Skin I'm In*
    Written by Sharon G. Flake

GHOST

Written by Jason Reynolds

*"You can't run away from who you are, but what you
can do is run toward who you want to be."*

....

Castle Cranshaw, aka Ghost, is recruited for an elite middle school track team after the coach sees him casually challenge his best runner to race. Ghost and his teammates are good enough to compete in the Junior Olympics if they can learn to work well individually and as a team, but Ghost struggles to let go of his past. His father is in prison for domestic violence, and even though his mom works hard to give him a better life, other kids can tell that Ghost doesn't have much, and they bully him. Ghost needs to stay out of trouble, at least until race day, and this book chronicles the ups and downs of the weeks leading up to the race.

WHY I CHOSE THIS BOOK: This is the first book in the Track series, a well-written chronicling of four of the newest runners on the Defenders track team. Ghost is a complex character teetering between harnessing his energy toward activities that will bring him life and succumbing to the trauma-induced pain that haunts him. The author shows the direct power of mentors in a young person's life, and he sends an important message: You can change your mind. You can be different than you have been once you realize that there's a better path forward. The other idea that comes through loudly is for adolescents to step lightly with one another because they never know what a person is going through. Finally, this book revolves around track and field, one of the many sports where talented Black athletes have dedicated themselves to training for and dominating the world's most elite races.

THOUGHT STARTERS

1. "Running for his life or running from it?" is on the cover of this book. What do you think that means? What does running mean for Ghost initially, and how is it different in the end? What is your most remarkable talent, interest, or hobby? What led you to pursue it, and how does it serve you?

2. How do Ghost's relationships with Mr. Charles and Coach help him remain

focused? Who inspires you to dream big, do the right thing, or feel confident? What do you like most about that person?

3. Describe Ghost's neighborhood. How does it compare to where you live? Does the type of neighborhood someone lives in determine their character? Why or why not?

DIGGING DEEPER

1. Have you ever seen anyone with albinism? Research the types, causes, and treatment for albinism. How do you think having albinism impacts people's lives?

2. Ghost's desire for an expensive pair of new running shoes leads to lousy decision-making on his part. What do you think it's like for a teen who can't afford something to be around others who seem to have everything? What could he have done differently? Reach out to a high school track coach, tell them you're researching a project based on this book, and ask them what a runner should do if they don't have money for running shoes but want to be on the team. What do you think of their answer?

3. What are your thoughts about how *Ghost* ended? What do you think happened next? Write an alternate ending to the story.

SECOND HELPINGS

» *Ghetto Cowboy*
   Written by G. Neri
   Illustrated by Jesse Joshua Watson
» *Once in a Blue Moon*
   Written by Sharon G. Flake

HARBOR ME

Written by Jacqueline Woodson

"If the worst thing in the world happened, would I help protect someone else? Would I let myself be a harbor for someone who needs it?"

Six students are invited to chat in an empty classroom each Friday afternoon with no adults listening. They bond in the ARTT room ("A Room to Talk") by sharing and accepting their personal stories. They captivatingly tell of family hardships, incarceration, deportation, grief, loss, and struggles with race and class. Even though their stories differ, the kids find that they hold the same values and hopes while creating a compassionate support system for one another.

WHY I CHOSE THIS BOOK: The children form healthy friendships rooted in trust. They don't gossip or bully; their mature relationships demonstrate the power of community. Woodson's writing validates the idea that societal issues and racial tensions weigh heavily on kids, and they have as much of a need to discuss them as adults.

THOUGHT STARTERS

1. Why do you think the children initially resist the ARTT room and what it represents?
2. How did you feel when you read each student's story? Which of their stories resonates with you most and why?
3. Haley's uncle says that we should forgive and forget. Do you agree? Why or why not?

DIGGING DEEPER

1. What does Ms. Laverne mean when she wants each student to say, "I will harbor you"? What does it mean to be a harbor for someone? Is there someone for whom you are a harbor or that harbors you? Write them a note letting them know how you feel about them or how they've helped you.
2. Why does Haley want to record the stories of the friends in the ARTT room? Why is it important to preserve memories? Record a critical or pivotal story from your life that you want to remember, and interview three others willing to let you document their stories. What do the stories have in common? How are they different?
3. What are some arguments for and against allowing immigrants into the U.S.? Research the position and rationale of both sides. Why do you think immigration has been the focus of such intense debate throughout American history?

SECOND HELPINGS

» *Locomotion*

Written by Jacqueline Woodson

» *Hush*

Written by Jacqueline Woodson

GHOST BOYS

Written by Jewell Parker Rhodes

"Wake. Only the living can make the world better.
Live and make it better. Don't let me (Or anyone else)
Tell this tale again."

. . . .

This gripping narrative gives voice to twelve-year-old Jerome, who returns as a ghost after being shot and killed by a police officer. The story is told through alternating chapters that switch between living and spirit Jerome as the narrator. While a ghost, Jerome watches the preliminary hearing of the officer who shot him and witnesses his family grieving their loss. Interestingly, Jerome meets the ghost of Emmett Till, who helps him make sense of what's happened, and in the end, he calls on the living to change the world so stories like his don't repeat themselves.

WHY I CHOSE THIS BOOK: The topics addressed in this book can be difficult for parents to discuss with their kids, but the discussions need to be had anyway. Through an engaging fictional story tinted with actual history, the author lays the intersection of past racialized violence and current debates on police brutality at the readers' feet while leaving space for them to wrestle with their thoughts and ideas. This cannot be the only take on such critical topics, but it's a compelling start.

THOUGHT STARTERS

1. In the afterword, the author explains that "bearing witness" means using your personal or cultural story to testify against inequities, injustice, and suffering. How did Jerome bear witness in this book? Have you ever had an opportunity to bear witness to something, or have you seen someone else do it?
2. Why does Carlos bring a toy gun to school? Do you agree with Jerome's decision not to tell his family he is being bullied at school? Have you ever bullied

someone? Have you ever been bullied? Tell about how either experience made you feel.

3. Why do you think Sarah is the only one who can see the ghost boys?

DIGGING DEEPER

1. Research the Civil Rights Movement and the Black Lives Matter movement. What do they have in common? What are their major differences?

2. Research the case of Tamir Rice. How is his story similar to or different than Jerome's?

3. Write a letter to author Jewell Parker Rhodes with three things you enjoyed about the book and three questions you have after reading it. You can find her mailing address on her website (jewellparkerrhodes.com).

SECOND HELPINGS

» *The Awakening of Malcolm X: A Novel*
   Written by Ilyasah Shabazz and Tiffany D. Jackson
» *A Good Kind of Trouble*
   Written by Lisa Moore Ramée

OUT OF MY MIND
Written by Sharon M. Draper
"Words have always swirled around me like snowflakes—each one delicate and different, each one melting untouched in my hands."

. . . .

Melody is a nearly eleven-year-old girl whose parents are her biggest supporters. Despite their attempts to provide her with a full life of experiences and love, Melody is consistently frustrated by her inability to move or speak due to cerebral palsy. When she begins communicating with the world through a new computer, everyone in her environment discovers just how much of Melody and her funny and brilliant mind they've never known. However, this new awareness doesn't always protect her from feelings of hurt and rejection from people who still don't fully accept her.

WHY I CHOSE THIS BOOK: First, this is just a darn good story. It also shows a different aspect of Black culture that is typically marginalized and overlooked. It highlights Melody's strength in breaking down the stereotypes and assumptions people made about her. Be sure to check out the sequel *Out of My Heart* for a continuation of Melody's inspiring story.

THOUGHT STARTERS

1. What did Melody want others to know or understand about her? Have you ever experienced the pain of being misunderstood or underestimated? What is one thing that you wish others knew about you?
2. Why was Melody's relationship with her little sister, Penny, so complicated? How would you describe your relationship with your siblings (or cousins or friends if you don't have siblings)?
3. How has reading this story changed any assumptions you may have made about people with disabilities?

DIGGING DEEPER

1. Research cerebral palsy to better understand its causes and symptoms and learn about the impact on those living with it. Create a video that explains what you learned about CP to other kids clearly and engagingly. Raise awareness by sharing it with as many people as you can.
2. How did the Medi-Talker change Melody's life? Why does she name her computer Elvira? Create a magazine ad or TV commercial advertising the device. Be sure to include the pros and cons and compare it to other options on the market.
3. Why is music so important to Melody? What kind of music do you enjoy most? Put together a soundtrack to go with your three favorite scenes from the book.

SECOND HELPINGS

» *Blended*
   Written by Sharon M. Draper
» *From the Desk of Zoe Washington*
   Written by Janae Marks
   Interior illustrations by Mirelle Ortega

CROSSOVER

Written by Kwame Alexander

"A loss is inevitable, like snow in winter.
True champions learn to dance through the storm."

Josh and Jordan Bell are twin brothers and basketball stars whose bond is tested throughout the season. Though they share an undeniable connection, their different personalities, experiences, and a new crush threaten to pull the brothers apart as they deal with changing family dynamics. Written in verse, this book incorporates the electric rhythms of basketball and the power of language to communicate messages of love, loyalty, loss, and redemption.

WHY I CHOSE THIS BOOK: Though written over a basketball soundtrack, this is ultimately a story on the importance of family and friendship. It gives voice to young teen boys who are balancing their relationships with each other and the world and gives them a complexity that's rarely found in sports-centered books.

THOUGHT STARTERS

1. Many people expect twins to be exactly alike. Is that the case with Josh and Jordan? How are they similar? How are they different? Which one would you most want to be friends with and why?

2. Basketball is a meaningful part of Josh's and Jordan's life. Which extracurricular activities are important to you and why?

3. What prevents their dad, Chuck Bell, from going to the doctor? Do you think his concern is legitimate?

DIGGING DEEPER

1. Have you ever had to forgive someone you love? Have you ever hurt someone and needed to ask forgiveness? Write a letter as the forgiver or the forgiven explaining what the experience was like for you. You don't have to mail the letter unless you want to.

2. Why do you think Josh writes an ode to his hair? Pick a part of yourself and write a poem about it in the same style.

3. Watch author Kwame Alexander's TEDx talk on "The Power of Yes."[3] What does

he mean when he says that the word "yes" creates the perception, but the work creates the reality?

SECOND HELPINGS

» *New Kid*
    Written by Jerry Craft
    With color by Jim Callahan
» *The Season of Styx Malone*
    Written by Kekla Magoon

BROWN GIRL DREAMING

Written by Jacqueline Woodson

"I believe in one day and someday and
this perfect moment called Now."

· ·

This award-winning memoir-in-verse takes readers on a mesmerizing ride from Woodson's birth amid the Civil Rights Movement to her early childhood in South Carolina with her grandmother and her later years in Brooklyn, where she reunited with her mom. Alongside her story of family and community, readers experience her development from a young girl who loves stories to her fully developed realization that "words are my brilliance."

WHY I CHOSE THIS BOOK: Aside from being a phenomenal piece of literature, this book presents a moving glimpse at the author's cherished childhood memories. In doing so, she demonstrates the fluidity of belonging as she warmly describes how deeply influenced we are by our pasts. Her detailed story helps personalize some shared history in Black American families and delivers a touching account of her growth and becoming amid joys and trials.

THOUGHT STARTERS

1. *Brown Girl Dreaming* was a Newbery Honor book and won the Coretta Scott King Award, the National Book Award, and the NAACP Image Award, among many other accolades. What do you think makes this book so special?

2. Jacqueline's mother tells her children they will experience a "moment when you walk into a room and no one there is like you." Have you experienced this? If so, what did it feel like? If not, how do you imagine it might feel?

3. Jacqueline Woodson was raised in the American South and the North. How were her experiences different in these varied geographies? Do you think Black people experience differences between the two regions today?

DIGGING DEEPER

1. At times, Jacqueline feels more comfortable in South Carolina and, at other times, in New York, not feeling fully at home in either place. Eventually, she accepts that home can be found in many places. Where do you think that you belong most? Using dance, rap, poetry, music, writing, or visual art, create something representing the word "home" to you.

2. Woodson struggles to find her place in the world until she realizes she has a gift for words and writing. What makes you feel most alive? Find a way to share your art, talent, or interest with others.

3. While writing this memoir, Woodson couldn't include every memory she had of her family and childhood; she had to select the ones that told her story best. What three stories from your life best represent you and your most central experiences? Find a way to record them through verse, journaling, audio, video, or drawing.

SECOND HELPINGS

» *Zora and Me*
   Written by Victoria Bond and T. R. Simon

» *One Big Open Sky*
   Written by Lesa Cline-Ransome

IT'S TREVOR NOAH: BORN A CRIME: STORIES FROM A SOUTH AFRICAN CHILDHOOD (ADAPTED FOR YOUNG READERS)

Written by Trevor Noah

"I became a chameleon. My color didn't change, but I could change your perception of my color. I didn't look like you, but if I spoke like you, I was you."

In this young reader's version of his bestselling memoir, South African comedian Trevor Noah tells of growing up as the child of a white Swiss-German father and Black Xhosa mother during and after apartheid. Told through a series of heartbreaking and hilarious stories, readers witness the evolution of a boy raised under the wing of his mother's unwavering love within a system of institutionalized racism and segregation, the devastating effects of which are still widely seen today.

WHY I CHOSE THIS BOOK: Children need to understand the parallels between segregation in the United States and apartheid in South Africa. It's not something commonly discussed in most school curricula, but understanding the similarities and differences helps us see how racialized traumas have harmed Black communities across the diaspora. Yet we're still standing, just like Trevor, able to find joy in all of life's funny little moments.

THOUGHT STARTERS

1. What does Trevor Noah mean when he says he was born a crime? What would it feel like if your life was proof that your parents broke the law?
2. Describe 3–5 ways that Trevor's childhood significantly differed from yours. What do you have in common?
3. How is Trevor similar to his mom? How is he different? Which relative or friend are you most like? How does that impact your relationship with that person?

DIGGING DEEPER

1. What do you know about apartheid? Research how it has affected the lives of South Africans, and write a paragraph about the differences and similarities between apartheid and Jim Crow laws in the United States.
2. Who were the most influential people in Trevor Noah's life? How did the relationships impact him? Write a poem, rap, song, or script about the most influential person in your life and how they've influenced you.
3. Trevor Noah has the unique ability to make people laugh without avoiding difficult (sometimes even devastating) topics. Retell some of Trevor's funniest stories in your own words.

SECOND HELPINGS

NOT AN EASY WIN

Written by Chrystal D. Giles

"He doesn't hate you," Mr. Dennis said. "He is you."

....

Ever since being evicted and moving from Charlotte, North Carolina, to his grandma's house in a small town, nothing has worked out for Lawrence. His father is incarcerated, he's being bullied at school, and he feels incredibly misunderstood. He gets expelled from school for fighting, but his grandma makes it clear that he must find something to do with his time. Lawrence starts helping his neighbor at a local recreation center, where he's introduced to new people and chess. These newfound relationships and his interest in the game begin to inform his perspectives on life and how he's dealt with the bullies trying to pull him down.

WHY I CHOSE THIS BOOK: I love the redemptive aspect of this story. It shows kids that despite the challenges that life can and will bring, they can decide how they respond and work through them, even when they can't always control their circumstances. The author adds depth and dimension to people often stereotyped and disregarded while remaining honest about the complex nature of decision-making and relationships. The impact of parental imprisonment on children is an important societal topic for children to understand and grapple with, and this book brings big doses of humanity to the kids impacted in the story. The spotlight on intergenerational living is another reason that I selected this book.

THOUGHT STARTERS

1. How does learning the complex rules of chess help Lawrence make better choices and remember to be more strategic in other areas?

2. Music helps Lawrence focus and feel self-assured when playing chess. What are some things that help you feel better when you're under pressure or feeling anxious?

3. How do you think having an incarcerated parent impacted Lawrence and Deuce? How did the loss and social stigma make them feel about themselves? Read the author's note. How did her personal experience impact this story? How did you or would you feel when meeting a peer with an incarcerated parent? Or if your parent is incarcerated, how much do you relate with the characters in this book?

DIGGING DEEPER

1. At the beginning of the book, Lawrence attends a school named after former President Andrew Jackson. In the end, he's planning to attend a different school named after educator Booker T. Washington. Why do you think the author chose those names for each school? Research both men and make a video comparing the two.

2. Watch the movie *Queen of Katwe* and write a letter from Lawrence to Phiona (or the other way around, if you prefer), encouraging her based on what he's learned from playing chess.

3. What does the title *Not an Easy Win* mean? Consider three different titles you would recommend for this book and explain why you think each one would work well.

SECOND HELPINGS

» *Operation Sisterhood*
    Written by Olugbemisola Rhuday-Perkovich
    Illlustrations by Brittney Bond

» *Fast Pitch*
    Written by Nic Stone
    Illustrated by Noa Denmon

10

HIGH SCHOOL (AGES 15–17)

NO CRYSTAL STAIR: A DOCUMENTARY NOVEL OF THE LIFE AND WORK OF LEWIS MICHAUX, HARLEM BOOKSELLER

Written by Vaunda Micheaux Nelson

Illustrated by R. Gregory Christie

"When a man is doing a thing, he has to do it the way he sees it."

. . . .

This is an engaging documentary novel written by Lewis Michaux's niece, a fictional work bathed in historical research and primary documents. It's an inspiring story of a man with a vision to build a bookstore that became the intellectual center of Harlem and how his tenacious commitment ultimately touched and served so many.

WHY I CHOSE THIS BOOK: Michaux's bookstore was an essential meeting place for the Black community. Many of the historical figures and writers we read and admire spent time there, and yet it's virtually unknown by most young people. This book rights that wrong. The author gives readers a vision of the deep ties within Black communities, something many of us lack and may not even realize how to form or why it's important to sacrifice for and hold on to.

THOUGHT STARTERS

1. Lewis Michaux's niece wrote *No Crystal Stair*. If you were to write an article, or maybe an entire book, about an ancestor or someone you know, who would you choose and why? How would you begin your research?

2. This documentary novel has a unique format: a hybrid of nonfiction and fictional elements used to fill in unknowns and increase engagement. What do you like best and least about this literary format?

3. Most of the images in the book are photographs and documents, but R. Gregory Christie's black-and-white drawings are sprinkled throughout. What do you think those drawings bring to the book? Which picture stood out to you most and why?

DIGGING DEEPER

1. The book's title comes from a poem called *Mother to Son* by Langston Hughes. Turn to page 67 to reread the poem. Why do you think the author chose that title for the book? What would you call it if you could rename the book? Be sure to pick something that will interest the intended audience (teens). Create a new book cover in the style of R. Gregory Christie's drawings with your new title and explain the design choices to someone who has (or should!) read the book.

2. Choose one of the historical figures from the book that interests you most and research their life. Find primary sources that help tell their story and illuminate the place and time during which they lived. Look for original records or accounts recorded by people with firsthand knowledge. This can include interviews, government documents, newspapers, photographs, audio recordings, etc. Examine the materials you've collected. What story do they tell about the person and the world they lived in?

3. Contact an indie bookstore and ask if you can schedule a time to interview the owner. Tell the owner about Lewis Michaux, and ask them questions about their journey with books, entrepreneurship, what keeps them going, things they like most and least about running the shop, their favorite books and authors, and whether any famous people have ever come in to purchase books or hang out.

SECOND HELPINGS

» *X: A Novel*
   Written by Ilyasah Shabazz and Kekla Magoon
» *The Fire Next Time*
   Written by James Baldwin

ORLEANS

Written by Sherri L. Smith

"Some choices, once you make them, they stay made."

. . . .

In this captivating dystopian novel, sixteen-year-old Fen de la Guerre works to survive as part of a primitive society in what's left of a lawless New Orleans after a string of hurricanes ravages it. A horrific outbreak of the Delta virus threatens lives, so the area was quickly quarantined and cut off from the rest of the United States by a sizeable, guarded wall. Those with the virus do what they can to survive by banding into tribes by blood type to slow transmission. It's now 2056, Fen's tribe is attacked, and she's left raising her leader's new-born until she teams up with a scientist who snuck in from the Outer States. Together, they try to make a way forward. Contains abuse, rape (not in detail), and violence.

WHY I CHOSE THIS BOOK: *Orleans* was published in 2013, so the horrific 2020 virus outbreak Smith writes about is eerily prescient considering COVID-19. A fictional look at the destruction caused by climate change following Hurricane Katrina and the impact of natural disasters (beyond the apparent physical damage) on the communities they devastate is a relevant topic addressed by today's environmental justice leaders, many of whom represent Black communities. There's no way to read this book without considering medical ethics, and that's a great entry point for teens to follow up by learning about the Tuskegee experiment and Henrietta Lacks. The division of people by blood type offers an opportunity to examine social hierarchies and injustice outside the realm of race.

THOUGHT STARTERS

1. What's one thing you would have done differently than Fen if you were in her situation?
2. If there was a sequel to this book, what would you like to see happen? Who or what would you want to know more about?
3. What do you think of the government's response to the hurricanes and the resulting Delta virus in the book?

DIGGING DEEPER

1. Daniel compares the underhanded research he finds at the former institute to the Tuskegee experiment (1932–1972). Research this instance of medical racism and abuse and compare it to what Daniel learned about the professors' research in *Orleans*. How are they similar or different?

2. When Daniel looked inside the Superdome, he saw the meticulous results of countless hours of work the nuns put into preserving the bones of the tens of thousands dead. In real life, at least twenty thousand people sheltered in the Superdome when Hurricane Katrina hit New Orleans in 2005. Watch this poem by New Orleans poet Shelton Shakespeare Alexander: "Hurricane Katrina: Superdome Poem" on the HISTORY Channel's YouTube page. What parts of Superdome reality connect with the fictional events in *Orleans*?

3. Blood typing is a significant element of this book. Draw a chart or digitally animate a tutorial that lists the possible blood types and shows which transfusions each blood type can receive. Given what you've learned, why was Fen's tribe among the most hunted?

SECOND HELPINGS

» *Parable of the Sower*
   Written by Octavia E. Butler
   Sexual violence is evident but not graphically depicted.
» *Sing, Unburied, Sing: A Novel*
   Written by Jesmyn Ward

PRIDE: A PRIDE AND PREJUDICE REMIX
Written by Ibi Zoboi
"Lifeboats and lifelines are not supposed to just be a way for us to get out. They should be ways to let us stay in and survive. And thrive."

• •

In this fantastic reimagining of the Jane Austen classic, an Afro-Latina teen named Zuri Benitez grapples with gentrification when wealthy Darius Darcy and his siblings move into her beloved Bushwick, Brooklyn, neighborhood. Her sisters are enamored by the Darcy brothers, but Zuri is more impressed by their classmate Warren. Eventually, Zuri and Darius overcome her pride and his prejudice to fall in love despite the complications inherent in their match-up.

WHY I CHOSE THIS BOOK: A modern twist on an established story is a fun way to bridge old and new, and the remix may spark ideas for how teens can reimagine other well-known books. I love how Zoboi kept the broad ideas from the original text but otherwise created something entirely new and incredibly authentic at the same time. The author's inclusion of gentrification in the storyline offers a significant learning opportunity, as do the conversations regarding class and social standing. Through the Benitez family, readers get a taste of Haitian-Dominican culture that rarely appears in books for young people, and the contemporary love story will capture their attention.

THOUGHT STARTERS

1. Throughout the book, food is used to signify familial and community culture and class distinctions. What does the food your family prepares or the options you find most available in your community say about your culture and environment?

2. If you wrote a sequel to this book, what would happen next in Zuri's and Darius's lives, and how would they change or grow?

3. What do you think the "pride and prejudice" in the title means? What are some examples of where you see pride and prejudice show up in your own life?

DIGGING DEEPER

1. Zuri observes that gentrification not only prices families like hers out of the neighborhood but also makes the area less and less diverse. Research how gentrification is impacting your city (or a nearby location). What should be done to maintain these neighborhoods' socioeconomic and cultural diversity?

2. Select one of Zuri's poems to reread. What is the poem's central message, and how does that relate to the rest of the book? Consider reading the poem aloud in front of a small audience in the spirit of spoken word. If you're unfamiliar with the art form, try to attend a live spoken word performance or watch videos online to get the groove of it.

3. Read Jane Austen's *Pride and Prejudice*. What parallels do you see between the two stories? How are they most different? Why do you think Zoboi called this book a "remix" rather than simply a retelling?

SECOND HELPINGS

- » *So Many Beginnings: A Little Women Remix*
  Written by Bethany C. Morrow
- » *A Raisin in the Sun*
  Written by Lorraine Hansberry

JUST MERCY: A STORY OF JUSTICE AND REDEMPTION
Written by Bryan Stevenson

"You can't effectively fight abusive power, poverty, inequality, illness, oppression, or injustice and not be broken by it."

Attorney Bryan Stevenson argues for compassion as he shares his experiences pursuing justice for people victimized by the justice system, including children and adults who have been wrongly convicted or unfairly sentenced. His nonprofit organization, the Equal Justice Initiative, challenges the death penalty and provides services to formerly incarcerated people. This book tells of his work in terms of how far they've come and how far they have left to go. Though he discusses multiple cases, he focuses on Walter McMillian, who was sentenced to death for a crime he didn't commit. Alternative for younger teens: *Just Mercy (Adapted for Young Adults): A True Story of the Fight for Justice.*

WHY I CHOSE THIS BOOK: Stevenson offers teens a rare opportunity to see the inner workings of the United States criminal justice system from the perspective of an attorney who represents death row inmates. He's not shy about the toll that fighting on behalf of those without a voice has taken on him and others, and that raw honesty helps readers understand just how far-reaching the grip of injustice can be. This book is timely and imperative if we hope for teenagers to be informed citizens willing to educate themselves on the issues most impacting our society today.

THOUGHT STARTERS

1. After Walter is diagnosed with advanced dementia and Jimmy Dill is executed, Bryan Stevenson thinks about quitting because he is emotionally exhausted from the pervasive suffering and injustice he regularly witnessed. What kept him

in the game? What helps you keep going when you feel like giving up on things, people, or even your dreams?

2. Stevenson's grandmother profoundly impacted him, especially her advice that to understand something, "you have to get close" to it. What did she mean by that, and what are some examples of things you may need to get close to in order to better understand something in your own life?

3. Stevenson believes that severe punishments perpetuate violence rather than deter it. He writes, "The death penalty is not about whether people deserve to die for the crimes they commit. The real question of capital punishment in this country is, Do we deserve to kill?" Do you agree or disagree? Support your answer with evidence.

DIGGING DEEPER

1. Watch Bryan Stevenson's TED Talk, "We Need to Talk About Injustice." How has your perspective changed after immersing yourself in Stevenson's book and talk? What are you more curious about now and why?

2. Collect money from friends, family, or strangers (or work and save your own!) to donate to Stevenson's Equal Justice Initiative. Please research before asking for donations so you can speak passionately and with authority about the work and why it's essential.

3. Stevenson frequently references the parallels between Walter's case and the book *To Kill a Mockingbird* by Harper Lee. Take the time to read Lee's book critically as a historical artifact—not just a story—and draw conclusions about the similarities between the actual and fictional cases. Walter and Harper Lee were born in Monroe County, where Walter was tried. What do you make of that connection?

SECOND HELPINGS

» *The Sun Does Shine: An Innocent Man, a Wrongful Conviction, and the Long Path to Justice (Young Readers Edition)*
   Written by Anthony Ray Hinton with Lara Love Hardin and Olugbemisola Rhuday-Perkovich

» *Punching the Air*
   Written by Ibi Zoboi and Yusef Salaam
   Illustrated by Omar T. Pasha

RIOT

Written by Walter Dean Myers

*"I think that if we can't go back, then we
should try even harder to go forward."*

In July 1863, a terrible race riot broke out in New York City when an angry Irish mob looted, destroyed, and burned property in Lower Manhattan while attacking and murdering Black people. Fifteen-year-old Claire, who is biracial but can pass for white if she chooses, is caught in the middle as the life she's always known crumbles around her. Readers witness Claire's struggles with the war and the riot and their impact on her community as she examines her identity and finds a way to move forward. This book is creatively written in a screenplay format with character dialogue and script directions.

WHY I CHOSE THIS BOOK: Though the treatment is fictional, this story sheds light on a little-known historical tragedy, the Manhattan draft riots, which remain among the worst episodes of racial violence in United States history. That alone makes it valuable for young people to learn about. Still, the added perspective of a girl with an Irish mom and an African American dad brings complexity to the story that readers will appreciate and learn from.

THOUGHT STARTERS

1. How does Claire's biracial family background impact how she sees the riot? How do you think your family background influences how you view modern-day riots?
2. Which character in this book do you most identify with and why?
3. Did the screenplay format help you better visualize the scenes, or did you find it distracting? Why do you think the author presented the book in this format?

DIGGING DEEPER

1. The Colored Orphan Asylum, one of the first in the United States to take Black children, was burned down on the first day of the riots. The U.S. later exchanged orphanages for group homes and foster care families. Research our current child welfare system and discuss ideas for improvement with a peer.
2. Choose a historical event that interests you and create a document or video pitching your idea for a screenplay to an imaginary movie executive.

3. If you'd been in Manhattan during the riots, what do you think you would've done? Write a diary entry as if you were there.

SECOND HELPINGS

» *Monster*
Written by Walter Dean Myers
Illustrated by Christopher Myers
» *A Few Red Drops: The Chicago Race Riot of 1919*
Written by Claire Hartfield

COPPER SUN

Written by Sharon M. Draper

"Freedom is a delicate flower, like a pretty leaf in the air: It's hard to catch and may not be what you thought when you get it."

Fifteen-year-old Amari lives happily with her family in Ghana until the day their village is attacked; Amari is kidnapped and forced to endure the Middle Passage to the Carolinas. A white teen girl, Polly, is an indentured servant on the same plantation, and much to her disappointment, she's instructed to "civilize" Amari. After enduring and witnessing devastating abuse, the girls eventually form a friendship as they escape together before settling in at Fort Mose, the first legally sanctioned free Black settlement in the United States. Contains mild sexual content that highlights the rape and sexual violence of enslaved women.

WHY I CHOSE THIS BOOK: In terms of learning about enslavement in the United States, this historical fiction novel offers everything. Draper writes unflinchingly about Amari's grave losses throughout the story. Still, we see hope in her connection with her fictive kin or chosen family and in her determination to maintain her sense of self despite all odds. By including Fort Mose as the girls' final destination, readers are introduced to an essential historical Black history site in Florida while witnessing multiple characters' humanity (and inhumanity) throughout the journey. The fictional aspect of this story brings to light the pain and beauty in Amari's life with extraordinary clarity.

THOUGHT STARTERS

1. How does Amari survive the multiple horrors she encounters from Cape Coast Castle to Mr. Derby's plantation to the journey toward Fort Mose? While most of us will never have to endure an ordeal as harrowing as Amari's, we do all experience painful circumstances. What are some of your coping mechanisms? How can you weather the storms you've encountered in your life?

2. What are the similarities and differences between Amari and Polly? How are they seen differently by society and each other? In which ways do they need each other? How do the differences between you and your friends impact your interactions? How do your similarities or shared experiences draw you together?

3. What did you learn about Black American history through this book that you didn't already know? Were you surprised by anything?

DIGGING DEEPER

1. Watch the video *FORT MOSE—St. Augustine Florida* by the Fort Mose Historical Society. How does what you learn in the video help you picture Amari, Polly, and Tidbit's new life?

2. This book offers many opportunities for further research. Choose an intriguing topic from the story, and learn more about it through other books, articles, videos, and primary sources. Ideas include the role of South Carolina's rice crop, the art of weaving, or indentured servitude versus enslavement.

3. Afi shared what we sometimes call "mother wit" with Amari, which helped her survive a grueling ordeal, while Teenie offered many cultural sayings that Amari grew from. Research Southern sayings online and ask adults with ties to the South which expressions they recall from their upbringing. Which phrases grab your attention most? What role does the wisdom offered by Afi and Teenie play in Amari's life?

SECOND HELPINGS

» *African Town*
    Written by Irene Latham and Charles Waters
» *Incidents in the Life of a Slave Girl*
    Written by Harriet Jacobs
    Includes sexual abuse at the hands of enslavers.

ALL THE DAYS PAST, ALL THE DAYS TO COME

Written by Mildred D. Taylor

"A gentle wind stirred and the branches began to sway,
swaying like giant green fingers strumming at a guitar . . . nothing
ever again would be the same."

This story follows Cassie Logan after she moved from the Jim Crow South and headed north and west to pursue educational and career opportunities during World War II. The storyline carries her through the Civil Rights Movement. Readers witness heartbreak and hope while learning that grave injustice can't stop inevitable redemption. The culminating book in Taylor's unparalleled series on the lives of the Logan Family in Mississippi, this book can be enjoyed by readers who've never met the protagonist Cassie, but it's most satisfying to those who read *Roll of Thunder, Hear My Cry* first.

WHY I CHOSE THIS BOOK: Knowing the Logan family is a rite of passage for young people, and this was a satisfying end to their story. With historical facts woven throughout the fictional tale, teens will walk away more knowledgeable about the Black American experience while thoroughly enjoying the unpredictable plot and characters. Though both are searingly poignant works of historical fiction, this book serves an older audience than its predecessors, *Roll of Thunder, Hear My Cry* and *Let the Circle Be Unbroken*, due to the age of the characters and the more complex and mature circumstances in which they find themselves.

THOUGHT STARTERS

1. Many people have called Mildred D. Taylor's books "Black classics." What is a classic book, and do you think this book fits that description? Who decides which books are the best of the best? What's the difference between a classic and a Black classic, and are those the best labels for each?

2. How does Cassie change throughout the book? What are the most defining points of her journey? What have been your most defining moments up to this time?

3. If you entered the world of this book for a day, where would you want to be dropped in and why?

DIGGING DEEPER

1. Cassie's involvement in the voting rights movement is prominently featured in this book. Research the current debates around voter registration laws and redistricting. Pretend you're running for local office and make a campaign video explaining your stance on these issues.

2. Watch the 1996 film *Ghosts of Mississippi*. How does the film carry elements of the book forward?

3. If you could change one scene in the book, what would you change and why? Rewrite that scene in your own words while integrating your suggested revisions.

SECOND HELPINGS

» *The Davenports*
   Written by Krystal Marquis
» *Crossing Ebenezer Creek*
   Written by Tonya Bolden

THE BEAUTIFUL STRUGGLE:
A MEMOIR (ADAPTED FOR YOUNG ADULTS)

Written by Ta-Nehisi Coates

"But we died for sneakers stitched by serfs, coats that gave props to teams we didn't own, hats embroidered with the names of Confederate states. I could feel the falling, all around . . . But Dad pledged to sire us through."

The author Ta-Nehisi Coates's early life memoir details his experiences growing up in Maryland, focusing on his brother and father, an Afrocentric book publisher and former Black Panther, who is intimately profiled throughout the story. His father's tough love and determination to instill discipline and embrace Black culture in his children are echoed throughout the book. Some older teens may prefer the adult version: *The Beautiful Struggle: A Memoir*.

WHY I CHOSE THIS BOOK: This view of a Black American family, penned by one of our time's leading voices on culture and race, is really a look at many African American families in one way or another. The overt expressions of

Black life seen in Coates's story will be familiar to some. The subtle portrayals and experiences that appear to be sidenotes, or even go unnoticed by those unfamiliar with Black family life, speak quite loudly. This is a story of hardship and hope, and the storytelling is as authentic as it comes.

THOUGHT STARTERS

1. The author refers to Howard University, one of the historically Black colleges and universities (HBCUs), as "the Mecca." Why does he do this? What are the closest HBCUs to your home? Why were they started, and what role do you think they play in the lives of young Black Americans today?

2. Black culture is seen as a liberatory force throughout the book. From his dad's African books to the music and the Black Panthers, Coates is soaking in Black cultural influences. How do these inputs impact him and his future? How does your culture influence your choices and dreams for your life?

3. His family strongly influences Coates, and though he first resists the "Conscious Man" and "the Great Knowledge," he eventually embraces their strengths in his own way. How are your family relationships molding you today? What family traits or priorities do you resist, and which do you find most desirable or enlightening?

DIGGING DEEPER

1. Music, especially rap and the djembe ("jem-bay"), is prominently featured throughout Coates's coming-of-age experience. He even included song lyrics throughout. Create a soundtrack that best accompanies this book and explain why each piece was chosen.

2. Write a letter to someone who has profoundly influenced your life. This can be a family member, community leader, or maybe even someone you've never met. Be sure to express what you've learned from this person and how the knowledge or inspiration has fueled you.

3. How do you think the Coates family's love of literature molded their perceptions and impacted their actions? Choose one of the African American literary greats named in the book and read a piece of their writing. It could be a novel, memoir, short story, poem, or any other format you find appealing.

SECOND HELPINGS

» *Dreams of My Father: A Story of Race and Inheritance*

Written by Barack Obama

» *Becoming*
Written by Michelle Obama

VICTORY. STAND!: RAISING MY FIST FOR JUSTICE

Written by Tommie Smith and Derrick Barnes
Illustrated by Dawud Anyabwile

"If the rain poured down and the thunder rang out, echoing for miles across the valley and hills—Daddy would work. Our protector. Provider."

In the 1968 Mexico City Olympic Games, athlete and activist Tommie Smith took a stand against racism and injustice in the United States by raising his fist on the podium after receiving the gold medal for the 200-meter race. Bronze medal winner John Carlos joined him, and both men were forced to forfeit their awards and leave the Olympics. Following the expulsion, they received violent threats and were discriminated against throughout their remaining careers. This graphic novel memoir tells of Smith's childhood in rural Texas, record-shattering career, and his sacrifice for what he believed in.

WHY I CHOSE THIS BOOK: Through Tommie Smith's experience, the book explores the incredible influence and substantial cost of athletes using their platforms to stand against injustice. In the wake of Colin Kaepernick taking a knee during the national anthem and the resulting furor it caused, *Victory* is a timely examination of how Black athletes have always found opportunities to protest and how they and others resiliently confront the resulting ostracization.

THOUGHT STARTERS

1. Tommie Smith balanced his athletic giftedness and social activism, and though he was once shunned for his choice at the Olympics, he's since been applauded. What do you think about Smith's form of protest?

2. When considering the risks versus rewards of activism, is speaking out ever worth the price? What questions should a person ask themselves before making that decision?

3. Why do you think Smith and John Carlos used a glove versus their bare hands? What did the gloves represent?

DIGGING DEEPER

1. What topic or cause, if any, would be worth taking a risk for if you had a high-profile platform? Describe how you would use your public image to bring attention to the situation.

2. How would people in your family feel about Tommie Smith's protest if it happened today? Interview a few family members or other adults of different generations to learn more about how they've processed these protests. Try to understand better the arguments of the people whose opinions differ from yours.

3. Read another graphic novel memoir, *Colin Kaepernick: Change the Game* by Colin Kaepernick and Eve L. Ewing (illustrated by Orlando Caicedo). What parallels do you find between Tommie Smith raising a fist and Colin Kaepernick taking a knee during the anthem?

SECOND HELPINGS

» *Forty Million Dollar Slaves: The Rise, Fall, and Redemption of the Black Athlete*
   Written by William C. Rhoden
» *The Narrative of the Life of Frederick Douglass*
   Written by Frederick Douglass

YOU'RE BREAKING MY HEART

Written by Olugbemisola Rhuday-Perkovich

"The longest silence winds its way around the room, above and below and through me, closing in on every part of my body."

. . . .

Harriet Adu's life spins as she tries to find peace in the aftermath of her sixteen-year-old brother's death. The tragedy happened to occur the day they had a huge blowup that ended with her wishing he was dead. She certainly didn't mean it, and now she'll do anything to turn back the hands of time. When a new girl shows up at school, Harriet is drawn to her and finds immense comfort in their shared passions and quirks. The new friend offers Harriet a way around the pain in her heart, but it requires a leap of faith beyond anything Harriet thought possible.

WHY I CHOSE THIS BOOK: Teens haven't had enough options for speculative fiction centered on Black characters, so this delightfully strange story and its seamless bending and blending of reality are a welcomed addition. The pulsating storyline keeps readers engaged lest they miss a critical blip in the story. With multiple references to Nigeria (language, names, stories, instruments, food) and life in New York City—both head nods to the author's background—this book offers a strong sense of place and culture within Harriet's family and community. Various degrees of religious beliefs and adherence are shown across a range of characters; this impressive demonstration of diverse spiritual thinking within a primarily Black cast of characters is rare within young people's literature.

THOUGHT STARTERS

1. Harriet was riddled with guilt. In chapter 2 we learn, "Sometimes hope snuck up on her, and she forgot for a moment that it was her duty to bludgeon it back." Though no one else was blaming her, she was unable to forgive herself for wishing the worst for Tunde. We often talk about forgiving others who have harmed us, but what does it look like to forgive ourselves? Have you ever had to do that, and how were you able to move forward? If there's something that you haven't forgiven yourself for, what steps can you take in that direction?

2. What type of traits or vibe do you look for in a person when you're considering whether to invest in a friendship? At the end of chapter 8, Alisia suggests that she and Harriet hang out and get maduros (sweet ripe plantain), roast chicken, or bubble tea. What's your ideal destination or activity for meeting up with a new friend? What are some things you'd like to do or try if you had someone interesting to go with?

3. Nikka once told Harriet that her parents were "fakers" who constructed a story of their background that didn't really belong to them. Where do you see the line between someone faking a connection with their ancestral homeland and reclaiming a lost identity? What are the dangers of going too far or not going far enough?

DIGGING DEEPER

1. According to a USA Swimming Foundation study, there's only a thirteen percent chance that a child will learn how to swim if their parent doesn't know how to swim. Sixty-four percent of Black American children cannot swim, placing them at a higher risk for drowning. Research the cultural and historical factors behind this statistic, and create a public service campaign (video, poster, brochure, ad, program, etc.) to reduce drowning rates in your community.[1]

2. People grieve in phenomenally varied ways. Interview several people who have lost a loved one and ask them to describe their grieving process to you. What made or makes them feel better when they think of the loss? What did or could others do to best comfort them?

3. Read the poem "The Lady of Shalott" by Alfred, Lord Tennyson. Harriet tears up when Mrs. Barclay, the English teacher, recites this poem. Why do you think the author chose to include a reference to this particular poem, and why does it make Harriet emotional?

SECOND HELPINGS

» *Untwine*
   Written by Edwidge Danticat
» *The Voice in My Head*
   Written by Dana L. Davis

ANGEL OF GREENWOOD
Written by Randi Pink

"While kissing him, there was only the two of them. Standing in the middle of idyllic Greenwood, surrounded by beauty and Blackness and excellence and kindness and gossip and loved ones and loss and hope for the future."

....

Seventeen-year-old Isaiah and sixteen-year-old Angel have always known each other, but sparks fly for the first time in the twelve days leading up to the 1921 Greenwood Massacre in an area of Tulsa, Oklahoma, known as the "Black Wall Street." When their favorite teacher hires them to run a mobile library together, they find out how much they have in common despite their differences: She favors Booker T. Washington's ideas, while he greatly admires W.E.B. Du Bois. The violence disrupts their sweet romance, but even then, their shared ideals and priorities bring them together while facing the unimaginable.

WHY I CHOSE THIS BOOK: I greatly appreciate the innocence of the romance between Isaiah and Angel, and I think it sets a standard for age-appropriate relationships explored in young adult fiction. The characters' shared love of foundational Black literature and traditional classics is an inspiring path for young people to enthusiastically pursue. The countdown to the massacre is an artful approach to storytelling as each chapter brings readers closer to a heartbreaking historical event that many have never heard of.

THOUGHT STARTERS

1. Isaiah asks Dorothy Mae, "What do you dream of becoming?" and he's genuinely interested in her response. What do YOU dream of becoming?

2. When Muggy teases him about distributing books on Blue, Miss Ferris's mobile library bike, Isaiah thinks about how wrong Muggy is because "books changed lives." Do you agree with that statement? What is a book that has impacted you and how?

3. Despite being one of the most horrific instances of racial violence in our country's history, nearly all textbooks leave the Tulsa Race Massacre out. Why do you think students aren't generally taught about this history? Who benefits from that history being forgotten, and why is it important to remember?

DIGGING DEEPER

1. There are multiple documentaries about the Tulsa Race Massacre, including *Tulsa Burning: The 1921 Race Massacre, Dreamland: The Burning of Black Wall Street*, and *Tulsa: The Fire and the Forgotten*. Watch one or more of them and compare what happened in real life to what occurred in the book.

2. Isaiah has the realization that he's beginning to forget things about his dad that he wants to remember—his voice, eyes, laugh, and most of all, his aphorisms: When cobwebs are plenty, kisses are scarce; gluttony kills more than the sword; and a friend to all is a friend to none. Write an original poem like Isaiah using one of these sayings as inspiration and the first line of verse.

3. Isaiah's mom makes morning glory muffins for breakfast, and Miss Ferris makes

red soup and cornbread for Isaiah and Angel. Research these recipes and choose one to prepare and share with family or friends.

SECOND HELPINGS

» *The Souls of Black Folk*
   Written by W.E.B. Du Bois
» *Up from Slavery*
   Written by Booker T. Washington

LOVE IS A REVOLUTION

Written by Renée Watson

"I don't know why people try not to cry, why we hold it in.
I have decided to cry as much and as hard as I need to."

. . . .

This sweet love story tells of a budding romance between seventeen-year-old Nala and Tye, a community activist she meets at an open mic event. While Nala falls for him, she navigates a journey of self-discovery that culminates positively despite her initially misleading Tye to get his attention. It's not your stereotypical teen story; in this book, a beautiful, dark-skinned, plus-size girl gets the hot guy, and the "in" crowd isn't superficial but has solid beliefs and integrity, even to the point of being self-righteous at times.

WHY I CHOSE THIS BOOK: Many teens appreciate a good novel where likable people fall in love, and this one is well written, fun, and age-appropriate. It highlights numerous healthy relationships, including Black girl friendships alongside Nala and Tye's innocent romance. But ultimately, the book's message is one of acceptance and confidence rather than purely romance.

THOUGHT STARTERS

1. How does Nala's summer end up differently than she expected? Describe an experience when the outcome varied from your initial expectations.
2. Nala misrepresents herself to get closer to Tye but ultimately finds that authenticity is the best path. Have you ever felt that you needed to change your image

to fit in or be liked? How were you able to move beyond that place or what can you do now to move forward?

3. Nala cares about her community but doesn't show it in the same way as some of the other characters. Is there any value in Nala's approach? What are the ways that you're most suited to help others? Which forms of helping come naturally to you?

DIGGING DEEPER

1. The cute guy's love interest in this book looks different than in most teen romance novels. Research colorism and body shaming to learn more about why this is such a big deal.

2. Nala learned lessons in kindness, forgiveness, and patience toward herself and others. Choose one of these lessons and write down realistic ways to practice it.

3. How are the women at the senior residence important in Nala's life? Reach out to a local senior center or home in your area to volunteer. Journal about your experiences afterward. Who did you meet? What did you talk about? How did you feel in that environment? What do you wish you'd done differently? Would you volunteer there again? Why or why not?

SECOND HELPINGS

» *All the Things We Never Knew*
    Written by Liara Tamani
    Contains profanity and a make-out scene with descriptive heavy petting. The couple stops short of having sex because they don't have a condom.

» *Love Radio*
    Written by Ebony LaDelle
    Contains profanity, a descriptive make-out session, and a recollection of an assault.

CHILDREN OF BLOOD AND BONE
Written by Tomi Adeyemi
"As it fades, I see the truth—in plain sight, yet hidden all along. We are all children of blood and bone. All instruments of vengeance and virtue."

Seventeen-year-old Zélie, her elder brother, Tzain, and rebel princess Amari work to bring magic back to their kingdom while inspiring a new generation of magi a decade after the king ordered all divîners over the age of thirteen to death. The trio sets out on a perilous mission to gather specific artifacts, participate in a ceremony, and restore magic. However, the crown prince mercilessly pursues them because he thinks divîners will threaten the monarchy if they can harness their magical powers.

WHY I CHOSE THIS BOOK: This is a Black fantasy book. That alone puts it in a lonely (but rapidly growing) class of books in which Black characters are seen having magical powers in imaginary worlds. Intriguing elements like mystical flying creatures, powerful magi, and the fictional West African kingdom of Orïsha bring an incredible thrill to this captivating story that examines race, colorism, power, and injustice amid a stellar storyline.

THOUGHT STARTERS

1. Zélie, the other divîners, and even those who associate with them are subject to discrimination and prejudice at every turn. What impact does this treatment have on their lives?

2. If you were a magi character in this book, which unique power would you want to possess and why? Examples: grounder, burner, reaper, connector, healer, seer, etc.

3. Though this book is set in a fantasy world of magic and intrigue, there are parallels between this story and the real world. What similarities do you see, and what are some of the ideas you think the author intended to convey?

DIGGING DEEPER

1. Orïsha is a fictional kingdom influenced by West African culture. The book also mentions places like Lagos, Ibadan, and Ilorin. Pretend you're being interviewed by someone interested in visiting the area and describe what they should expect to see and experience there, including clothing, food, and language.

2. Sweet Binta's death was a catalyst for the divîners' revolution, but we don't know much of her back story. Write a prequel chapter to this book written in Binta's voice that tells her history and perspective.

3. Students are often expected to learn about Greek, Roman, and sometimes Norse mythology, but African mythology is rarely studied. Research Yoruba

mythology and list similarities and differences from well-known myths you've learned or heard about previously.

SECOND HELPINGS

» *Akata Witch*
Written by Nnedi Okorafor
» *Beasts of Prey*
Written by Ayana Gray

RHYTHM RIDE: A ROAD TRIP THROUGH THE MOTOWN SOUND

Written by Andrea Davis Pinkney

"This music's urban doo-wop spread its harmonies into the city streets, inviting neighbors to throw open their windows to let the doo-wops and croons fly into their living rooms."

Narrated by an informed voice that the author calls "the Groove," this book is a fantastic history of the influential Black music that captured the hearts (and radios) of Americans and the story of Berry Gordy, the visionary behind the Motown sounds and the meteoric rise of its artists. The author paints a strong picture of the times by weaving details on the Civil Rights Movement and more into the music story.

WHY I CHOSE THIS BOOK: This is the story of some of the most popular Black American music ever. Black parents and grandparents grew up singing these songs. Today's young people can sometimes hum along, but they rarely realize Motown's impact on American music. This introduction to the people who created a unique sound and packaged it for world consumption is essential, even as we grapple with what we gain and lose when our art is curated for and sometimes appropriated by the mass market.

THOUGHT STARTERS

1. What were some of Berry Gordy's big decisions that helped catapult his company to such success? Are there decisions you've made or will need to make soon that will heavily influence your future?

2. How did Berry Gordy's work at Ford Motor Company inspire what he did with Motown? Have you ever gotten a great idea from seeing how someone else gets a job done or approaches a situation? Explain how the concept inspired you.

3. What impresses you most about the story of Motown? What do you find most surprising?

DIGGING DEEPER

1. Select some artists mentioned in the book (the Supremes, Smokey Robinson, the Four Tops, the Temptations, Marvin Gaye, Martha Reeves and the Vandellas, the Jackson Five, etc.) and watch videos of their performances online. What do they do differently than today's top music acts? What do you recognize as aspects of their performance or sound that may have influenced current music chart toppers?

2. The eight-hundred-dollars loan Gordy received from his family would be valued at about nine thousand dollars today. Write a business plan for a product or service company you would launch and manage if someone gave you a similar loan.

3. Intense "finishing school" work and choreography influenced the Motown groups' signature performance styles. Give Cholly Atkins's singing pantomime moves a try by following the instructions on pages 57–58. Be sure to record yourself to check out your smooth moves when you're done.

SECOND HELPINGS

» *Notes from a Young Black Chef (Adapted for Young Adults)*
    Written by Kwame Onwuachi with Joshua David Stein
» *Spoken Word: A Cultural History*
    Written by Joshua Bennett

CASTE: THE ORIGINS OF OUR DISCONTENTS (ADAPTED FOR YOUNG ADULTS)

Written by Isabel Wilkerson

"And only recently have circumstances forced us, in this current era of human rupture, to search for the unseen stirrings of the human heart, to discover the origins of our discontents."

Isabel Wilkerson deftly traces the history of caste systems globally while highlighting the invisible hierarchy and infrastructure governing American racial and ethnic relationships. By drawing comparisons to the ancient Hindu caste system in India and that of the Nazi party during the Third Reich, she calls out parallels between caste systems across time and place. Though different, they all dehumanize people deemed inferior. Wilkerson argues that it will take collective societal effort to overcome the caste problem and offers hope in that direction. Older teens may be interested in the adult version of this book (same title) and the movie *Origin* directed by Ava DuVernay.

WHY I CHOSE THIS BOOK: Looking at the history of Black people in America through the lens of global caste systems is jarring, eye-opening, and validating. Wilkerson shows teens how to use research, draw conclusions, and think critically while examining a familiar concept in new ways and telling an extraordinarily compelling story. Teens will learn much about hierarchical societies and how they're developed and maintained. They'll be well prepared for entering civil discourse on the topic after wrestling with Wilkerson's work.

THOUGHT STARTERS

1. Throughout the book, Isabel Wilkerson weaves personal anecdotes about her experiences as a Black woman into the historical context of how the caste system began and how it shapes American society. Which one of her personal stories stood out to you most and why?

2. What did you learn about caste systems that you didn't know previously? Are there any parts of her research that did *not* surprise you? If so, what was it and why were you not surprised?

3. Wilkerson compares the American caste system to that of Nazi Germany. How are they similar and different? Do you think it's a fair comparison? Why or why not?

DIGGING DEEPER

1. This book is subtitled "The Origins of Our Discontents." Listen to Dr. Martin Luther King's famous "I Have a Dream" speech to hear his reference to the "Negro's legitimate discontent." Also, check out the opening lines of Shakespeare's *Richard III* for another connection. Why did MLK refer to that part of Shakespeare, and why did Wilkerson pull from those concepts in her book? What is the relationship?

2. Create an infographic explaining caste systems in easy-to-understand terms based on what you learned in the book and reputable outside sources.
3. What would you do first if you had the opportunity to initiate changes that would eliminate caste systems? Make a presentation outlining your key points and prepare for anticipated counterarguments.

SECOND HELPINGS

» *Black Birds in the Sky: The Story and Legacy of the 1921 Tulsa Race Massacre*
Written by Brandy Colbert
» *Revolution in Our Time: The Black Panther Party's Promise to the People*
Written by Kekla Magoon

THINGS FALL APART
Written by Chinua Achebe
*"Among the Ibo the art of conversation is regarded very highly,
and proverbs are the palm-oil with which words are eaten."*

Published in 1958, this was one of the first African books to be read globally and is considered an essential contribution to world literature. It depicts pre-colonial life and the influences of European colonialism in a fictional clan in Igboland, as seen through the story of Okonkwo, a clan leader. The book takes place in the late nineteenth century, beginning with a deep exploration of Okonkwo's life and the customs of his people before delving into how colonialism and the involvement of Christian missionaries impacted his family and forever changed the culture and dynamics of Igbo society.

WHY I CHOSE THIS BOOK: While visiting West Africa with my family, I was stunned by the European influences visible in nearly every area of society, from the books in the library and the history taught in schools to the political environment and altered customs. Though I knew the history of colonialism, the far-reaching and insidious nature of its devastating impacts had been lost on me and, therefore, my children. This book provides the African perspective of European invasion, a rare but essential view for young people.

THOUGHT STARTERS

1. Much of this book focuses on Okonkwo's inability or unwillingness to adapt to the changes happening to his clan due to European colonialism. Do you think he was right to resist the changes? Should he have worked harder to conform? Why or why not?
2. How does the role of family and community change in the story after the arrival of the missionaries?
3. Were you surprised by the ending? Why or why not? What message do you think the author tried to share with the novel's conclusion?

DIGGING DEEPER

1. The title of this book comes from "The Second Coming," a poem by Irish poet William Butler Yeats. Take a moment to read the poem. Why do you think Achebe chose this as the title for his book?
2. Igbo proverbs feature prominently throughout this book. The characters use them when speaking to one another, and the narrator relies on them to describe aspects of the clan's culture. Look up a list of Igbo proverbs and select a few to write about. Do you see the wisdom in them? How could they be applied to your life circumstances?
3. Achebe was criticized for writing the novel in English instead of his native language, and some schools have censored or banned the book because of its negative portrayal of colonialism. Research these debates and write a paragraph or make a video explaining your opinions on each.

SECOND HELPINGS

» *They Poured Fire on Us from the Sky: The True Story of Three Lost Boys from Sudan*
   Written by Alephonsion Deng, Benson Deng, and Benjamin Ajak, with Judy A. Bernstein
» *Kaffir Boy: An Autobiography—The True Story of a Black Youth's Coming of Age in Apartheid South Africa*
   Written by Mark Mathabane
   Includes a disturbing scene depicting the prostitution of young boys under the direst of circumstances.

THE GIRL WITH THE LOUDING VOICE

Written by Abi Daré

"Then I swim deep inside the river of my soul, find the key from where it is sitting, full of rust, at the bottom of the river, and open the lock. I kneel down beside my bed, close my eyes, turn myself into a cup, and pour the memory out of me."

• •

Adunni, a fourteen-year-old girl living in rural Nigeria, wants to attend school and become a teacher, but the customs of her village dictate her future. She's forced to marry an older man with multiple wives before being indentured to an abusive home, making her dreams feel farther away than ever. In Big Madam's household, she's mistreated at every turn but finds friends in Kofi, the cook, and Tia, a neighbor who helps Adunni gain independence. Contains profanity, nonexplicit sexual and domestic violence, and child marriage.

WHY I CHOSE THIS BOOK: All the tragedy and abuse in Adunni's life make this unforgettable story challenging to read and process at times, but the way the teenager persistently clings to hope regardless of her circumstances offers a strong message of resiliency and perseverance. Adunni's ability to envision a different future prevents resentment from festering, ultimately giving her the motivation and determination to break free.

THOUGHT STARTERS

1. Why was education so important to Adunni, and what did she mean when she said she wanted to have a "louding voice"?
2. What are the gender dynamics in rural Nigeria? Think of the differences between what's expected of Adunni versus her brothers. How do those dynamics compare to what Adunni encounters in Lagos?
3. Learning about the history of European colonialism in *The Book of Nigerian Facts* teaches Adunni what it means to be free. Which book has been most impactful in your life and why?

DIGGING DEEPER

1. Visit a Nigerian restaurant or find a recipe to prepare a traditional Nigerian meal to share with others.
2. Besides Adunni, who would you most want to meet from this story? Write that person a letter telling them about yourself and asking questions to help you get to know or understand them better.
3. Search for this article online: "Trafficked, beaten and abused: The life of a Nigerian house girl." Some critics have said that *The Girl with a Louding Voice* exaggerates the experiences of house help in Nigeria. Based on the article, do you think Adunni's fictional story is a realistic depiction of how some girls live?

SECOND HELPINGS

» *Buried Beneath the Baobab Tree*
    Written by Adaobi Tricia Nwaubani
» *The Girl Who Smiled Beads: A Story of War and What Comes After*
    Written by Clementine Wamariya and Elizabeth Weil

MARCH

Written by John Lewis and Andrew Aydin
Illustrated by Nate Powell

"But sometimes going to school was a luxury my family couldn't afford. When planting and harvesting seasons arrived, the reality of those fields displaced any dreams about the future."

· ·

Congressman John Lewis's personal life story is used as a springboard to tell of the Civil Rights Movement across a trilogy of graphic novels. Starting with his childhood on a sharecropping farm in Alabama and traveling through to his election as a congressman in Georgia District 5, the story includes many intervening experiences that inspired his work and furthered the mission to which he and many others committed their lives.

WHY I CHOSE THIS BOOK: This series gives readers a solid introduction to a man who knew from an early age that he wanted to make a difference and moved forward with indomitable determination. And by examining his life, teens will get a front-row seat to his civil rights journey. One that led to Lewis receiving the Presidential Medal of Freedom in 2010 and becoming the first Black American lawmaker to lie in state in the U.S. Capitol's rotunda, reminding us of the power held in his commitment to justice.

THOUGHT STARTERS

1. Why do you think John Lewis chose the graphic novel format to tell his story, and do you think he made the right choice?
2. John Lewis follows the philosophy of nonviolent direct action. Describe this concept and give examples of where this philosophy has been applied in recent times. Do you think it's an effective approach? Why or why not?
3. How would you describe the relationship between civil rights activists and the media during the time in which *March* takes place? What about today?

DIGGING DEEPER

1. Research civil rights movements occurring today in other parts of the world. How do they compare to what Lewis experienced?
2. What role did education play in Lewis's journey? Find a relative or another adult who attended segregated schools and interview them about their experiences. Be sure to ask them how the reality of desegregation compared to their initial expectations.
3. In 2018, John Lewis posted this message on social media: "Never, ever be afraid to make some noise and get in good trouble, necessary trouble."[2] Knowing his philosophy of nonviolence, what do you think he meant? What are some ways that people can get in *good* trouble?

SECOND HELPINGS

» *Wake: The Hidden History of Women-Led Slave Revolts*
   Written by Rebecca Hall
   Illustrated by Hugo Martínez
   Contains mature content. Best for older teens.
» *The Black Panther Party: A Graphic Novel History*
   Written by David F. Walker
   Illustrated by Marcus Kwame Anderson

DEAR MARTIN

Written by Nic Stone

"When it comes down to it, the only question that matters is this: If nothing in the world ever changes, what type of man are you gonna be?"

Seventeen-year-old Justyce McAllister turns to the teachings of Dr. Martin Luther King, Jr., to process the incongruencies between who he is and how others perceive him. He increasingly faces physical and emotional threats and violence despite his efforts to keep his head down and do the right thing. One night, while riding around with his best friend, an off-duty police officer shoots and kills his friend and injures Justyce because they wouldn't turn down their music. Both boys were innocent, and the officer was put on trial. The book analyzes what led to what they call "The Incident" and its aftermath with heart-wrenching honesty. Contains some profanity.

WHY I CHOSE THIS BOOK: This is a timely look at multiple tensions that many of today's teens have to grapple with: lack of understanding in interracial friendships, racially charged police profiling, finding belonging in non-diverse environments, resisting peer pressure, microaggressions, pervasive racism, injustice, forgiveness, and redemption. The main character's letters written to MLK, Jr., add another layer of intricacy to this story, as does the troubling fact that others recognize Justyce as not being one of "those" Black people: He's a prep school kid at the top of his class, headed to Yale in the fall. Yet he still faced challenges and racism as a young Black man. The book does a stellar job of including the role of the media and public discourse, a topic young people need to explore critically.

THOUGHT STARTERS

1. Dr. Dray ("Doc") is Justyce's debate team coach and a positive role model in Justyce's life. What do you think about the way he runs his class? What would you change if you were him? What would you keep the same?
2. After The Incident, Justyce thinks his bruises may never fade. What does the author mean by that? If you knew Justyce, what would you say or do to help him heal emotionally?

3. If you wrote a series of letters to someone you think could offer wisdom related to problems in your life or community, who would you write and why?

DIGGING DEEPER

1. Stone was inspired to write this book as a response to the numerous cases of police brutality, including the shooting of Michael Brown, Jr., in 2014. Research Brown's story and write a letter to Dr. Martin Luther King, Jr., sharing your thoughts about what happened and asking any questions you wish he could answer.

2. Read Stone's follow-up book, *Dear Justyce*, which follows Manny's cousin Quan Banks. Write a review of both books online and make a book trailer video to encourage other teens to read the book you enjoyed most.

3. At Blake's party, Justyce notices racist paraphernalia and minstrel décor reflecting ugly stereotypes about Black people in the home. Take the time to watch a few videos or read articles about the way mammy jars, lawn jockeys, and Jim Crow propaganda exploit Black suffering. Visit the Jim Crow Museum of Racist Imagery online (www.jimcrowmuseum.ferris.edu) and take the virtual self-tour. How would you feel, and what would you do if you saw these things in a friend's home?

SECOND HELPINGS

» *The Hate U Give*
   Written by Angie Thomas
   Contains profanity and a descriptive make-out session.

» *Long Way Down*
   Written by Jason Reynolds
   Contains some profanity.

THE BOY IN THE BLACK SUIT
Written by Jason Reynolds

"And sometimes . . . I can lose and lose and lose and I don't know why. But there's nothing I can do but just keep flipping the cards. Eventually, I'll win again. As long as you got cards to keep turning, you're fine."

Matt Miller is having a rough senior year: He desperately misses his mom, who passed away from breast cancer, and his dad has been admitted for a lengthy hospital stay after drinking too much and getting into a car accident. This upheaval leaves Matt to cope with his overwhelming loss alone until he meets a girl named Lovey while working at a local funeral home. She's lost her grandmother, who was raising her, and they quickly form a bond rooted in their shared grief.

WHY I CHOSE THIS BOOK: While working at the funeral home, Matt finds comfort in being around others who have suffered similar losses, even strangers, and in many ways, this mirrors the connection many Black Americans have due to unspoken shared experiences. The book offers a unique treatment of that cultural connection, and despite the tragedy in their circumstances, both characters find joy together.

THOUGHT STARTERS

1. After his mother's death, Matt feels like he's too mature to be in high school. Why does he say that? Are there times that you feel out of place at school or somewhere else? When or where do you experience your most substantial feelings of belonging?
2. Lovey helps Matt embrace the reality that life can be beautiful despite the pain of losing loved ones. Have you ever lost someone you love? What thoughts, items, or activities bring peace when you think of that person?
3. What is the meaning behind the book's title? What would you call it if you were asked to rename the book? Why did you choose that title?

DIGGING DEEPER

1. Jason Reynolds does a terrific job bringing the Bedford-Stuyvesant neighborhood of Brooklyn to life. Take a moment to write a descriptive paragraph or two about your community. Who lives there, what type of housing exists, what are some of the businesses or nonresidential buildings in the area, who works at them, what are the rhythms and vibe of your neighborhood, etc.?
2. Photographs play a recurring role throughout the book. Matt, Lovey, and Mr. Ray all have photos they treasure, and Matt and Lovey take pictures of each other and the Sempervivum plant. Scroll through your device and select three of your most meaningful images. Why are they special to you?

3. Lovey took Matt on a date to the botanical gardens, where her grandmother always took her to see beauty after her mom passed away. If you have a botanical garden in your area, take a visit and soak in the beauty.

SECOND HELPINGS

» *Slay*
  Written by Brittney Morris
  Contains profanity, and Keira mentions having previous sexual experiences with her boyfriend, though there are no scenes depicted within the book.
» *Saving Savannah*
  Written by Tonya Bolden

HOME IS NOT A COUNTRY
Written by Safia Elhillo
*"so busy looking / at my one empty hand
I almost missed everything / filling the other"*

Nima is a fourteen-year-old Muslim girl contextually indicated to be a Sudanese American who lives in suburban America with her single mom and near her best friend, Haitham, who is terribly injured in a hate crime. Nima wishes she had been named Yasmeen, and she takes on the persona as an escape in a turn of magical realism.

WHY I CHOSE THIS BOOK: Looking at America through the eyes of a Black immigrant is a rare turn in young people's literature. The language and structure of novel-in-verse expose teens to a unique form of storytelling, and the exploration of home and what it means to people who feel displaced or unwelcomed is compelling.

THOUGHT STARTERS

1. What does Nima learn about home? When do you feel your greatest sense of home and belonging?
2. What is the significance of the names Nima and Yasmeen in the book? What does your name mean? Do you know why it was chosen?

3. What does it take to help someone feel welcomed in an environment you already find comfortable? Do you think people should go out of their way to pull others in? Why or why not?

DIGGING DEEPER

1. In "A Life" (page 169), Yasmeen lists what she wants in her life. Make a list of what would make you feel more "fluent in your body."
2. Select a poem from the book and create a new version on the same topic using your own life experiences and thoughts.
3. Haitham calls Nima a "nostalgia monster." What does he mean, and what are you most nostalgic about? Create a mood or vision board that represents nostalgia in your life.

SECOND HELPINGS

» *How You Grow Wings*
   Written by Rimma Onoseta
» *Purple Hibiscus*
   Written by Chimamanda Ngozi Adichie

BLACK WAS THE INK
Written by Michelle Coles
*"Black like the ink used to write the laws intended to protect his people,
but also like the ink used to strip their rights away."*

....

Sixteen-year-old Malcolm is more than annoyed that he must spend the summer on a farm with his extended family. Little does he know that his life is about to turn inside out when he travels back in time as his ghostly ancestor Cedric during 1870s Reconstruction. There, he meets real-life Black statesmen who fought for change during Reconstruction while trying to save his family's land in present-day Mississippi.

WHY I CHOSE THIS BOOK: This time-travel story bridges the modern struggles faced by some of today's Black teens with the brief period of promise for Black citizens during Reconstruction, a fascinating time in American history. The novel's structure provides a clear view of how the past informs the future, making the historical part of the story even more relevant. Contains profanity.

THOUGHT STARTERS

1. What parts of Malcolm can you relate to most? Do certain thoughts, feelings, or actions remind you of yourself?
2. If you could go back in time as an ancestor, which year would you pick to visit and why?
3. What do you think the newly freed enslaved people should have received at the close of the Civil War? Do you think their descendants should receive reparations today? Why or why not?

DIGGING DEEPER

1. Describe what happened during Reconstruction. What do you find most surprising about that period? Write a poem or draw a picture about how you imagine American life today if the progress Black people made during that time had been allowed to flourish and the Jim Crow era had never taken place.
2. Watch the video titled *Black Was the Ink: Using Fiction to Investigate Reconstruction and Its Legacies* on the NMAAHC YouTube channel (Smithsonian National Museum of African American History and Culture). What new insight did you gain from the author that you didn't get from the book?
3. Read the "Meet the Statesmen" section in the back of the book. If you could meet one of the profiled men in person, which one would you select, and what three questions would you ask him?

SECOND HELPINGS

» *Fly Girl*
Written by Sherri L. Smith
» *The Overground Railroad: The Green Book and the Roots of Black Travel in America*
Written by Candacy Taylor

CONCLUSION

Black children deserve to be imagination-busting heroes, beautiful and daring princesses, fantastical magic-wielding warriors, and techy sci-fi explorers. We owe them the chance to star in coming-of-age stories filled with complex relationships, transformative journeys, and everyday happenings. To experience the joie de vivre of ordinary life. To see children and teens like them being tenderly loved by family, friends, and communities.

Our kids enjoy fishing, getting lost in museums, building forts, taking road trips with grandparents, and traversing magical worlds as much as the next kid, and they relish stories that they recognize as their own. They need to hear the voices of their ancestors in the tales of our nation and the world. To know that their people have always existed, that their lives are contributing to today's stories, and that the most exciting, mundane, and tender parts of their adventures and disappointments will be marked for the ages.

Soul School offers children a phenomenal chance to experience the emotional tension and overwhelming joys of Black American culture while directly witnessing the often-imitated-never-duplicated creativity bursting from every seam of our literature.

But miraculously, these books offer so much more.

Our collective children belong together, and we owe them every opportunity to intimately sense each other's humanity. These Black stories are indeed human stories, and every child who touches them will be changed, regardless of color or culture. Books themselves are not magic; they won't fix everything, but the priceless power they hold to delight hearts, heal hurts, and bond lives is piercingly magical.

Right down to the very soul.

ACKNOWLEDGMENTS

To my husband, Scott, and our four beautifully soulful children, Nina, Sasha, Beckett, and Brooks, thank you for your patience and enthusiasm for the things that make my heart sing. The hours we've spent reading together are among my most coveted moments and precious memories, and I hope you will always feel the same.

To Anna Knutson Geller, thank you for helping me organize my thoughts and dream big with this book. You're more than I ever imagined an agent could be, and I love having you in my corner.

To Joanna Ng, even though we didn't ultimately get to work on this project together, your belief in my idea gave me courage and made it possible.

To my new secret weapon and editor, Nina Shields, your insights and recommendations catapulted this book to new heights. Thank you!

To Olugbemisola Rhuday-Perkovich, your eager willingness to contribute the foreword to this labor of love is something I'll cherish forever. Your work has profoundly impacted my children, evidenced by your many books that I regularly see scattered around my home. Thank you for the beautiful words you are putting into the world.

To Raygen Samone (aka Libby), you endured endless hours of painstakingly detailed discussions on books (and oh so much reading) as you came alongside me during the hardest part of this journey. You are a fantastic encourager and lover of people.

To the Black authors and illustrators highlighted in this book, your work is lifegiving and absolutely stunning. You are brave and beautiful, and I'll never stop singing your praises to everyone who will listen (and especially those who will not). You deserve more respect and recognition than you've received, but please don't stop. We are here, reading and appreciating every word, line, and stroke.

To the many Black creators who are producing incredible books that haven't been included here, please know that I'm still mourning the books that I missed or had to cut, even though it felt impossible to do so. You're absolutely deserving of honor. In some cases, your books were out of print while I was writing or came out after my manuscript was submitted. Incredible new books were launching while I was in the trenches, and there was simply no way to enjoy them all. I'm woefully finite and may not have encountered your work (yet), no matter how spectacular or powerful it may be. I've agonized over missing your contributions and will continue to do so until I find ways to recognize your talent and contributions to our grand story.

To the parents of non-Black children: Reading this book and using it to share fun and inspiring stories about Black people with your kids is a revolutionary act. You're getting it right; I sense your commitment and salute you. Thank you for diving in and honoring the wonder and spirit of Black American culture.

To the parents of Black children, this is my most precious gift to your family. It's for your extraordinary and often overlooked babies (even the ones who have grown taller than you!) who need to know that they are our everything and that there's nothing we won't do to show it. There are so many things that were left unsaid on these pages, but I know that you know. May these books plant seeds of confidence, hope, and pure, unadulterated joy in the hearts of your children, one page at a time.

NOTES

INTRODUCTION

1. **I PLUCKED MY SOUL**: McKay, Claude. "I Know My Soul," Poets.org. Accessed December 21, 2023. https://poets.org/poem/i-know-my-soul.
2. **REALLY GOOD BOOKS FOR CHILDREN**: Rollins, Charlemae Hill. *We Build Together: A Reader's Guide to Negro Life and Literature for Elementary and High School Use* (Champaign, IL: National Council of Teachers of English, 1967), ix.
3. **WITH THE IDEAS AND THE PROVOCATIVE THOUGHTS**: Jackson, Miles M., Jr. *A Bibliography of Negro History & Culture for Young Readers* (Atlanta: Atlanta University, 1968), xx.
4. **IF THERE'S A BOOK**: Morrison, Toni. Speech at the annual meeting of the Ohio Arts Council (United States, Ohio, 1981).

CHAPTER 1: BLACK IS BEAUTIFUL

1. **A CIRCUMSCRIBED COMMUNITY**: Jones, Arthur C. *Sweet Chariot: The Story of the Spirituals*, 2004. https://web.archive.org/web/20150725040520/http://www.spiritualsproject.org/sweetchariot/History.
2. **SOULFULLY COOKED FOOD**: Ferguson, Sheila. *Soul Food: Classic Cuisine from the Deep South* (New York: Grove Press, 1993), 8.
3. **FRIED CHICKEN, FRIED CATFISH, OR CHITLINS**: Miller, Adrian. *Soul Food: The Surprising Story of an American Cuisine One Plate at a Time* (Chapel Hill: University of North Carolina Press, 2013). https://www.google.com/books/edition/Soul_Food/Od8VAAAAQBAJ?hl=en&gbpv=0.
4. **WE YOUNGER NEGRO ARTISTS**: Hughes, Langston. "The Negro Artist and the Racial Mountain." Essay. In *The Collected Works of Langston Hughes*. Columbia: University of Missouri Press, 2002. Accessed October 12, 2023. https://www.poetryfoundation.org/articles/69395/the-negro-artist-and-the-racial-mountain.
5. ***THE DIRTY SOUTH***: "The Dirty South: Contemporary Art, Material Culture, and the Sonic Impulse." MCA Denver. Accessed December 9, 2023. https://mcadenver.org/exhibitions/dirty-south.
6. **ART DOES NOT NECESSARILY**: Jonnalagadda, Akhil. "In Dialogue: What Is Misunderstood About Blackness?" Princeton University, February 27, 2023. https://press.princeton.edu/ideas/in-dialogue-what-is-misunderstood-about-blackness.
7. **BLACK ENGLISH SPEECH**: Luu, Chi. "Black English Matters." JSTOR Daily, February 12, 2020. https://daily.jstor.org/black-english-matters.
8. **THE BLACK CHURCH**: Gates, Henry Louis, Jr. "How the Black Church Saved Black America," *Harvard Gazette*, March 9, 2021. https://news.harvard.edu/gazette/story/2021/03/the-history-and-importance-of-the-black-church.

9. **THE QUALITY OR AGGREGATE**: "Beauty Definition & Meaning." *Merriam-Webster*. Accessed December 9, 2023. https://www.merriam-webster.com/dictionary/beauty.

10. **A FEVER OF AFFIRMATION**: "Black Is Beautiful: The Emergence of Black Culture and Identity in the 60s and 70s." National Museum of African American History and Culture, April 24, 2020. https://nmaahc.si.edu/explore/stories/black-beautiful-emergence-black-culture-and-identity-60s-and-70s.

11. **CULTURE OF ANY KIND**: Simien, Justin. "5 Things to Know About Black Culture Now." CNN, February 25, 2014. https://www.cnn.com/2014/02/25/living/justin-simien-black-culture-now/index.html.

CHAPTER 2: INTANGIBLE ASSETS

1. **NOBODY CAN DO FOR LITTLE CHILDREN**: Zuckerman, Marilyn R., and Lewis J. Hatala. *Incredibly American: Releasing the Heart of Quality* (Milwaukee, WI: Asq Pr, 1992), 13.

2. **MOTHER WIT**: Angelou, Maya. *I Know Why the Caged Bird Sings* (New York: Random House, 1969), 83.

3. **BLACK IMMIGRANTS**: Tamir, Christine. "The Growing Diversity of Black America." Pew Research Center, March 25, 2021. https://www.pewresearch.org/social-trends/2021/03/25/the-growing-diversity-of-black-america.

4. **FOR BLACK PEOPLE**: Finney, Carolyn. "The Perils of Being Black in Public: We Are All Christian Cooper and George Floyd." *The Guardian*, June 3, 2020. https://www.theguardian.com/commentisfree/2020/jun/03/being-black-public-spaces-outdoors-perils-christian-cooper.

5. **BLACK AMERICAN POPULATION**: "Black Population by State 2023." World Population Review. Accessed December 8, 2023. https://worldpopulationreview.com/state-rankings/black-population-by-state.

6. *THE SIGNIFYING MONKEY*: The Editors of Encyclopedia Britannica, eds. "Henry Louis Gates, Jr." Britannica, November 10, 2023. https://www.britannica.com/biography/Henry-Louis-Gates-Jr#ref810274.

7. **I KNOWED A MAN SO SMART**: Neale Hurston, Zora, and Christopher Myers. *Lies and Other Tall Tales* (New York: Harper Collins, 2005), 30.

8. **HERE ON THIS BRIDGE**: Clifton, Lucille. "Won't You Celebrate with Me." Poetry Foundation. Accessed December 8, 2023. https://www.poetryfoundation.org/poems/50974/wont-you-celebrate-with-me.

CHAPTER 3: PAIN, PROTEST, AND PRIDE

1. **THE RECORD OF HUMAN ACTION**: Du Bois, W.E.B., and David L. Lewis. *Black Reconstruction in America: An Essay Toward a History of the Part Which Black Folk Played in the Attempt to Reconstruct Democracy in America, 1860–1880* (Oxford: Oxford University Press, 2007).

2. **VOMITING UP ALL THE FILTH**: Baldwin, James. "They Can't Turn Back." *James Baldwin: Collected Essays* (LOA #98) (New York: Library of America, 1998). Accessed online: https://www.historyisaweapon.com/defcon1/baldwincantturnback.html.

3. **NEGRO IN HISTORY**: Woodson, Carter G. "The Celebration of Negro History Week, 1927." *The Journal of Negro History* 12, no. 2 (April 1927). https://doi.org/10.2307/2714049.

4. **THE MAN OF AFRICAN BLOOD**: Woodson, Carter G. *The Mis-Education of the Negro*. Associated Publishers, 1969. https://www.google.com/books/edition/The_Mis_education_of_the_Negro/zF6J8Zge4XgC?hl=en&gbpv=0.

5. **DECADES OF DISAPPOINTMENT**: Quarles, Benjamin. *The Negro in the Making of America* (New York: Simon & Schuster, 1964), 150.

6. **THE RACIAL MOUNTAIN**: Hughes, Langston. "The Negro Artist and the Racial Mountain." Essay. In *The Collected Works of Langston Hughes*. Columbia, MO: University of Missouri Press, 2002. https://www.poetryfoundation.org/articles/69395/the-negro-artist-and-the -racial-mountain.

7. **BLACK AESTHETIC**: Frederick, Candice. "On Black Aesthetics: The Black Arts Movement." The New York Public Library, July 15, 2016. https://www.nypl.org/blog/2016/07 /15/black-aesthetics-bam.

8. **DEADLY OPPRESSION**: "Herstory." Black Lives Matter. Accessed December 8, 2023. https://blacklivesmatter.com/herstory.

9. **LARGEST MOVEMENT IN U.S. HISTORY**: Buchanan, Larry, Bui Quoctrung, and Jugal K. Patel. "Black Lives Matter May Be the Largest Movement in U.S. History." *The New York Times*, July 3, 2020. https://www.nytimes.com/interactive/2020/07/03/us/george-floyd -protests-crowd-size.html.

10. **RELEVANCY AND SUPPORT OF BLM**: Hatfield, Jenn. "8 Facts About Black Lives Matter." Pew Research Center, July 12, 2023. https://www.pewresearch.org/short-reads/2023/07 /12/8-facts-about-black-lives-matter/.

CHAPTER 4: BIRDS WITH WINGS

1. **BIRDS WITHOUT WINGS**: Collier, Andrea. "Why Telling Our Own Story Is So Powerful for Black Americans." *Greater Good Magazine*, February 27, 2019. https://greatergood .berkeley.edu/article/item/why_telling_our_own_story_is_so_powerful_for_black _americans.

2. **A STORY TOLD BY A BLACK PERSON**: Collier. "Why Telling Our Own Story Is So Powerful for Black Americans."

3. **OTHER THAN PROPERTY**: Collier. "Why Telling Our Own Story Is So Powerful for Black Americans."

4. **THE TALE OF HOW WE SUFFER**: Baldwin, James. "Sonny's Blues." *The Oxford Book of American Short Stories*, ed. Joyce Carol Oates (Oxford: Oxford University Press, 2013), 512.

5. **BLACK CULTURAL LENS**: "Afrofuturism." National Museum of African American History and Culture, December 8, 2023. https://nmaahc.si.edu/explore/exhibitions /afrofuturism.

6. **ROOTED IN AFRICAN CULTURE**: Wabuke, Hope. "Afrofuturism, Africanfuturism, and the Language of Black Speculative Literature." *Los Angeles Review of Books*, August 27, 2020. https://lareviewofbooks.org/article/afrofuturism-africanfuturism-and-the-language -of-black-speculative-literature.

7. **A PEOPLE DISPLACED**: Woo, Celestine. "Towards a Poetics of Asian American Fantasy: Laurence Yep's Construction of a Bicultural Mythology." *The Lion and the Unicorn* 30, no. 2 (2006): 250–64. https://doi.org/10.1353/uni.2006.0027.

8. **BOOKS AND MOVIES**: Thomas, Ebony Elizabeth. "Why We Need More Black Characters in Fantasy." *YES! Magazine*, May 8, 2019. https://www.yesmagazine.org/social-justice /2019/05/08/fiction-fantasy-imagination-magic-black-characters.

9. **SUFFERED IN BEAUTIFUL LANGUAGE**: Hughes, Langston. *The Big Sea: An Autobiography* (New York: Macmillan, 1993), 16.

10. **IF A MAN KNOWS NOTHING:** Klein, Colton. "The Symbolism Behind Horace Pippin's Fantastical Biblical Vision." Sothebys.com, November 11, 2019. https://www.sothebys.com/en/articles/the-symbolism-behind-horace-pippins-fantastical-biblical-vision.

11. **OWN DISTINCTIVE FEATURES:** Cooper, Anna Julia. Letter to the editor, *The Southern Workman and Hampton School Record* (Hampton, VA: Hampton Normal and Agricultural Institute, January 1894).

12. **BEAUTY AND INJUSTICE:** Young, Kevin, ed. *African American Poetry: 250 Years of Struggle & Song* (New York: Library of America, 2020), xxxix.

13. **KEY THEMES IN AFRICAN AMERICAN POETRY:** "5 Key Themes in African American Poetry." Lift Every Voice. Accessed December 8, 2023. https://www.africanamericanpoetry.org/themes.

14. **OPPRESSIVE LANGUAGE:** Morrison, Toni. "Nobel Lecture." Speech. NobelPrize.org. Accessed December 23, 2023. https://www.nobelprize.org/prizes/literature/1993/morrison/lecture/.

15. **BLACK POETS HAVE CONSISTENTLY:** Shockley, Evie. "Essay." In *Black Experience in History and Memory.* Accessed December 8, 2023. https://assets-global.website-files.com/5eed2ad14b809188d9fc0869/5f61564e635a100955316550_LEV_black_experience.pdf.

16. *FREE WITHIN OURSELVES*: Bishop, Rudine Sims. *Free Within Ourselves: The Development of African American Children's Literature* (Portsmouth, NH: Heinemann, 2007), 273.

CHAPTER 5: ROCKSTARS AND READERS

1. **AS SOMEONE WHO GREW UP:** Noah, Trevor. "Jacqueline Woodson—'Red at the Bone' and Creating Empathy via Complex Stories." *The Daily Show*, 2019.

2. **THE FORCE FROM SOMEWHERE:** Hurston, Zora Neale. *Dust Tracks on a Road* (New York: Harper Perennial, 1996), 175–76.

3. **BOOKS TRANSMIT VALUES:** Myers, Walter Dean. "Where Are the People of Color in Children's Books?" *The New York Times*, March 15, 2014. https://www.nytimes.com/2014/03/16/opinion/sunday/where-are-the-people-of-color-in-childrens-books.html.

4. **BOUNDARIES OF IMAGINATION:** Myers, Christopher. "The Apartheid of Children's Literature." *The New York Times*, March 15, 2014. https://www.nytimes.com/2014/03/16/opinion/sunday/the-apartheid-of-childrens-literature.html.

5. **TEMPTS US TO WISH:** "Books for Children." *The New York Times*, October 23, 1932. https://archive.nytimes.com/www.nytimes.com/books/01/04/22/specials/hughes-popo.html.

PART TWO INTRODUCTION

1. **BECAUSE I WRITE:** Barnes, Derrick. "Black Joy Matters: Why Kids Need to See Black Protagonists in Children's Books." Today.com, September 16, 2021. https://community.today.com/parentingteam/post/black-joy-matters-why-kids-need-to-see-black-protagonists-in-childrens-book.

2. **I CHEATED:** Giovanni, Nikki. Introduction to *The 100 Best African American Poems* (Naperville, IL: Sourcebooks, 2010).

CHAPTER 6: THE EARLY YEARS (AGES 2–4)

1. **IN AN INTERVIEW:** "All Because You Matter | Tami Charles and Bryan Collier." YouTube, July 17, 2020. https://www.youtube.com/watch?v=zWQhFhunqh0.

CHAPTER 8: LATE ELEMENTARY (AGES 8–10)

1. **CEDAR HILL**: "Frederick Douglass National Historic Site (U.S. National Park Service)." National Parks Service. Accessed December 7, 2023. https://www.nps.gov/frdo/index.htm.
2. **BESSIE COLEMAN VIDEO**: "Bessie Coleman: Unladylike2020." PBS LearningMedia, February 23, 2022. https://gpb.pbslearningmedia.org/resource/ull20-bessie-coleman/unladylike-2020.
3. **MAP AN IMAGINARY TRIP**: "Navigating the Green Book." Navigating the Green Book. Accessed December 7, 2023. publicdomain.nypl.org/greenbook-map/.
4. **DIGITAL COLLECTIONS**: *The Green Book*. New York Public Library Digital Collections. Accessed December 7, 2023. https://digitalcollections.nypl.org/collections/the-green-book#/?tab=about.
5. **KINOBE KALIMBA PERFORMANCE**: Kalimba, Kinobe. "Kinbe Kalimba Performance." World Beat 101, September 8, 2014. https://www.youtube.com/watch?v=Yr-P5sWx-V0.

CHAPTER 9: MIDDLE SCHOOL (AGES 15–17)

1. **LITTLE BROWN BABY**: Weaver, Afaa Michael. "Afaa Michael Weaver Reads and Discusses Paul Laurence Dunbar's 'Little Brown Baby.'" Library of Congress. https://www.loc.gov/programs/poetry-and-literature/audio-recordings/poetry-of-america/item/poetry-00000832/afaa-michael-weaver-paul-laurence-dunbar.
2. **GREAT MIGRATION: CRASH COURSE**: Smith, Clint. "The Great Migration: Crash Course Black American History #24." Crash Course. YouTube, November 6, 2021. https://www.youtube.com/watch?v=Woh63FlFDBk.
3. **THE POWER OF YES**: Alexander, Kwame. "The Power of Yes." TedxHerndon. YouTube, June 13, 2017. https://www.youtube.com/watch?v=tkTn3l2FnIY.

CHAPTER 10: HIGH SCHOOL (AGES 15–17)

1. **REDUCE DROWNING RATES**: Mondick, Lindsay. "Why Are Black Youth at Highest Risk for Drowning?" YMCA.com, March 25, 2021. https://www.ymca.org/blog/why-are-black-youth-highest-risk-drowning.
2. **GET IN GOOD TROUBLE**: Lewis, John. Twitter post, June 27, 2018. https://x.com/repjohnlewis/status/1011991303599607808?s=20.

INDEX OF BOOKS BY TITLE

INDEX OF AUTHORS AND ILLUSTRATORS

ABOUT THE AUTHOR

Amber O'Neal Johnston is a home education expert and mother of four who speaks and writes about including diverse voices in traditional curricula and infusing ethnic and family culture into the home environment. She is the author of *A Place to Belong: Raising Kids to Celebrate Their Heritage, Community, and the World* and passionately shares Black books, art, music, poetry, people, things, and ideas at HeritageMom.com. She regularly speaks at education, homeschooling, and parenting conferences around the country and lives in Georgia, nestled among pine trees, hammocks, and zip lines with her husband and four children.